NOVEL FORMATIONS

The Indian Beginnings of a European Genre

NOVEL FORMATIONS

The Indian Beginnings of a European Genre

edited by

SAMBUDHA SEN

BAIDIK BHATTACHARYA

permanent black

Published by

PERMANENT BLACK

'Himalayana', Mall Road, Ranikhet Cantt,
Ranikhet 263645

perblack@gmail.com

Distributed by

ORIENT BLACKSWAN PRIVATE LTD

Bangalore Bhopal Bhubaneshwar Chandigarh Chennai
Ernakulam Guwahati Hyderabad Jaipur Kolkata
Lucknow Mumbai New Delhi Patna
www.orientblackswan.com

ISBN 978-81-7824-536-2

Typeset in Adobe Garamond Pro
by Guru Typograph Technology, Crossings Republic,
Ghaziabad 201009
Printed and bound by Sapra Brothers, Noida

Contents

Acknowledgements

THIS BOOK BEGAN taking shape several years ago, when the two of us and Udaya Kumar were colleagues at the English Department of Delhi University. We found ourselves drawn together by our common interest in the novel form and our conviction that the sheer range of discursive energies that went into the making of the early Indian novel had never been fully understood.

This conviction was strong enough for us to continue to meet and discuss the early Indian novel even after two among us left Delhi University. It was at this stage that we managed to get Vasudha Dalmia interested in our project. Vasudha's enthusiastic participation, her work ethic and wisdom, were instrumental in turning what might have remained merely a set of engaging ideas into a book. Udaya and Vasudha are thus much more than contributors to this collection of essays. Without their constant support at every stage this book simply would not have existed.

Aniket Jawaare's comments on several individual essays in this volume, as well as his more general ideas on the novel form, have helped to sharpen many of the arguments we make here. We thank him for these important contributions.

We also thank Rochelle Pinto and Madhava Prasad not only for sticking to deadlines and responding promptly and professionally to queries but also for helping us sustain several lines of continuity that underpin this book as a whole.

This book would not existed in its present shape without Rukun Advani's deep engagement with it from the moment he took it on. Rukun's editorial skills are widely known and having borne the brunt of them, we now know why!

BAIDIK BHATTACHARYA
SAMBUDHA SEN

1

Introduction

SAMBUDHA SEN and
BAIDIK BHATTACHARYA

Babu: What's up?

Wife: Reading, what else?

Babu: What do you read?

Wife: Whatever I can. Unlike you I can read neither English nor French, so I read whatever is in my lot.

Babu: Why do you read those rubbishy Bengali books? Instead, it's better not to read anything at all.

Wife: Why?

Babu: They are all *immoral, obscene, filthy.*[1]

Wife: And what are they?

Babu: You know what *immoral* is – well, you know – I mean anything that goes against *morality.*

Wife: Is that a four-legged animal?

Babu: No, no – it is something like – how do I translate this into Bengali? I mean whatever is not *moral.*

Wife: What is "moral"?[2] Is it the swan?

[1] Italicised English words are in italics in the original.

[2] *Moral* in Bengali is the word for swan – the wife is deliberately playing on phonetic similarity.

Babu: Shame! *O woman! Thy name is stupidity.*

Wife: Then what is it?

Babu: It's impossible to explain so much in Bengali – but the crux of the story is that Bengali books are bad.

Wife: But this book isn't bad – interesting story.

Babu: Is it the story of a king with two wives? Or is it the story of Nala and Damayanti?

Wife: Isn't there anything else?

Babu: Do you really have anything else in Bengali?

Wife: This one is different. It mentions cutlet, brandy, widow marriage – even songs by a *vaishnabi*.

Babu: Exactly. That's why I said you shouldn't read that trash.

Wife: Why? What's the big deal if I read it?

Babu: You will be *demoralized.*

[. . .]

Wife: Even Englishmen don't detest this book as much as you do. I have heard that they are reading it in translation.

Babu: Are you out of your mind?

Wife: Why?

Babu: Bengali book in English translation? Where do you get these absurd stories from? I hope the book isn't *seditious*. In that case it is possible for the *government* to get it translated. What book is it?

Wife: *Bishbriksha.*

Babu: *Bish* [numeral] – you mean twenty?

Wife: No – it's the other *bish* [poison], which I will have one day to get rid of you.

Babu: Oh! *Poison! Dear me!* And a *briksha* of that – well I must say it's an appropriate title. Now throw it away!

Wife: Tell me what *briksha* in English is.

Babu: *Tree.*

Wife: Now join these two words together.

Babu: *The Poison Tree!* Oh, I see. I read about a book called *Poison Tree* in the newspaper. So is it a translation from Bengali? Well, now that the English translation exists why should I fall for the Bengali version?

Wife: Yes, it's better to fall for anything in the English way – whether it's a book or a drink. I ask you to follow the English way. Please have a look at this book. This is translated from English – the author testifies as much.

Babu: It's better to read such books. What's the English book – *Robinson Crusoe* or *Watt on the Improvement of the Mind*?

Wife: I don't know the English title, the Bengali one is *Chhayamayee*.

Babu: *Chhayamayee?* What's that? Let me see (takes the book), *Dante, by Jove.*[3]

THIS EXTRACT FROM Bankimchandra Chattopadhyay's satirical text "Bangla sahityer ador" (1884), written as a conversation between a westernised babu and his self-consciously Bengali wife, brings into focus a set of concerns that lie at the heart of *Novel Formations*. Like the conversation, this book is concerned with novels, and specifically with the many ways in which the early novel in India negotiated its inescapable relationship with colonial modernity. Thus we follow Bankim in probing the novel's role in one of colonialism's central cultural transactions: to promote the modern English-educated woman who will make an intelligent, capable, and companionable wife. Bankim, as is obvious, satirises the imported ideal of companionate marriage by complicating its internal assumptions.[4] But other

[3] Chattopadhyay, "Bangla sahityer ador", in *Bankim Rachanabali*, vol. II, 41–2; translation ours.

[4] See Bhadra, *Nyara battalay jay kabar?*, 86–7.

writers discussed in this volume found it impossible to dissociate the modernity of the novel form from modern ideas about how a husband should relate to his wife, as well as from the more public authenticating discourses of post-Enlightenment Europe.

As several contributors to this volume show, the anxiety to be modern demonstrated a familiarity with modernity's knowledge-producing protocols and it often ended up cramping rather than facilitating the free development of the early Indian novel. But their essays – which document some of the ways in which the early Indian novel negotiated modernity – do not in any sense reduce the modernising projects of the novels they discuss to the antics of Bankim's caricaturised babu. Indeed, Bankim's own sense of the interlinked unfolding of the novel and modernity was more complex than the words of the babu would suggest. His *Bishbriksha* – which the wife is reading – itself suggests this complexity. Thus, far from being projected as an embodiment of pure tradition, the book being read is shown to have freed itself from the inaccessibility of the older Sanskrit-laden Bangla and to be fully equipped to deal with the contemporary – pithily summarised by the wife as "cutlet, brandy, widow marriage".

The first essay in this book links Bankim's quest for a novelistic Bangla that would be both accessible and contemporary with his interest in philology, but it also probes the cultural incommensurability implied in the wife's witty misunderstanding of English words such as "moral" and "immorality". Not all early Indian novelists followed Bankim in separating the culturally embedded life that he embodies in the figure of the wife from the swirl of the modern – out of which Bankim's own novelistic language emerged. Indeed, following the many transactions that take place even in the conversation we are discussing –

between languages, novels, commodities, and worldviews – the present book tracks a third trajectory along which the early Indian novel moved through its negotiation with colonial modernity. This was a mode of writing energised neither by the dream of a uniformly enlightened India of the future, nor by confidence in the resilience of traditional ways of life, but by unthinkable admixtures that erupted out of the cauldron of colonial modernity and which pushed some early Indian novels in a direction very different from canonical realistic novels of nineteenth-century Europe.

Novel Formations is thus interested not so much in focussing on the chronology or regional spread of early Indian novels as in uncovering the relationships between them and colonial modernity, and more specifically with the discursive fields that this modernity brought into existence. We do in fact discuss novels from a range of regions in India, but, while working always with details specific to Kerala or Bengal or Maharashtra or Karnataka we are interested, above all, in the ways by which technologies, values, languages, and discourses set into circulation by colonial modernity collaborated to produce the new formation called the novel. Indeed, if there is a single defining move that this book makes, it is to locate the novel at the discursive crossroads of colonial modernity, and to study its formation in relation to other discourses, both literary and non-literary. Enlarging the scope of our investigation thus, we hope to show how the formation of the novel is separable neither from the intermixture of languages that colonialism accelerated, nor from the new knowledge-producing systems such as journalism, ethnography, and philology that it brought into existence.

The discursive instability that this way of understanding assumes as the heart of the early Indian novel also suggests our point of departure from the traditional literary orientation towards this corpus of writing. This volume is not interested in thinking of the early Indian novel as a self-sufficient or unified whole, nor in evaluating its aesthetic achievements when judged by the standards of nineteenth-century European realism, nor even in explaining the social factors and cultural anxieties that prevented novels like *Gobinda Samanta* or *Indirabai* from attaining the psychological depth or formal elegance of, for example, Jane Austen's fiction.[5] Rather, we envisage the early novel in India as a discursive formation characterised by a certain formal indeterminacy and semantic open-endedness which made it capable of reactivating and reworking the ideas, expressive resources, and formal possibilities that circulated within the inscriptive fields in which it took shape.

These circumstances explain the paradox which the reader will confront throughout this book. On the one hand, excepting Bankim's work, no novel discussed by the contributors can be said to attain the aesthetic excellence of a *Pride and Prejudice* or a *Middlemarch*. On the other hand, as the conversation with which we began suggests, the early Indian novel took shape in relation to many more elements than were available to its English counterpart: not only a multiplicity of tongues as against the single language available to *Robinson Crusoe*, but also a world whose traditional customs and dietary habits made brandy, cutlets, and widow marriage strange new additions. Thus, although almost invariably underdeveloped as individual forays in the art of novel-writing, nineteenth-century Indian novels hold enormous promise for the later development of the novel form.

[5] For examples of this type of scholarship, see Mukherjee, *Realism and Reality*; Joshi, *In Another Country*; and Kaviraj, *The Invention of Private Life*.

New Directions in Novel Studies

Some recent works on nineteenth-century literary cultures, sharply regional in their focus, have made it possible for us to think of the early novel as a discursive crossroads and as a site of colonial modernity. Vasudha Dalmia, for instance, has suggested that early Hindi novels like Srinivasdas' *Pariksha Guru* (1882) needs to be read both in terms of its "embeddedness [. . .] in the multilingual Indo-Persianate literary culture that characterised North India, as also [in terms of] the rupture brought about by the radical changes in social and cultural sensibilities that it both explored and anticipated."[6] To tease out the implications of this formulation, she expands her inquiry beyond the traditional frameworks of literary history and explores the complex intertwining of "self and sociality", not only in *Pariksha Guru* but also in an early-modern text set in a similar milieu of the merchant communities of northern India – Banarasidas' *Ardhakathanak* (1641). This comparative method is then structurally positioned to raise a series of questions that encompass the modern Hindi literary idiom as it developed in the Delhi–Agra region, with special attention given to the Hindi–Urdu debates and a shared linguistic ancestry, and of course to the changes that colonialism forced upon a largely traditional merchant community in the late-nineteenth century. What emerges through Dalmia's juxtaposition of the two texts is not so much a narrative continuity across time as a comparative sense of the life-worlds both inhabit, and the ways in which issues such as domesticity, subjectivity, and sexuality display such considerable similarity across narrative genres. Dalmia shows, for instance, that despite parallels deriving from the merchant communities in the two works, and despite the recurrence of various themes across

[6] Dalmia, "Merchant Tales", 43.

them, it is the modern sensibility of Srinivasdas' novel that sets it apart "from the vast range of life stories grouped formerly under *charita* or *bat*" (of which *Ardhakathanak* is an eminent example). This sense of modernity is not simply an external attribute of the novel but a characteristic feature of the way *Pariksha Guru* thematises North India, especially the Delhi–Agra region as it changed under colonial rule. A case in point is the way the new political dispensation affected the "merchant ethos", and the way Srinivasdas responded to such changes in his novel. The central idea of merchanthood that exists in *Ardhakathanak* – resting on the typical figure of the frugal merchant who could reasonably expect "credit and creditability" – was still intact in the nineteenth century, but Srinivasdas also realised that the "'new climate of social and moral experience' asked for a new kind of morality tale for the merchants of the city." Hence, the sense of merchant community invoked in *Pariksha Guru* is no longer dependent on traditional mechanisms such as religious institutions (temples and charity) and caste panchayats, but made up of new technologies and institutions like the newspaper and law courts presided over by British judges. Within the novel this newness is staged through contrasting characters: the dilettante merchant Madanmohan and the upright lawyer Brajkishor representing the older and newer moral universes.[7]

Such an inquiry is particularly important because of the way it makes the novel as a genre infiltrate a range of issues, literary and otherwise, and because it constitutes for us a sense of the public sphere within which early novels took shape and participated. In recent years, the scholarship on colonial North India and its public sphere has sprung to life, especially in relation to the second

[7] Ibid., 51–2.

half of the nineteenth century. Dalmia herself has written about the intertwining histories of the novel and pre-colonial cities like Banaras, Lahore, and Agra after 1857.[8] While the novels she examines represented the changing world of colonial North India, they also circulated through the public sphere constituted by popular print, and often referred to this other world as a foil.

In Francesca Orsini's work one encounters the "highly intertextual world" of popular print, leading to a "heterogeneous linguistic and aesthetic repertoire".[9] Dubbed by the British as "bazaar trash", this is the world of *barahmasas* or "songs of the twelve months", popular songbooks, *qissas* (both *dastan* and *naql*), serialised novels, detective fiction, and so on.[10] Especially important in the context of the present volume is what Orsini calls the "novel experience", comprising texts like the first serialised Urdu novel, Pandit Ratannath Dar "Sarshar"'s *Fasana-e Azad* (1878–85), and Devkinandan Khatri's somewhat Hinduised *dastan* titled *Chandrakanta* (1887–91), which represent a vital extension of popular print culture. These folk texts, she tells us, "subordinated ideas of social reform to a combination of pleasures and aesthetics: the older pleasures and aesthetics connected to tales and poetry and the new pleasures [of] suspense, uncertainty regarding character and plot, verisimilitude of setting and character."[11] What arrests our interest is the approximately parallel history of canonical Hindi novels that Dalmia describes and this world of popular print that Orsini tracks – the interplay

[8] Dalmia, *Fiction as History.*

[9] Orsini, *Print and Pleasure*, 104.

[10] The analogous popular and pulp literature in Tamilnadu, called "*gujili*", is the subject of ch. 5: "Songsters of the Crossroads", in Venkatachalapathy, *The Province of the Book.*

[11] Orsini, *Print and Pleasure*, 162.

between two different forms and their participation in a shared market for print and visual entertainment make it difficult to sustain a neat boundary between the elite canonical tradition and subaltern commercial publishing. Moreover, it was this overlap, and easier access to commercial print, that created the mental habits necessary for reading novels, especially in a neo-literate reading community of young people and women.

What we see in recent work by Orsini and others in this broad area is an eclectic mix of book history and the more traditional methods of close reading. Indeed, as Ulrike Stark points out, over the last couple of decades or so scholarship on South Asia has taken book history, and especially the book and its attendant material culture, as an object of serious intellectual inquiry. While earlier historians of print culture were primarily concerned with the newspaper (for a number of reasons), more recent work has placed the printed book at the centre of attempts to retrieve "factual knowledge of material, infrastructural, and operational aspects of the regional-language book trade, of author–publisher and publisher–bookseller relations, of readership and consumption practices", and so on.[12] Her own work on the influential nineteenth-century publishing house of Lucknow, the Naval Kishore Press, is a significant addition to this growing body of scholarship. Similar works on Hindi–Urdu, Bangla, Tamil, Konkani, and other Indian languages have also appeared.[13] The relevance of this new body of work for the essays in this volume is not very far to seek. As many of them argue, the materiality of

[12] Stark, *An Empire of Books*, 7.

[13] Orsini, *The Hindi Public Sphere*; Blackburn, *Print, Folklore and Nationalism*; Ghosh, *Power in Print*; Chatterjee, *Empires of the Mind*; Pinto, *Between Empires*; Venkatachalapathy, *The Province of the Book*; also see Chakravorty and Gupta, *Print Areas*; idem, *Moveable Type*; idem, *Founts of Knowledge*; Orsini, *History of the Book in South Asia*.

print culture, including the circulation and reception of books, publishing houses and public libraries, and reading habits form a substantial part of this new trend in book history; and in trying to understand the early histories of the novel in India these institutions and practices are remarkably illuminating. This is in fact a part of the lateral expansion of research mentioned earlier, because these sites, institutions, and practices produced networks of "novel experience" that introduced the novel into various literary cultures. Across these networks, and along with the novel, a variety of material also circulated – indeed, newspaper reporting, biographical writing, essays, and discursive prose on society, philosophy, science, and politics seem to have exerted a significant influence on what was exchanged in the public sphere; and the novel, as a significant mode of public articulation, not only participated in this public sphere of print and commerce but appropriated its forms in several ways. As we shall see in a number of contributions that follow, this materiality of print found unexpected ways into a number of early novels in India. Working always within a comparative frame, alert always to the ways in which ideas and expressive strategies enter into and are transformed by the early Indian novel, the contributors here bring out this materiality of print culture by reading their resources in new and often unpredictable ways.

A second line of inquiry into early Indian novels has been suggested by Sudipta Kaviraj and Udaya Kumar. Kaviraj's work on Bankim, one of the first major novelists in India, is not restricted to his novels but shows how a complex and gifted novelist like him needs to be read with reference to his immediate context – colonial Bengal.[14] At the centre of Bankim's novels Kaviraj locates a sense of liminality, a continuous struggle between the moral world of

[14] Kaviraj, *The Unhappy Consciousness.*

a society dependent on permissions and prohibitions, and on the other the darker and unfathomable world of human desire which relentlessly pushes the limits of the ideal moral universe. Indeed, Kaviraj suggests that this is the governing principle of Bankim's novels, leading to an inevitable sense of the tragic: "Bankim's art creates life stories of individuals to express wonder at this primeval darkness, this peculiar problematicity of life that is much easier to think of through art than through conceptual thought."[15] However, this tragic sense of life, constituting a new subjectivity under colonial rule (he calls it the "unhappy consciousness"), cannot be understood through Bankim's novels alone: it has to be situated in the contact zones of differing genres, within the porous boundaries between novels like *Durgeshnandini* (1865) and *Indira* (1873) on the one hand, and on the other satirical pieces like *Kamalakanta* (1875, 1885), as well as discursive prose works like *Krishnacharitra* (1886). One of the central clues in this regard, Kaviraj suggests, is Bankim's use of language – or rather, the way he created specific linguistic worlds to suit his characters and contexts, and used the same sort of language in his non-fiction. What we encounter in this mixed and complex world of Bankim are the first signs of colonial modernity, a world that his texts both captures and evaluates: "Bankimchandra fashioned the Bengali sense of modernity, because he was the first to teach them to wonder at this phenomenon of history reflexively. He was the first to create something like the rasa of modernity, for which the earlier primary colours of the palette of feelings was inadequate."[16] In his more recent work, Kaviraj has extended this "rasa of modernity" beyond Bankim into the print culture of nineteenth- and

[15] Ibid., 26.

[16] Ibid., 159.

early-twentieth-century Bengal. As he puts it, "modern Indian literature [is] a primary field of theoretical-philosophic reflection on the nature of modern times, and particularly the experiential interior of it. Literature is so essential for the understanding of modernity precisely because it deals with experience."[17]

The essence of the rasa of modernity, which Kaviraj describes as a broadly romantic and tragic view of life, is reformulated within this fundamental generic form of a modern sensibility, the novel. Indeed, Kaviraj identifies the novel and autobiography as *the* quintessentially modern genres and argues that they played a crucial role in "persuading individuals to own a modern life-ideal, and to live by its rules."[18] One of the central threads running through Kaviraj's work on Bengali literature is the argument that the experience of modernity was internalised by colonial subjects not so much through its classic philosophical accounts by Kant or Mill, but through the gradual impact of modern literature. He shows striking parallels between philosophical debates on the nature of modernity and the modern self in Europe, and the same set of ideas vigorously discussed in Bengali literature. This invests a modern literary form like the novel with an unusual responsibility – we have described it earlier as a discursive cross-roads – and at the same time suggests the fluid nature of the genre. One can begin to fathom the issues involved by juxtaposing Kaviraj's gloss on the characters Bankim created in his novels – especially vibrant and dynamic women like Ayesha and Indira who push at the limits of transgression – and his reading of the Brahmo reformer Sibnath Sastri's autobiography, with its painstaking chronicling of a modern subject with a clearly defined

[17] Kaviraj, *The Invention of Private Life*, 4.

[18] Ibid., 6.

interiority. Kaviraj does not suggest that these different forms consciously created models for each other to emulate, but he does indicate a larger cultural milieu of modernity – a discursive complex and its material conditions – that produced cognate sensibilities across different genres. Such a framework allows us to ask fresh questions about the modern self that the early novel was critically dependent on: how can we revisit the figures of subjectivity and interiority represented in the novel in light of the complex discursive heritages of the novel and the reading practices and habits they provoked? How do the figures of the body and of the individual's inner self that circulate in the public sphere – in literature but also in non-literary texts and visual culture – shape the field within which characters in novels are conceived and articulated? What is the role of caste, class, gender, and sexuality in this formation of modern subjecthood?

Udaya Kumar's work on modern Malayalam autobiographies, and varying modes of self-articulation more broadly, take us further into this complex world of modern subjectivity and sensibility. Kumar charts a world of overlapping forms, genres, and modes of writing as characteristic of colonial modernity in Kerala. His search for modern autobiographies led him inevitably, he says, to other forms of writing because many techniques of self-articulation were developed not in works identifiable as "autobiographies", but in adjacent areas of writing and public discourse.[19] This plurality and porosity was neither accidental nor perfunctory; as the evidence from Kerala shows, different aspects of modern selfhood were fashioned through varying documentations of the self across novels, lyric poetry, devotional tracts, legal papers, and so on. Kumar argues that

[19] Kumar, *Writing the First Person.*

narrative heterogeneity was also helpful in articulating different aspects of the modern self and its interiority, as also its agential components, and that it offered a more comprehensive view of the relationship between an individual and written practices of self-representation, autobiographical or otherwise. Within the world of early Malayalam novels, however, this technique of inter-generic representation met another mechanism to represent the modern individual, which Kumar calls a "scopic regime". Once again, this was a method that drew on various visual registers like photography, painting, and photolithography, and constituted a visual field that depended, almost in equal measure, on both visual and verbal representations. The point of the detailed documentation of a variety of modes of seeing and showing in novels like Appu Nedungadi's *Kundalata* (1887), O. Chandu Menon's *Indulekha* (1889), Cheruvalathu Chathu Nair's *Meenakshi* (1890), and C.V. Raman Pillai's *Premamrtam* (1913), Kumar suggests, is to indicate the new terrain of the early novel:

> [T]he space inhabited by these divergent representations defines the emergent genre of the novel. These early novels produced a new field of perception and enunciation precisely through unresolved diversities. They reveal no simple concatenation of the indigenous and the colonial, or the traditional and the modern; they produce a new discursive space where ideas and tropes from varied resources – from Sanskrit *kavyas* to English political treatises – acquire vernacular contemporaneity.[20]

He details the forging of these relationships between the novel and established literary conventions (both Sanskrit and English), new technologies of print and photography, the new world of

[20] Ibid., 163–4.

objects and ideas, and eventually the arrival of a new sense of public space and articulation. It was within this "configuration of visibility" characterised by its liminality and "unsteady luminosity" that early novels in Kerala imagined the new subjectivities and interiorities of colonial modernity.[21]

A case in point is the eponymous heroine of Chandu Menon's *Indulekha*, a novel which employs a range of narrative techniques to describe the newness of both Indulekha as a character as well as her world, and often, through self-reflexive passages, guides its imagined reader over this new world. If, for instance, the novel relies rather heavily on the Sanskrit *kavya* tradition to marshal an adequate language to describe the first appearance of the heroine in the second chapter, it quickly shifts gear to underline her Western education, going as far as stating that her education by the age of sixteen was comparable to that of "a girl in England". Again, the novel posits an opposition between Indulekha's distinguished aesthetic taste and Suri Namboodiripad's rather dissolute love of gold by describing their respective dress and appearance – while Indulekha's "elegantly clean white clothes" with gold borders embody "aesthetic discrimination", Suri's bizarrely golden attire signifies vulgar opulence.[22] Gradually, and with copious help from the narrator, we begin to see a semiological pattern inscribed on individual bodies of the characters in the novel, and while this technique depends on different resources it unmistakably points towards a new regime of "novel experience". Kumar's central argument about the heterogeneity of writing that characterised colonial modernity in nineteenth-century Kerala, alongside these varied resources and a certain sense of publicness, together offer

[21] Ibid., 164.

[22] Ibid., 137, 153, 160.

an interesting contrast to Kaviraj's description of the similar heterogeneity in Bengal which facilitated the appearance in prose of the modern individual with an inner life. The point is not to suggest that the form in Kerala is exclusively geared towards a public perception of modern subjects while the version in Bengal chiefly concentrates on inner turmoil; rather, both confirm our central point that the early novel in India opened up a space to different languages, registers, and techniques to mesh with and influence each other without any inevitable feeling of the genre reaching formal resolution or closure.

Novel Formations aims to take forward some of the methods and insights developed in the best work on the early Indian novel which we have tried summarising. Cutting across regions, we hope to show that the early novel emerged out of the proliferating discursive fields that colonial modernity brought into existence, and that, unlike the canonical novels of nineteenth-century England, it was constituted by its location at – to use Bakhtin's words – "the boundaries of individual genres and not the places where these genres have become enclosed in their own specificity."[23]

This interdisciplinary and multilingual orientation necessitated by our material and method allows us to examine several issues that have not received sufficient attention in the existing scholarship on the Indian novel. We hope that our account of the individual essays that follows will show some of the ways in which such novels came by their connections with colonial modernity, and by doing this we hope to locate some of the formal, expressive, and thematic possibilities that have not adequately been explored critically.

[23] Bakhtin, *Speech Genres*, 2.

The Novel in India and the Discourses of Colonial Modernity

In "Novel as Social Form: Gulvadi Venkatrao's *Indirabai*", Madhava Prasad invokes an important moment in a novel by Achintyakumar Sengupta, when a character comments, metatextually, on the ability that contemporary novels generally have to organise themselves around communities which, despite their internal differences, show signs of modernity. This character, the father of the heroine, overrides conservative objections to the ways in which his daughter conducts herself by arguing that the modern way of life has become, for people like him, an inescapable condition of being. He then justifies his view by drawing attention to the modern community of novel readers. Those who read novels, he asserts, may criticise this or that particular novel, but not novel-reading itself.

Significantly, though, the modernity that Sengupta claims both to embody and bring into existence has to do with social practices, and not with the articulation of interiority that had been at the heart of the novel's modernising project in Europe and England.[24] Indeed, with the exception of Bankim's fiction, the early Indian novel, as a number of contributors to this volume show, seems uninterested in the very elements that many would consider inseparable from the novel as a form – the gradual unfolding of psychologically complex characters and the dense network of interpersonal relationships which they enter. Thus, unlike what happens in *Pride and Prejudice* (1813), for example, romantic love

[24] On the relationship between the English novel and making of the self-conscious "deep subject", see McKeon, *The Origins of the English Novel*; Armstrong, *Desire and Domestic Fiction*; and Gallagher, *Nobody's Story*.

in the early Hindi novels of Mallikadevi does not, as Vasudha Dalmia shows in "Another Genealogy of the Hindi Novel: Mallikadevi of Banaras", so much stimulate the language of inner feelings as generate some powerful satire against a corrupt, unproductive, and greedy patriarchy, even as it makes a case for the modern woman who will be a "literate and cultivated companion and mother". Similarly, in Gulvadi Venkatrao's *Indirabai* (1899) the activation of inner life by the experience of love is staged rather than elaborated. And if that staging results in the momentary and secretive freeing of desire, the novel ensures there is no conflict between such desire and the quest for a virtuous modern life in which women do not wear the veil and are allowed to learn English, mathematics, and history. K. Narayana Kurukkal's *Udayabhanu* (1911), as Udaya Kumar demonstrates, self-consciously subsumes the language of inner life within the more urgent imperatives of nationalist politics. When the heroine Devi is finally reunited with her lover after a long separation, she experiences no inner turmoil or joy. Instead, her response takes the form of a political speech.

The essays in this volume thus engage in a sustained way, but from differing perspectives, with the paradoxical modernity of the Indian novel: on the one hand its lack of interest in the introspective modern subject at the heart of the European novel, and on the other its self-conceptualisation as both embodiment and midwife of modernity. Indeed, *Indirabai*'s engagement with modernity is so direct that it ends up *retarding* a crucial dynamic that drove European realism. Madhava Prasad shows that Venkatrao had little interest in replicating in India the possibilities that the novel form had offered in Europe: i.e. serve as a neutral ground from which to observe how the tensions of colonial modernity play out in the changing inner lives of characters. In fact, reading the novel in terms of a tension between "the desires and aspirations of [the modernising middle] class and the social context in which it is enmeshed" – and by extension between "the two sides of the colonial game of power" – erases the real stakes in a novel like *Indirabai*. These stakes are far more instrumentalist: they involve fashioning "the very middle ground of the colonial order, the small but growing society of modern Indians who are now engaged in exploring their own place in the world."

The instrumentalist orientation towards reform which underpins some early Indian novels explains an important shift in the internal workings of the form as we move from Europe and England to India. Rather than absorb the language of inner life from the works of Jane Austen or George Eliot, the early Indian novel internalised the discourses of public life set into circulation by the colonial government: the new idioms of public address as they emerged from journalism, the protocols of the police report or the public petition, and most significantly those of the newly developed discipline of ethnography. In fact, several essays here demonstrate the restraints that these discourses, which staked their value on "authenticity", put on the free imaginative improvisation that was always possible within the novel.

Udaya Kumar, for instance, engages with the complex ways in which the techniques of scandal journalism affected a novel like K. Narayana Kurukkal's *Udayabhanu*. Kumar delineates a well-developed practice in the early Malayalam novel whereby novelists, borrowing techniques from scandal journalism, insinuated without fully revealing the identity of the powerful people they were criticising. So the movement from scandal journalism to the freer domain of the novel offered possibilities for heightening the emotive impact of exposure. For example, Kurukkal used a whole system of allusions, made available by the Indian epics, as well as a range of literary devices – metaphor, exaggeration, satiric devaluation – to manipulate and heighten the reader's aversion to a corrupt politician. Yet, in their capacity as documents that sought to make an impact in real life, these early novels also encouraged readers to recognise and disdain the politician or person against whom the novelist sought to mobilise public opinion. This inhibited any full elaboration of the "purely" fictional, free from the responsibility to replicate existing and recognisable real-life circumstance. This is what Catherine Gallagher demonstrates in her classic work on the rise of the English novel. Gallagher anticipates Kumar's focus on the transition from the scandal sheet to the novel but she also shows that the full expressive potential of the novel could not be brought into play until the recognisable "somebody" of the scandal sheet had fully mutated into a purely fictional "nobody" unconstrained by irreversible real-life circumstance, and not responsible to anything except the "truth" of the author's imagination.[25]

Rochelle Pinto's reading of *Govinda Samanta* (1874), in her essay "*Govinda Samanta*, or the Threat of Ethnography in the Colonial Novel", again demonstrates how the anxiety of authentication *inhibits* the free unfolding of expressive possibilities available to the novel form. For her novel's author, Lal Behari Dey, however, this authenticity is produced not by real-life figures whom readers will instantly recognise, but by the protocols of modern science. Thus he casts his description of Indian villages and villagers in the language of scientific classification that colonialists habitually used to categorise everything in the subcontinent – from its flora and fauna to its communities and castes. As Dey moves from one authorised representational regime to another – from botany to ethnography – classifying a village tree by its Linnaean

[25] See Gallagher, *Nobody's Story*.

term or casting a peasant as a "specimen" of Indian peasants – he cramps "the play of structure or meaning within the novel by a prior authorised version of reality". The resulting impoverishment of literary and imaginative possibilities is, in fact, Pinto argues, openly acknowledged: "the reader will please remember," the novel confesses at one point, "that nothing very striking does, in point of fact, ever occur in the history of . . . a Bengali peasant boy."[26]

Despite the affiliation to modernity and to the knowledge systems that it set in motion, the early novel in India could never completely flatten out and make homogeneous either its own expressive system or the field in which it was constituted, since such homogenisation was impossible under the conditions of what has come to be called colonial modernity. As so many scholars have shown, colonialism enforced intermixtures: it set in motion the intersection of objects, images, languages, time frames, and expressive energies that originated in dramatically disparate cultures. It's true, of course, that European thinkers classified the heterogeneous elements brought together by the colonial encounter into the more or less "developed". As Dipesh Chakrabarty and others have shown, nineteenth-century European historians had no difficulty accommodating the cultures and practices of the colonised within a conception of time that was linear and oriented towards progress, and where colonialism itself became the opportunity for "backward" or "barbaric" cultures to enter history and participate in its progressive trajectory. But irrespective of how it was conceptualised, in practice it was impossible for the colonial subject to get away from the experience of a time where dramatically different historical trajectories had

[26] Dey, 186.

become entangled in what Chakrabarty calls a "constant and shared 'now'." This "synchronicity of the non-synchronous" – to use a phrase Chakrabarty borrows from Ernst Bloch – makes it impossible to conceptualise the modernity that the early Indian novel was both reflecting and helping to bring into existence as a homogeneous entity.

The massive disjunctions of colonial modernity, the idea of "a time that is out of joint with itself",[27] spring into dramatic relief if we juxtapose the modern feminine ideal that Mallikadevi advocates in both her novels – the ideal of the woman as an educated wife, companion, and mother – with the increasing desperation of Mallikadevi's own situation in a deeply conservative society where women with intelligence and talent are accorded no value at all. As Vasudha Dalmia suggests, Mallikadevi's education, intelligence, and abilities were recognised by the well-established Bharatendu Harischandra: for a time she flourished under his benign and enlightened patronage. But she had arrived in Banaras as a single woman without social credentials, and once the patronage evaporated after Harischandra's death, she gradually sank into destitution and then disappeared, possibly into the life of an abandoned widow.

The simultaneous coexistence of the modern and the not-modern that comes into view when we bring together Mallikadevi's novels with her life is of great interest to this volume. Although many essays in it uncover the ways in which early Indian writers sought to replicate, within the novel form, the European conception of time as a linear movement towards progress and modernity, we are interested also in the non-modern modes that persist in the Indian novel. Even more are we interested in the aesthetic

[27] Chakrabarty, *Provincializing Europe*, 112–13.

possibilities that emerge out of the coexistence, within a single text, of representational modes, systems of allusion, and languages originating in widely disparate literary and cultural traditions.

The powerful reactivation of Sanskrit poetic conventions within, for example, Marathi prose narratives, enables us to think of the early Indian novel as a form that could accommodate expressive strategies, idioms, tropes, and systems of allusion that had originated *both* in Europe and in the subcontinent. This jostling of incommensurate modes is evident in the contrary claims that traditional religious recitation and European "mleccha" books make on the mindspace of the heroine of *Indirabai*; in the deployment within *Udayabhanu* of both the language of modern scandal journalism and a whole system of allusions to the *Mahabharata*; and in the references to Valmiki, Vyas, and the compilers of the Puranas as well as to Swift and Rabelais in a single sentence within *Govinda Samanta*. But it was the massive ferment in the languages of an already multilingual culture now exposed to English and to modernisation which provided the early Indian novel with one of its most powerful and far-reaching expressive energies.

Novel Formations indeed demonstrates that there were no limits to the experiments writers were willing to make in their search for a language that would meet the ever-expanding demands of the early Indian novel. At one end of these experiments is the identitarian intervention of Bankim. As Baidik Bhattacharya shows, Bankim's interconnected interests in ethnography and philology were oriented to the twin projects to which he devoted himself. On the one hand he sought to fabricate an elegant modern Bangla comparable with any modern European language, and purged of its over-dependence on Sanskrit as well as of the rustic vulgate. On the other hand he hoped that this new language would become a means of rejuvenating the fallen Bengali race repeatedly humiliated by conquests. Bankim's novels thus became his means of imagining an alternative (and more heroic) history of Bengal, even as he sought to make modern elegant Bangla a marker of Bengali identity.

As is well known, Bankim succeeded brilliantly. The aesthetically evolved quality of his novels and his innovative Bangla provided the initial impetus to the development of an autonomous Bengali literary tradition. It is equally important to recognise, though, that autonomy and purity were not the only possibilities open to Bangla and other Indian languages as they developed in relation to each other and to English through the second half of the nineteenth century. Venkatrao, for example, used three languages in *Indirabai*: Kannada, of course, but also the English in which well-educated and Anglicised young men conversed, and the Konkani which is, in *Indirabai*, the language of the lower classes. Venkatrao chose to provide Kannada translations every time he used Konkani or English rather than let the three languages collaborate seamlessly. On the other hand, Lal Behari Dey did not hesitate to seize the opportunity to relieve the bleak atmosphere of *Govinda Samanta* with bilingual puns, enabled by English and Bangla being both part of the everyday life of educated Bengalis.

But it is only in the last book discussed in this volume that we see the full linguistic efflorescence which erupted when tropes, conventions, idioms, phrases, and words from the English language and English literature infiltrated a literary Bangla already cross-fertilised by Sanskrit, Arabic, and Persian. This infiltration, as Sambudha Sen shows in "*Hootum Pyanchar Naksha*, Colonial Modernity, and the Making of the Postmodern Novel in India", did not happen in an orderly manner. Rather, what Kaliprasanna Sinha offers in his Bengali work of that name is a prose that has absorbed English words and phrases, overlaid them with accents of Bangla speech, joined them to other words, and in this way created for itself an unprecedented allusive and semantic reach. Sinha's polyglot Bangla could, for example, produce a range of effects from the comic to the profound by conjuring unexpected rhymes or alliteration that worked only on multilingual levels. Similarly, it could awaken a derisive connotation within an authoritative English word or phrase of colonial administration with a bilingual pun intelligible only to Bangla readers.

For Sen the linguistic innovations of *Hootum* are symptomatic of a larger and more comprehensive, although of course incompletely developed, novelistic aesthetic. This aesthetic – based on the unprecedented and unimaginable juxtapositions forced by the shock of colonialism – involved ways of conceptualising time, and of plotting and characterisation that did not conform to the norms prescribed by realism as it had developed in nineteenth-century Europe. Driven underground by the dominance of realism, the expressive strategies that had germinated in *Hootum* found no room for development in Indian novels until quite recently. But they remained part of what Bakhtin would call the novel's "generic memory",[28] liable always to being reactivated and elaborated, as indeed they were in the third quarter of the twentieth century when an aesthetic based on hybridisation and intermingling came to enjoy universal acceptance.

Novel Formations thus demonstrates that the early novel in India engaged with and was affected by the modern – the sign under which it was born – in multiple and sometimes contradictory ways. First, several of the novels discussed below saw themselves both as midwives and embodiments of the modern – not just as

[28] See Bakhtin, *Problems of Dostoevsky's Poetics*, 106.

vehicles of change, but also as texts with the formal capacity to internalise the knowledge systems of modernity. Bankim, however, pushed the novel in a contrary direction. He modernised the Bengali language to assert its autonomy, deploying the protocols of ethnography not as a means of scientific knowledge production but to underline the superficiality of the modern when seen in relation to the deeply embedded and unchanging life of rural Bengal. Finally, this book, by engaging with *Hootum*, grapples with a text that had realised colonialism not as the catalyst propelling the non-modern into the modern, but as a life-world that had guaranteed their tense coexistence within the everyday.

The diversity of ways in which the early Indian novel negotiated colonial modernity points to paradoxes that we have sought to uncover. On the one hand there is the anxious identification, in the minds of many nineteenth-century Indian novelists, between Western modernity and authentic (sometimes scientific) knowledge, which, we suggest, inhibited the free fictional improvisations that lay at the heart of European realism. On the other hand the frequency with which novels from nineteenth-century India internalise protocols not normally associated with the novel form suggests the range of discursive and formal orientations to which they were open. Thus, apart from deploying the idioms of knowledge-producing forms such as ethnography and the police report, the novels we discuss had access, in theory at least, to poetic conventions, and to a wide range of allusions that could refer to *Paradise Lost* or to the *Mahabharata* or to languages that had already mingled with other languages in the very process of their formation. Similarly, if some of our novels are oriented towards the homogenised spaces of modernity, others pioneer expressive techniques to register the massive and chaotic intermingling of objects, attitudes, conceptions of time, value systems, and languages produced by the experience of colonialism. In these circumstances of constraints and confusions, it is hardly surprising that few writers, apart from Bankim, managed to produce aesthetically satisfying novels. Yet the sheer range of representational possibilities that remained open to Indian novels of that time suggests trajectories that would outflank the traditional European realistic novel, and subsequently animate the great new shapes the genre began to take after the third quarter of the twentieth century.

References

Armstrong, Nancy, *Desire and Domestic Fiction: A Political History of the Novel* (New York and Oxford: Oxford University Press, 1987).

Bakhtin, M.M., *Problems of Dostoevsky's Poetics*, trans. Caryl Emerson (Manchester: Manchester University Press, 1984).

———, *Speech Genres and Other Late Essays*, trans. Vern W. McGee (Austin: University of Texas Press, 2010).

Bhadra, Gautam, *Nyara battalay jay kabar?* (Calcutta: Chhatim, 2011).

Blackburn, Stuart, *Print, Folklore and Nationalism in Colonial South India* (Ranikhet: Permanent Black, 2003).

Chakrabarty, Dipesh, *Provincializing Europe: Postcolonial Thought and Historical Difference* (Princeton: Princeton University Press, 2000).

Chakravorty, Swapan, and Abhijit Gupta, eds, *Founts of Knowledge* (Delhi: Orient Longman, 2015).

———, *Moveable Type: Book History in India* (Delhi: Permanent Black, 2011).

———, *Print Areas: Book History in India* (Delhi: Permanent Black, 2004).

Chatterjee, Rimi B., *Empires of the Mind: A History of the Oxford University Press in India Under the Raj* (New Delhi: Oxford University Press, 2006).

Chattopadhyay, Bankimchndra, *Bankim Rachanabali*, vol. II, ed. Jogeshchandra Bagal (Calcutta: Sahitya Samsad, 2010).

Dalmia, Vasudha, *Fiction as History: The Novel and the City in Modern North India* (Ranikhet: Permanent Black, 2017).

———, "Merchant Tales and the Emergence of the Novel in Hindi", *Economic and Political Weekly*, 23 August 2008.

Gallagher, Catherine, *Nobody's Story: The Vanishing Acts of Women Writers in the Marketplace, 1670–1920* (Berkeley: University of California Press, 1994).

Ghosh, Anindita, *Power in Print: Popular Publishing and the Politics of Language and Culture in a Colonial Society, 1778–1905* (New Delhi: Oxford University Press, 2006).

Joshi, Priya, *In Another Country: Colonialism, Culture, and the English Novel in India* (New York: Columbia University Press, 2002).

Kaviraj, Sudipta, *The Invention of Private Life: Literature and Ideas* (Ranikhet: Permanent Black, 2015).

———, *The Unhappy Consciousness: Bankimchandra Chattopadhyay and the Formation of Nationalist Discourse in India* (New Delhi: Oxford University Press, 1995).

Kumar, Udaya, *Writing the First Person: Literature, History, and Autobiography in Modern Kerala* (Ranikhet: Permanent Black, 2016).

Mukherjee, Meenakshi, *Realism and Reality: The Novel and Society in India* (New York: Oxford University Press, 1994, rpnt).

McKeon, Michael, *The Origins of the English Novel: 1600–1740* (Baltimore: Johns Hopkins University Press, 1987).

Orsini, Francesca, *The Hindi Public Sphere, 1920–1940: Language and Literature in the Age of Nationalism* (New Delhi: Oxford University Press, 2002).

———, *The History of the Book in South Asia* (New York: Routledge, 2016).

———, *Print and Pleasure: Popular Literature and Entertaining Fictions in Colonial North India* (Ranikhet: Permanent Black, 2009).

Pinto, Rochelle, *Between Empires: Print and Politics in Goa* (New Delhi: Oxford University Press, 2007).

Stark, Ulrike, *An Empire of Books: The Naval Kishore Press and the Diffusion of the Printed Word in Colonial India* (Ranikhet: Permanent Black, 2007).

Venkatachalapathy, A.R., *The Province of the Book: Scholars, Scribes, and Scribblers in Colonial Tamilnadu* (Ranikhet: Permanent Black, 2015).

2

The Formal Unconscious

Ethnography, Seriality, and the Early Novel in Bengal

BAIDIK BHATTACHARYA

HOW DOES THE NOVEL travel across the boundaries of Europe?[1] How does it flourish in different cultural environments and still retain its distinctive features, making it possible to imagine the novel as a world literary phenomenon? Or, to look at it from the other end, what are the narrative signs or formal qualities that allow us to identify novels in non-European languages, and what historiographical resources can one mobilise to write adequate histories of the novel outside Europe? Can there be a world history of the novel that takes into account both its features across locations while also paying close attention to its reconfiguration of literary traditions away from European shores? Fredric Jameson answers some of these questions, with reference to modern Japanese novels, through a

[1] An earlier version of this essay was published in *South Asian Review*, 32:1 (2011). All translations from Bengali sources, unless otherwise noted, are mine.

framework of unhappy union or "compromise" between the "raw material of Japanese social experience and the abstract formal patterns of Western novel construction." The encounter between the "imported technology" of "the Western form of the novel" and the "content or social experience of the non-Western importing country," he suggests, will always lead to "systematic modification, or *Unfunktionierung* of the former in the context of the latter."[2] Since this phenomenon is not restricted to Japan and can be found in vastly different cultural contexts like India, Jameson insists, it needs to be taken as a general rule for the emergence of the novel in "alternate modernities".

In an influential essay, "Conjectures on World Literature", Franco Moretti turns Jameson's insight into a "law of literary evolution" and argues that since this is generally the case in almost every culture except England and France, it should be taken as the elementary rule of the novel's rise as a world literary form. He suggests English and French novels are in the minority here, and are therefore exceptions: "if the compromise between the foreign [form] and the local [content] is so ubiquitous, then those independent paths that are usually taken to be the rule of the rise of the novel (the Spanish, the French, and especially the British case) – *well, they're not the rule at all, they're the exception.*"[3] Alongside this bold and innovative claim about the rise of the novel, Moretti introduces a caveat. He tells us that Jameson's model is incomplete; to make it historically more accurate one needs to add the crucial element of "local narrative voice" to Jameson's binary of foreign form and local content. This third component grows in importance once we realise that only by it

[2] Jameson, "In the Mirror of Alternate Modernities", xiii.

[3] Moretti, "Conjectures on World Literature", 58, 61; emphasis original.

does the vital transaction between the first two take place – it is the narrator who negotiates this fateful "compromise" by providing copious comments, explanations, and evaluations.[4] Thus for Moretti the novel, beyond its core European territory, shows intense negotiations between foreign debt and local patrimony under the watchful eye of a local legislator who understands the nuances of both.

In Jameson as well as Moretti, however, the identity of the foreign form remains largely unexamined. In both, the assumption is that by the time the novel travelled out of Europe – Moretti gives a precise date, 1750 and after – it not only had a stable identity that could have been recognised in foreign locations, even its portability was largely aided by the irreversible completion of its formal history by then. This is a surprising claim on various counts. What trumps every other concern, however, is the way this argument militates against the long traditions of novel theory that have meticulously documented the European novel's formal uncertainty as an indispensable part both of its history as well as identity. Bakhtin is the most powerful chronicler of this fluidity as he takes the novel's generic question beyond its "formalistic" properties and calls for interpreting it "as a zone and a field of valorized perception, as a mode for representing the world."[5] Even in most other schools of novel theory – from Lukács to McKeon – the novel is characterised chiefly by its ability to formulate and appropriate instability, change, and displacement.[6]

[4] Ibid., 65.

[5] Bakhtin, *The Dialogic Imagination*, 28, and ch. 1 *passim.*

[6] See, for instance, Lukács, *The Theory of the Novel*, and McKeon, *The Origins of the English Novel.* For an overview on various theories of the novel that prioritise its historical instability, see the essays collected in McKeon, ed., *Theory of the Novel.*

Jameson and Moretti, in contrast, assume that this problem is settled the moment the novel is taken out of its point of origin and placed in a distant and dissimilar locale, or the moment a language other than English and French encounters the "abstract formal patterns" of novel writing. The task of the literary historian, they argue, is simply to narrate the compromises and concessions made in the non-European location, and investigate how the narrative voice shifts and adjusts the two in order to facilitate the novel's ambition of going native. Moretti in fact identifies the narrative voice as the "most unstable" element of the three and carefully avoids facing the inevitable conclusion of his own theory – that is, if the core European history is the exception and the rest of the world is the norm, and if this new theory is to be understood territorially and not through the temporal frame of origin and derivation, then it is logical to assume that the formal identity of the novel was settled elsewhere and with reference to non-European histories. It stands to reason, in other words, to use the world eminence of the form as a theoretical point of departure to rethink its formal stability.

Quite evidently, this cannot be done using just one archive or by one researcher. Therefore, I explore here one aspect of this formal resolution by looking closely at the conjunction between the new literary prose's simultaneous commitment to novelistic narration and ethnographic realism within one non-European context – colonial Bengal – to show how this encounter between different conventions of writing led to the consolidation of the novel in this particular case. My archive of nineteenth-century Bengal is particularly important not only because it developed one of the earliest and most robust traditions of novel writing outside Europe, but also because Bengali novels had a decisive influence on fictional practice in other Indian languages. For these reasons I argue the importance of examining how, in a number of ways, early novels in Bengal signalled this dual allegiance to the novelistic and the ethnographic: Pyarichand Mitra's *Alaler gharer dulal* (1858), often considered the first novel of note in Bengali, introduced itself in an English Preface as "illustrative of the condition of Hindu society, manners, customs, &c. and partly of the state of things in the Moffussil. The work has been written in a simple style, and to foreigners desirous of acquiring an idiomatic knowledge of the Bengali language and an acquaintance with Hindu domestic life, it will perhaps be found useful."[7] This was partly because Mitra was building on a tradition of social satire introduced by Bhabanicharan Bandyopadhyay in his "Babur upakhyan" (1821), *Kalikata kamalalay* (1823), *Nabababubilas* (1825), and *Nababibibilas* (1831) – a genre of satire that, while mocking modern educated Bengali men and women, employed a vivid sense of ethnographic realism to make its case.[8] However, Mitra's was not an isolated instance, for the attractions of this paradigm of a dual loyalty to two different modes of writing could be seen as late as 1884, when Bankimchandra Chattopadhyay's fourth Bengali novel, *Bishbriksha* (1872–3), was translated by Miriam S. Knight as *The Poison Tree: A Tale of Hindu Life in Bengal*.[9] I explore this particular conjunction of two styles of representation – the novelistic and the ethnographic – their

[7] Thakur (Pyarichand Mitra), "Preface", in *Alaler gharer dulal*, xiv.

[8] For a discussion on the profligate and foppish babu character in early Bengali prose, see Herder, "The Modern Babu and the Metropolis", 358–401.

[9] The ethnographic point was further accentuated in the Preface by Edwin Arnold, the poet and author of *The Light of Asia*, with his praise for the novel's "faithful picture of Indian life", detailing the "native life and manners [. . .] with the religious, domestic and social customs of Bengali houses." Arnold, "Preface", in Bankim Chandra Chatterjee, *The Poison Tree*, v–vi.

genealogies, and their subsequent configurations in early novels with reference to Bankim and his novel *Bishbriksha*.[10] I also situate this history of the early Bengali novel within the larger context of colonial modernity, including its investment in cultural and social reform, as well as in relation to the development of new areas of learning such as philology and ethnology. In Bankim's case, many of these concerns merged within his voluminous comments on contemporary Bengali culture's reliance on a hybrid literary prose, and its expression in the public sphere of print. It is the development of this new literary prose during the colonial era that Bankim saw as chiefly responsible for the emergence of new forms like the novel, and for a more general rejuvenation of Bengali culture.

The Prose of Modernity

It is a truism in Bengali literary criticism that the novel was intimately tied to the appearance of modern literary prose somewhere in the final decades of the eighteenth century, and through its development during the first few decades of the nineteenth. Furthermore, literary prose in Bengal was mostly

[10] The case of *Bishbriksha* is particularly important for my argument. As Tagore suggested in 1931, the publication of Bankim's fourth novel was widely seen as a radical event in Bengali literature. While his earlier prose narratives, such as *Durgeshnandini*, *Kapalkundala*, and *Mrinalini*, were "romances", *Bishbriksha* offered a new narrative form that Tagore defined as "*akhyan*" (lit., "narrative/story"; but the implied sense is of the novel), that was part of one's lived world and yet which translated the everydayness into innovative and pleasurable aesthetic experience. It was also a break from popular print entertainment such as *Golebakawali* and similar fantastic tales. See Bagal, "On Novels", 32–3.

seen as a break in history, a sign of the language's modernity itself. The classic account came from the linguist Suniti Kumar Chatterji's magisterial *The Origin and Development of the Bengali Language* (1923):

> Modern or New Bengali: from 1800. Prose is written for the first time seriously, but for fifty years the literary language is under the tyranny of Sanskrit. Out of the large number of forms, dialectal and archaic, which prevailed in Middle Bengali, specially in the verb, documentary and epistolary Bengali of the three centuries 1500–1800 was evolving a standard language for prose in which only a few recognised forms were used; and this documentary and epistolary Bengali, based as it was on the speech of the 15th century, or it may be of the 14th, was adopted as the language of ordinary prose composition, when the advent of Western learning brought in a sudden demand for a prose style.[11]

Chatterji also pointed out the "stilted" nature of this new language: "Literary Bengali of prose, during the greater part of the 19th century, was thus a doubly artificial language; and, with its forms belonging to Middle Bengali, and its vocabulary highly Sanskritised, it could only be compared to a 'Modern English' with a Chaucerian grammar and a super-Johnsonian vocabulary, if such a thing could be conceived."[12] In subsequent accounts, this central scheme of an artificial literary prose emerging at the turn of the century was repeated with minor variations. Thus, in an influential account from 1934, the literary historian Sukumar Sen cited a range of prose narratives between the sixteenth and the eighteenth centuries, including tracts by Portuguese

[11] Chatterji, *The Origin and Development of the Bengali Language*, vol. 1, 134.

[12] Ibid.

missionaries as well as mystic sects of Gaudiya Vaishnavism, but concurred with Chatterji that the new Bengali literary prose was fashioned in the early decades of the nineteenth century, especially as a consequence of colonial rule. He largely subscribed to the argument about the "stilted" nature of the new prose, identifying William Carey, Mrityunjay Vidyalankar, and Rammohun Roy as heralding this new phase.[13] In conclusion, Sen argued that the earlier, and livelier, traditions of prose writing were lost because missionaries like Carey or Company pandits like Mrityunjay were either ignorant of such traditions or had little interest in reviving prose styles that grew out of local practices and religious sects.[14] This became the standard narrative in literary history, and a range of commentators, including Sajanikanta Das, Asitkumar Bandyopadhay, and Ghulam Murshid worked on it in later decades, deploying a somewhat similar archive.[15]

In literary-historical terms, colonialism thus played a dual role – while the new political dispensation made possible the new prose through a mixed bag of "Western learning" and print technologies, it also made evident an essentially artificial "literary" language that had little in common with Bengali as ordinarily used in daily life. This was not an isolated development; it could be traced back to works on philology and ethnology by colonial officials in the eighteenth and the early-nineteenth centuries. Such works collectively constitute the colonial discovery of

[13] This genesis was tracked by Sen through Carey's *Dialogues, intended to facilitate the acquiring of the Bengali Language* (1801) and *Itihasmala* (1812); Mrityunjay's *Hitopodesh* (1802), *Batrish Singhasan* (1802), *Rajabali* (1808), and *Prabodh-chandrika* (1833), and Rammohun's *Vedanta grantha* (1815).

[14] Sen, *Bangala sahitye gadya*, 19–39.

[15] See Das, *Bangla gadyasahityer itihas*; Bandyopadhyay, *Unabingsha shatabdir prathamardha o bangla*; Murshid, *Kalantare bangla gadya*.

linguistic diversity in the subcontinent – especially its unearthing of Sanskrit texts – and the new phase of information gathering known as Orientalist knowledge on India.[16] For my purpose here, the central development in comparative philology was the way language, territory, and race were closely linked with each other, and the way India became a representative case in point of such a link. As Thomas Trautmann has suggested, philology's reliance on ethnology, or rather their entwined emergence in the early-nineteenth century, had a major impact on notions of race, language, and territory.[17] India's linguistic profusion provided fertile and legitimate grounds for some of the early experimental works in this conjoined field. It is evident from Bankim's own essays, especially from his rather speculative reflections on the origins of the Bengalis as a race/nation, that this conjunction could also be used as an effective way of getting around established historical narratives, especially in explaining the plight of colonial nations. Bankim repeatedly stressed the point that when proper historical evidence (both archaeological and textual) are difficult to come by, it is legitimate to turn to language as an effective archive since languages carry the historical traces of the races that spoke them.[18] Colonial modernity, in this sense, provided Bankim a new knowledge paradigm of philology-ethnology, on which he relied heavily to retrieve an alternative sequencing of history. As we shall see, he also extended this project into his novels in order to chart out a very different narrative of colonialism.

[16] See Mufti, "Orientalism and the Institution of World Literature"; Bhattacharya, "On Comparatism in the Colony".

[17] Trautmann, *Aryans and British India*, 131–64.

[18] Chattopadhyay, *Bankim Rachanabali*, vol. II, 297–8. Henceforth, Bankim's works are cited parenthetically with volume and page numbers.

Bankim's project becomes clearer as we realise how instrumental he was in the formulation of a rather hybrid Bengali prose – later shown to be so by scholars like Chatterji, Sen, etc. – which came to be recognised as an unmistakable mark of colonial modernity, as also a preparatory ground for modern Bengali literature. In his essay "Bangala bhasha" (1878), published in his journal *Bangadarshan*, Bankim argued that though a distinction was made almost everywhere between the written and colloquial forms of languages, in Bengal this distinction was specially stark. "To tell you the truth," he continued,

> until recently two different languages were in circulation in Bengal. One was called *sadhu bhasha* [polished tongue], and the other *apar bhasha* [other tongue]. The first was the written language, the second was primarily the spoken. Books were written almost exclusively in the first. In *sadhu bhasha* obsolete Sanskrit words were frequently conjoined with archaic forms of Bengali verbs. All that was not pure Sanskrit could find no entry into *sadhu bhasha*. Whether comprehensible or not, pure Sanskrit reigned. *Apar bhasha*, on the other hand, discarded this path altogether and embraced whatever was intelligible to all. (II, 317)[19]

[19] It seems this was the prevalent argument during Bankim's time. Take, for instance, another article of the same title by Haraprasad Shastri, again published in *Bangadarshan* (1881), which lamented the predominance of an artificial Bengali prose under the influence of three different languages – Persian, Sanskrit, and English. Shastri squarely blamed the company pandits for the heavily Sanskritised language: "It is our misfortune that those great Englishmen who took up the task of teaching Bangla to Bengalis happened to know pundits only from Sanskrit College, at that time an ostracised institution in Bengal. [. . .] These were the people appointed to write books in Bengali. And they, true to their pedantic vanity, took up the pen without sparing a thought for the seriousness of the task." Translated and quoted in Chakravorty, "Purity and Print", 200.

However, by such remarks Bankim was not advocating a random or wholesale rejection of such prose; he was careful to note that, despite their limitations, both versions expanded the scope of literary Bengali, stretched its limits, and exposed a certain flattening in its character to encompass more and more expressive resources. I shall return to this point about the flattening of a language and its history later, but want to note here that this complex response to prose was a precursor to Bankim's view of the novel. He imagined the novel – written in both *sadhu* and *apar* versions – to perform a similar stretching of the literary tradition of Bengal, marking its limits as well as possibilities.

Bankim was not alone in this. Finding strong support in the new colonial yoking of philology and ethnology, he arrived at an idea of a new hybrid prose as an expression of hybrid colonial modernity. In Halhed's *A Grammar of the Bengal Language* (1778), one of the earliest analyses of Bengali, this lack of stability of a pure Bengali language had been traced to the pre-colonial period. "Exclusive of the Shanscrit," Halhed claimed, "there are three different dialects applied (tho' not with equal currency) in the kingdom of Bengal: Viz. the Persian, the Hindostanic and the proper Bengalese." While the first two had distinct identities of their own, he said, Bengali was "intimately related to Shanscrit both in expressions, construction and character."[20] Halhed conceded the fact that the "grammatical part [of Bengali] is simple, tho' diffuse, and compleat without being complex," but cautioned his prospective readers about the "impossibility of learning the Bengal dialect without a general and comprehensive idea of the Shanscrit."[21] More than a century later, in the encyclopaedic *Linguistic Survey of India* (vol. 5, pt 1, 1903), Grierson repeated the point with a vigour reminiscent

[20] Halhed, *A Grammar of the Bengal Language*, viii, xiv.

[21] Ibid., xviii, xx.

of Bankim: "Literary Bengali, as now known, is the product of the present century. Its direct cultivators were Calcutta Pandits, who, however well-meaning, have ruined the language by their learning."[22] In order to support his claim about the destructive influence of the "Calcutta Pandits", Grierson quoted from the census commissioner J.A. Baines' *General Report on the Census of India for 1891*:

> . . . [*sadhu bhasha*] is the product of what may be called the revival of learning in Eastern India, consequent upon the settlement of the British on the Hooghly. The vernacular was then found rude and meagre, owing to the absence of scholarship and the general neglect of the country during the Moghal rule. Instead of strengthening the existing web from the same material, every effort was made in Calcutta, then the only seat of instruction, to embroider upon the feeble old frame a grotesque and elaborate pattern in Sanskrit, and to pilfer from that tongue whatever in the way of vocabulary and construction, the learned considered necessary to satisfy the increasing demands of modern intercourse. [. . .] The simile used by Mr. Beames is a good one. He likens Bengali to an overgrown child tied to its mother's apron-string, and always looking to her for help, when it ought to be supporting itself.[23]

To bolster this claim, Grierson cited an essay of 1877 in the *Calcutta Review*, entitled "Bengali, spoken and written" by Babu Shyamacharan Ganguli, who had more or less endorsed the point made by Baines.[24] In Grierson's view, the result of this reliance on the "Pandit-ridden language of the present century"

[22] Grierson, *Linguistic Survey of India*, 5:1, 14.

[23] Ibid. The reference in the final sentence is to Beames, *A Comparative Grammar of the Modern Aryan Languages of India*, 3 vols; see also Beames, *Grammar of the Bengali Language, Literary and Colloquial.*

[24] Grierson, *Linguistic Survey of India*, 5:1, 16.

was that literary Bengali lost touch with its precolonial "nervous" expressions and entered a phase where "all competent European scholars are agreed that no work of first class originality has much chance of arising in Bengal." Even an "excellent writer" like Bankim, Grierson lamented, "sometimes laboured under the fetters imposed upon him by a strange vocabulary."[25]

Despite this rather bleak prognosis, the Bengali publishing industry flourished well in the nineteenth century. In 1854, for instance, it was estimated that 571,670 Bengali books were printed in Calcutta alone and that nearly ten million such books were printed in the previous ten years or so.[26] By the time Bankim formulated his two-language theory in 1878, it is safe to assume that the urban public sphere was inundated by both varieties of prose writings.

Bankim responded to this proliferation of print in a number of ways. In an English address entitled "A popular literature for Bengal", delivered before the Bengal Social Science Association on 28 February 1870, he acknowledged that even a cursory look at the "quarterly returns published by Government" would convince anybody that the "Bengali mind is anything but unproductive," but "its productions are remarkable for quantity alone; the quality is on an average contemptible – often they are positively injurious" (III, 100). The reasons for this generally pitiable state of affairs were not far to seek and ranged from the typical apathy of educated Bengalis to compose books in their native tongue to the absence of any reliable or "intelligent" standards of criticism. A genuinely popular literature for Bengal, Bankim stressed throughout the

[25] Ibid., 17.

[26] Long, *Returns Relating to Publications in the Bengali Language in 1857*, vol. 23, xi.

speech, could only be written in Bengali, and the present public discourse on literature, as evident from contemporary print cultures, did not offer an encouraging picture (III, 100–1). This was, however, not isolated anguish. Bankim sought to place this public sphere of print and shared cultural taste within a schematic reading of history, attempting to explain its shortcomings and weaknesses as historically determined. As I have suggested above, the most remarkable aspect of this scheme of things was Bankim's almost uncritical reliance on the Orientalist narratives of his time, and his belief in the colonial ethnographies that recounted a tale of Aryanism across South Asia on the evidence of the supposed unity of linguistic groups and the insights offered by the discipline of comparative philology. It is important to recognise this interest in ethnology and philology, for it had a profound impact on history, not only in India but also in Europe and elsewhere. Bankim subscribed to this seamless mixing of philology and ethnology and found in it the groundwork for a literary history of Bengal.

This conjunction of philology and ethnology *vis-à-vis* literary history was the mainstay of Bankim's essay "Bidyapati o Jaydeva" (1876). At its outset, he stated his central notion of literary history: "Everything is determined by laws, including literature. Under different conditions or laws of the air and the earth, the same water may assume different forms, such as vapour, raindrops, dew, snow and ice, or cloud. Similarly, literature takes different shapes on account of the differences among regions, or differences among the conditions internal to a region, and myriad other similar laws" (II, 167).[27] Such laws were not, however, easy to arrive at,

[27] Bankim of course used the Sanskrit-derived "*sahitya*" which does not exactly correspond to "literature". The way he imagined the universality of *sahitya*, however, made it seem very close to a worldwide reality of literature,

and despite cognate models for science in the works of authors like Comte, Bankim argued, no one had had any real success enunciating the laws that had determined literature. After these preliminary and somewhat cautionary notes, he proceeded to establish a few broad features of "*bharatbarshiya sahitya*", or Indian literature. In his estimation, the Ramayana revealed an early stage of the Aryan conquest of non-Aryan people in the subcontinent; the Mahabharata documented how the post-conquest society was settled among the Aryans; the texts of the *darshan* and *bhakti* traditions evinced the peace and success in the following period; the plays of Kalidasa suggested the opulence and stability of his times. And then he turned to Bengal:

> At last the Indians settled in a region where they lost their natural spirit because of the climate of that place. The place was unbearably hot, its climate was filled with vapour, the soil was shallow but fertile, and its product was useless and dispiriting rice. Here the Aryan race lost its spirit, and gradually became soft, idle, and enamoured by domestic pleasure. Everyone will understand that we are here describing Bengal. A peculiar lyricism was born that was in perfect consonance with this non-ambitious, leisurely, pleasure-seeking, and domestic culture. This lyricism was likewise non-ambitious, leisurely, pleasure-seeking, and domestic in nature. This lyric poetry was extremely pliable, very harmonious, and was the ultimate embodiment of conjugality. This form of poetry imitated the racial characteristics, and by suppressing other forms became the national literature of Bengal for seven or eight hundred years. (II, 168)

Bankim had little difficulty imagining either a unified space called India or a close correlation between racial attributes

---

showing how many of these other ideas were being subsumed under the new identity of literature during the long nineteenth century.

and cultural production. Both these formulations, Trautmann demonstrates, were developed by early Company officials and Orientalists like H.T. Colebrooke and Alexander Hamilton. In the first instance, these officials appropriated an idea from their Brahmin teachers, namely the "*Vyakarana* doctrine of the unity of all languages as corruptions of the eternal and incorruptible Sanskrit language."[28] While accepting its larger contours, these colonial scholars then restricted it to India, arguing that only Indian languages derived from Sanskrit. It has in fact been possible to argue that this colonial philological moment found important elaboration in influential texts like Friedrich Schlegel's *Über die Sprache und Weisheit der Indier* (1808) and constituted "a mode of producing the *canon* of 'Indian literature,' that is, a conception of *the unique tradition* of the vast and complex society of the sub-continent, and grounded it in the notion of the Indo-European family of languages."[29] Bankim appropriated this argument since the idea of Sanskrit as the fount of linguistic unity suggested the geographical unity of India, and also provided the grounds for establishing a continuous literary history of India. During the course of the nineteenth century, this theory of a linguistic unity that mirrored its geographical counterpart faced serious challenges, especially after the publication of Bishop Robert Caldwell's *Comparative Grammar of the Dravidian or South-Indian Family of Languages* (1856), a work that firmly established the separate identity of the Dravidian family of languages in southern India. Bankim cited this other tradition elsewhere, but stuck to the earlier ideas of Company Orientalism to argue his case about Bengal.

[28] Trautmann, *Aryans and British India*, 136.

[29] Mufti, *Forget English!*, 107–8; emphasis original.

In a related argument, Bankim borrowed heavily from contemporary ethnological ideas that linked linguistic peculiarity with racial specificity while making the latter subservient to the former.[30] Additionally, the idea of racial emasculation and its cultural expression was tied to Bankim's thinking about colonialism and the possibility of anticolonial resistance. Partha Chatterjee has shown how Bankim's political project was predicated on a crucial link between "culture" and "power", and that this "moment of departure" in the history of Indian nationalism was the first step of anticolonial nationalism as a "derivative discourse". The central problem of such a project, Chatterjee argues, was to conceptualise a culture seen as responsible for political failure and as being in need of transformation, and which yet had to be situated within a framework of continuity through which the depleted culture would transform itself into a new yet recognisable domain of power. Chatterjee's reading shows Bankim overcoming this question of physical emasculation via his formulation of a social power that was needed to rejuvenate the cultural domain.[31]

The analogous transformation of literary history, however, could not be as programmatic, and was therefore less certain. In his 1870 address, for instance, Bankim picked up the twelfth-century poet Jaydeva's *Gitagovinda* as a typical example of the

[30] This overlapping of philology and ethnology was suggested by James Cowles Prichard in his influential study *Natural History of Man* (1843). "Prichardian ethnology," Trautmann observes, "was essentially a classification of peoples based upon the classification of languages by the methods of comparative philology. [. . .] In this conception language and physique tell the same story, but language comparison was believed to be the superior method by which to uncover the story, and the study of bodily features and structures was distinctly subsidiary." *Aryans and British India*, 133.

[31] Chatterjee, *Nationalist Thought and the Colonial World*, 57–65.

"Bengali character" and suggested that "it does not contain a single expression of manly feeling – of *womanly* feeling there is a great deal – or a single elevated sentiment" (III, 98; emphasis original). For Bankim this lack of masculinity was also a historical marker in need of proper contextualisation: "I do not deny him [i.e. Jaydeva] high poetical merits in a certain sense, exquisite imagery, tender feeling and unrivalled power of expression, but that does not make him less the poet of an effeminate and sensual race. Soft and mellifluous, feelingly tender and as often grossly sensual, his exquisitely sounding but not unfrequently meaningless verse echoed the common sentiments of an inactive and effeminate race" (III, 98). It is difficult to overlook Bankim's eagerness to read an ethnological structure as underpinning the cultural production of Bengal, and shaping its literary history in decisive ways. This ethnological principle served as a causal connection between a depleted and emasculated race on the one hand, and its political subjugation on the other, while also indicating continuity between racial characteristics and the prospect of future redemption.

It was here, through this ethnological moment, that Bankim sought to make an intervention in the public literary sphere. In his view, the "contemptible" or even "positively injurious" literary culture was the direct product of the emasculated race he traced through Jaydeva. In one of his most sustained interrogations of contemporary literary production – written as an introductory piece to a collection of the poet Ishwarchandra Gupta – he made a curious distinction between two sets of writers: while Ishwarchandra was a "*bangali kobi*" (Bengali poet), his own contemporaries such as Michael Madhusudan, Hemchandra, Nabinchandra, and Rabindranath were "*shikkhito bangalir kobi*" (poets for educated Bengalis). This was not a rhetorical distinction for Bankim – it suggested to him a fundamental, almost schizophrenic, division at the heart of colonial modernity, and that its proliferation through print was a sure sign of its power to shape the public domain. In his eagerness to establish Ishwarchandra as the quintessential Bengali poet, he distinguished two of his characteristic virtues – his "*khanti*" or authentic Bengali sensibility and his ability to express himself in a language recognised by every Bengali ("*bangalir praner bhasha*"). The first claim was a complex one and Bankim took some pains to explain the charge of *ashlilata* (obscenity) against Ishwarchandra. He maintained that it was the purity of the Bengali sensibility, untutored by either Sanskrit learning or English education, that seemed obscene in the new era, and if one discarded the genuinely bawdy in Ishwarchandra's poetry, what remained were simply the values of an earlier era. Bankim's obsession with the issue of obscenity requires a longer discussion (for which I lack space), but I will highlight how this argument about sensibility was supported by a second claim about Ishwarchandra's language. While describing his poetry, Bankim suggested that the "language he used for his poetry, authentic and heartfelt Bengali, was not used by anyone else for either poetry or prose. It does not show any corruption of either Sanskrit or English tutelage. It doesn't boast of its learning or purity. The language doesn't bend, or falter, or waddle – it reaches the reader's heart straightaway" (II, 785). What he sought to endorse in the poet's content, i.e. a pure and authentic Bengali sensibility, was reinforced through his language. Ishwarchandra was thus the purveyor of Bengali authenticity, and this distinguished him from his contemporaries.

It would be erroneous, however, to think of Ishwarchandra as Bankim's model. Indeed he said Ishwarchandra's brand of purity was not in tune with the contemporary era, and there was therefore no need for another Ishwarchandra. At the same time, this admiring piece on the poet tells us something very fundamental about Bankim's approach to literature, literary history, and even the novel. At the core of this approach resides the belief that the idea of authenticity had to be established in the language itself: though Ishwarchandra's language was anachronistic, it at least showed the possibility of carrying authentic cultural values in one's language. In an important sense, this was part of the ethnological argument Bankim championed, since language, along with race, provided a sense of community that was verifiable and popular at the same time. If there was a new Bengali language, according to this belief, it probably indicated a new beginning in racial history as well. As against many of his contemporaries, Bankim did not advocate a return to an earlier era with its purer sensibility and language; though he often cautioned against the widespread obscenity of public print culture, he maintained that this newness was an opportunity to renew racial energies buried for millennia. The philological investigations of his time assured Bankim of this essential twining of language and race, of linguistic innovation and racial regeneration.

Novelisation and Horizontal Time

Bankim's complex gloss on authentic Bengali sensibility, thus, was built on a central contradiction. Following his acceptance of an ethnological principle, he had to argue that this notion of purity, traceable from Jaydeva to Ishwarchandra, was an essential part of racial emasculation, and yet, to conjure a future for Bengali literature he had to resurrect the same purity in order to regenerate authenticity. This explains his frequent reiteration of the fact that there was little chance of encountering another pure Bengali poet like Ishwarchandra, and that Bengali literature was consequently better off. Instead, he argued, authenticity and purity lay somewhere else, away from the monotonous continuity of literary history.

The coevalness of the new prose and the new form, the novel, offered Bankim the grounds to resolve this contradiction. In his note on Pyarichand Mitra and his popular prose satire *Alaler gharer dulal, or The Spoilt Child* (1857), Bankim described the text as the first novel in Bengali and singled out its prose for special praise. *Alaler gharer dulal*, he says, established for the first time that the "Bengali that is commonly spoken and used could be the vehicle for serious writing, that such writing could be beautiful, and that such writing could easily reach everyone which the heavily Sanskritised language failed to do" (II, 863). In another essay written in English with the title "Bengali Literature" (1871), he observed:

> It was reserved to Tekchand Thakur [Mitra's pseudonym] to deal the first blow to this insufferable pedantry [of Sanskritised prose], and all honour to the man who did it. Endowed as he was with strong common sense as well as high culture, he saw no reason why this idol of unmixed diction should receive worship at his hands, and he set about writing *Alaler Gharer Dulal* in a spirit at which the Sanskritists stood aghast and shook their heads. Going to the opposite extreme in point of style, he vigorously excluded from his works, except on very rare occasions, every word and phrase that had a learned appearance. His own works suffered from the exclusion, but the movement was well-timed. In matter he scattered to the winds the time-honoured commonplaces, and drew upon nature and life for his materials. (III, 108)

Bankim did not advocate a complete break between Sanskrit and modern Bengali, nor did he suggest that Mitra's language must be the model for everyone writing after him. But he insisted on the newness of the language because of its reliance on the contemporary, the "now-time" that combined writing and representation. The interesting point in Bankim's formulation was the rejection of a strictly historicist model of literary tradition within which earlier versions of Bengali prose did not eventually culminate in Mitra's writing; what was more, he did not posit a teleology wherein these earlier stages were steps that gradually prepared the existing literary culture or readership for the novelty of Mitra's text. Rather, he argued that it was the violent insertion of the contemporary within literary history that allowed the newness of the form to consolidate itself.

The point about the contemporary is crucial here. Bankim related Mitra's novel to a generalised schema of modernity in Bengali literature; modernity in this formulation was distinguished on two accounts – its singular relationship with time, and its distinction from the popular print culture of *battala*. The new narrative form was distinctly different because of its investment in something akin to what Walter Benjamin calls *Jetztzeit* or the "now-time" of history – in the coevalness of narration and representation where narration began not so much within history but in a self-reliant stasis that existed outside history.[32] This exteriority was noticeable especially when Bankim described Mitra's efforts as without precedent or model – in both formal structure and content – and as affecting fundamental changes in literary tradition from outside, from beyond its regulatory principles. Bankim's formulation had serious consequences not only for the novel as a new form but also for literary history more broadly. Such a structure, for instance, allowed the new form to signal its newness by disrupting the continuity of history. The

[32] Benjamin, "On the Concept of History", 3.

now-time in Benjamin's account, as well as in our case, did not use history as a determining sequence of events that would eventually shape the present as a logical outcome of its immanent principles. It did not even allow the signs of history to form a coherent and rational chain that would manifest its potential in the fulness of the present. The moment of narration as now-time was introduced within the space of the text as a structure that initiated new engagements with history and its sequencing of events, but did so by disallowing its inherent logic within the shaping of the text. My point is not that Bankim's formulation did not allow history within the space of the new genre, nor that he did not recognise the role historical order played in shaping the plot or the story, but rather that he envisaged the starting point of the narration as standing away from historical time to conceptualise its own *bildung*. He did recognise the newness of Mitra's novel on the grounds that it marked its own genealogy outside available literary history and the regulations that such a history would enforce. The site of production was thus not historicist as such, or at least that was how it was offered within the context of literary modernity, and the newness of the genre or even the modernisation of the tradition was a direct result of this exteriority.

The second implication of now-time follows from the first. The exteriority that initiated the novel and structured its discursive protocols also imagined its own temporality as a flattening of time, or what I would call *horizontal time*, and used it to stage the paradoxical novel–history relationship I have charted above – i.e. the novel appropriated the protocols of history but did not submit its own genealogy to history's monopolised authority over time. Thus, horizontal time was both related to history at its edge and separated from it because it did not reproduce historical sequencing within its own domain. This duality was used to think through the temporality of the genre of the novel itself, as it simultaneously gestured towards and retreated from historical time, as it repeatedly invoked its contemporaneity only to mark how that notion of the contemporary was different from available historical discourses. This point was made repeatedly by Mitra in his Preface. He described the text as an "original Novel in Bengali being the first work of its kind" and also as the first such account of the "condition of Hindu society, manners, customs, &c."[33] Bankim's own novels, such as *Bishbriksha* or *Indira* (not romances), engaged with modernity through a similar notion of horizontal time, and, as we shall see below, reformulated modernity within the textual space as a question of differentiated temporal frames that competed with each other for prominence by exploiting the organising codes of flattened temporality. These frames were in various degrees related to historical time, but their own structures often deviated from the expectations of such temporal sequencing and produced a complex narrative reorganisation of time. In other words, now-time was an initiation into the complex temporal structure of these texts and was the governing principle as it was progressively assimilated into a further restructuring of time, but its function as a guardian of modernity needed special attention.

As may be evident by now, it was on these very grounds that Bankim claimed a different sort of authenticity for Mitra. His gloss on Mitra's writing style marked both continuity and departure from the tradition of Ishwarchandra, and established him as the

[33] Thakur, "Preface", *Alaler gharer dulal*, n.p. Contemporary critics also made the same point; a review in *The Calcutta Review* noted: "We hail this book as the first novel in the Bengali language. Tek Chand Thakur has written a tale the like of which is not to be found within the entire range of Bengali literature." Quoted in Oswell, "Preface", viii.

first major author of the novel in Bengal. While Ishwarchandra's authenticity depended to a large extent on his ability to give voice to a precolonial Bengali sensibility, and hence was historicist in nature, Mitra represented the deeply schizophrenic colonial modernity that, at the same time, alluded to a notion of innate purity and yet framed it in new idioms. Bankim maintained that

> Pyarichand Mitra was not the creator of ideal Bengali prose, but he was the chief reason behind the gradual progress of Bengali prose. [. . .] His other major achievement was that he first demonstrated that the genuine material for good literature was available with us, and we didn't need to beg in front of English or Sanskrit. He first showed that both in life and literature, our own belongings are far more preferable than borrowed ones. He first made it clear that if we wish to develop Bengal through our literary initiatives then we have to build that literature with material culled from Bengal. Indeed, *Alaler gharer dulal* is the beginning of our national literature. (II, 789)

Evidently, this was a very different notion of authenticity, and derived not so much from the promise of history as from what he saw as the evidence of ethnology. If Jaydeva represented the low point of racial emasculation, and if popular print continued that legacy, Mitra's novel reversed the process by initiating a national literature that was both vigorous and authentic.

This is a key point. Bankim's praise of Mitra hinged on the fact that he was successful in capturing the now-time of history, and also on the fact that for this he devised a prose capable of representing authentic Bengali material, or "*gharer samagri*". But the way he linked Mitra's novel with horizontal time needs some explanation. He proposed that Mitra's language marked one limit of contemporary literary Bengali, while the other was marked by Tarashankar Tarkaratna's translation of Banabhatta's

Kadambari (1865) into Bengali – a rendering into heavily Sanskritised prose (II, 789). In one move, he secured a curious flattening of time – on the one hand he retained the new Sanskritised Bengali that I have traced, and on the other he placed Mitra's prose not only as a counter-example but as a further exploration of the limits of the same language. Alongside, he selected a text that has often been seen as the paradigmatic prose novel in Sanskrit; by citing *Kadambari* and *Alaler gharer dulal* together, he stretched the very idea of the novel in Bengal. The most striking feature of this dual citation is thus a simultaneous invocation of history and its flattening, a gesture towards a longer frame of time and its reorganisation across a horizontal plane of language. This is why he was able to make the following point:

> The greatest value and the primary need of writing is lucidity. What everyone understands and what makes sense immediately, if it is worthwhile, is the best form of writing. The beauty of language comes next – one needs to blend beauty with lucidity and simplicity of writing [. . .] First you must select the language suitable for your purpose. If you know that everyday conversational language can express your ideas with utmost clarity and beauty, why should you go for something [supposedly] better? If the language of Tekchand or Hutom is best suited to your purpose you must use it. If the purpose is best served by the Sanskritised language of Vidyasagar or Bhudebbabu, then you must abandon the commonplace language and embrace it. If your subject requires something different from these two, you must hunt for it; if the subject demands so, there is no objection – an objection is only raised where there is no such demand. The subject should be elaborated with greatest clarity – you must elaborate as much as possible – and for that reason you must draw on English, Persian, Arabic, Sanskrit, lowly rustic, almost everything except what is obscene. (II, 373)

My contention is that this flattening of literary history and emphasis on horizontal time saturated Bankim's ideas of both the new language and the new form of the novel. He made these two interdependent and suggested that the former was directly responsible for the latter.

The point needs elaboration. In Bankim's scheme of things, the novel was concurrently an extension and the other half of what Kaviraj identifies as the production of "imaginary history" in his historical romances. Romances like *Mrinalini*, or later ones like *Rajsingha* and *Anandamath*, offered a surrogate sequencing of positivist history and in a nationalistic climate they became the "repository of truth which might otherwise be lost."[34] Such imaginary accounts of the nation's history were prompted by a deep dissatisfaction with the present state of the nation, with its status of being a subjugated colony of the British empire, and Bankim joined a host of others to retrieve alternative genealogies of the present in order to imagine a different future for the nation. The status of the present in this project is ambiguous. It is consciously avoided in an attempt to link the past and the future of the nation; on the other hand, the present remained a stumbling block as it was the beginning of narration and was the only addressee of such narratives. Though the novel was part of the collective reimagining of the nation, it was designed to inhabit this ambiguous present in its course, to articulate the *here and now* of historical time. The contested historical present of alternative retelling here became the exclusive material, and the novel turned into a momentous vehicle for it. Imaginary history and the novel shared a common ground of narration as both were involved in what Lukács described as the "form-giving" act or the formulation

[34] Kaviraj, *The Unhappy Consciousness*, 115.

of a form that calibrated the given material into a meaningful whole, but the novel performed such a role through the crucial principle of democratisation.[35] Bankim used the new language of literary prose as a model for this principle of democratisation and firmly anchored the new form within the newness of the language itself. This is partly why his response to the new prose and its relationship with the public sphere of print was much more complex than those of his contemporaries. He saw the new prose as representing the very core of colonial modernity – and hence a rejuvenation of cultural forces – and imagined the novel as a natural extension of it.

While this new literary prose signified a distinct phase of colonial modernity, it also signalled, at least for Bankim, a further phase of the ethnological query. In his encounter with ethnological writings, both European and Indian, he found a way of bypassing the highly partisan and often racist opinions of Company historians like James Mill on Indian history. He found the claims to "scientific" rigour of ethnology and anthropology, over their investigations into "primitive" cultures or into the dark crevices of ancient civilisations, extremely appealing. This is evident from his repeated invocation of contemporary works in anthropology and ethnology. But the recourse to these new disciplines entailed two different dimensions that he had to negotiate in his writings – on the one hand, these anthropological insights, especially when conveyed through the ethnographic accounts of various colonial officials, embodied a unique sense of contemporaneity that resonated with his emphasis on the horizontal temporal frame; on the other, they pointed towards an inevitable plurality, especially for the racial composition of either Bengalis or Indians, that

[35] Lukács, *The Theory of the Novel,* 51, and *passim.*

did not support any idea of a united nationalist imagining but foregrounded a distinctive sense of democracy. In one of his most sustained ethnological tracts, "*Bangalir utpatti*" (the origins of the Bengali people), Bankim addressed this duality and made extensive use of his contemporary philological and ethnographic researches; he cited European authorities from Friedrich Schlegel to Friedrich Max Müller, and local officials like John Muir, Edward T. Dalton, W.W. Hunter, and even the Census Reports of 1871.[36] He repeated the familiar nineteenth-century argument that for lack of historical data about ancient civilisations one must rely on ethnology and philology, and presented a summary of the philological schema of the Indo-European languages representing the "Aryan" languages and cultures. Alongside this, however, the ethnological data on race, especially in the reports by colonial officials, presented a far more disturbing picture because ethnology essentially negated any possibility of a unified Bengali identity. In his essays Bankim raises this point repeatedly, and laments the fact that this diversity threatened not only the Bengali identity but even the dream of a larger Indian nationhood.

The Formal Conundrum

Bankim's early novels were designed to respond to these complex and fractured possibilities of the present – that is, while the present held the promise of a racial rejuvenation through exploitation of the essentially hybrid nature of its constitution, its fundamental

[36] The works Bankim cites: John Muir, *Original Sanskrit Texts on the Origin and History of the People of India, their Religion and Institutions*, 5 vols (1858–70); Edward T. Dalton, *Descriptive Ethnology of Bengal* (1872); W.W. Hunter, *Statistical Account of Bengal*, 20 vols (1875–9); Census Reports of 1871 (II, 297–312).

ethnological diversity undercut the very foundations of the promise. Mitra's *Alaler gharer dulal* showed a clear precedent, this text and Bankim's novels being part of the same ethnological logic that treated the novel form as an intervention in, as well as an extension of, the social world. Both Mitra and Bankim exploited the democratic principle that ethnology made available about the contemporary social, and both employed ethnographic realism to flesh out their respective texts.

With Bankim, however, we enter a much more complex world of the novelisation of ethnology and encounter its consequences at multiple levels of the text. Bound by the structural requirements of the novel he devised a complex structure of seriality and constructed his plots by manipulating sequences, both for characters within the novel and for the reader. I shall demonstrate that it is in fact this construction of seriality that remained his most explicit debt to ethnographical writing, and that this same seriality allowed him to incorporate a hybrid and democratic modernity within his novels.

A good point to start this investigation is *Bishbriksha*, translated as *The Poison Tree*. The plotline of *Bishbriksha* is deceptively simple. It is the story of a polygamous man, Nagendra, who takes a second wife, Kundanandini, in spite of his apparently happy married life with his first wife, Suryamukhi. In the context of nineteenth-century Bengal, this central theme had obvious resonances with ongoing reformist movements concerning polygamy and widow marriage. Indeed, the novel can be read as an exploration of the vilified target of such reformist movements, i.e. the upper-caste male Bengali babu of the nineteenth century, and understood as a direct intervention in these debates of the time. With these three central characters and episodes involving them, Bankim constructs the novel's central serialisation of events. At this level, the plotline is fairly simple and generally accessible. However, the central triad is also placed within another serialisation, leading to complex subplots with a second set of characters – Debendra, Heera, Kamalmani, Shrishchandra, and Taracharan – and providing some necessary depth to the story. This second seriality is discontinuous, and at several points the author makes some of its components or episodes inaccessible to its three central characters. As a result, while the reader is from the beginning made aware of Debendra's sinister plans against his cousin Nagendra, within the novel Nagendra, Kunda, and Suryamukhi remain unaware of such machinations. To make things even more complex, the story of *Bishbriksha* is told twice in the novel, once as a condensed dream of Kunda that surfaces strategically at different junctures, and then as the main body of the novel. In its first appearance in the third chapter, the dream sequence gives a programmatic but highly symbolic version of the serialisations of the plot. The novel, from this chapter on, works out the details of this dream vision, often explaining its meanings in the more accessible forms of relationships, customs, and motives that proliferate through its body, and these bring the narrative closer to the reality of nineteenth-century social life in Bengal.

In *Bishbriksha* Bankim writes a novel which seems self-aware: it seems almost to show awareness of the fact that this new kind of serialisation is likely to baffle its readers and takes care to explain its meaning by pointing out and commenting on what it sees as the irregularities of its own formal structure. It seems the novel assumes a normative structure for itself and is anxious that it often has to deviate from such norms in order to make its point and to manipulate the serialisation of its events. Take, for example, the two following cases in the early chapters, where the novel breaks into self-reflexive mode in order to explain its serialised structure. In the first instance, it compares itself to Kalidasa's *Meghdut* and describes the early chapters as somewhat "tasteless" and similar to some of the early poems of *Meghdut* which form a preparatory ground for the unfolding of the main events.[37] In the second instance, in a short chapter entitled "The Reader has Cause for Great Displeasure", the novel again explains some of the irregularities in its structure:

> At this point the reader will be much annoyed. It is a custom with novelists to conclude with a wedding, but we are about to begin with the marriage of Kunda Nandini. By another custom that has existed from ancient times, whoever shall marry the heroine must be extremely handsome, adorned with all virtues, himself a hero, and devoted to his mistress. Poor Tara Charan possessed no such advantages [. . .]. The reader is no doubt much displeased, but in fact the tale is only begun.[38]

In each case what the novel attempts is a gloss on both its own structure and motivation, but simultaneously invokes a sense of the ideal or normative novel as one with a neat serialisation. In Bengal, however, the tradition of writing such a novel was in its infancy in 1872–73, so it is safe to assume that the primary reference here is to the European novel. And yet the novel assumes even the normative novel as incapable of capturing the social world of the colony, as falling short of its reputed obligation to provide realistic representation.

Such irregularities, *Bishbriksha* suggests, are part of its structure – they signpost the novelty of the form but, more important, allow it to inhabit the space of the social as its supplement as well as critique. One can even read the novel as an extension of

[37] Chatterjee, *The Poison Tree*, 32.

[38] Ibid., 47, 50.

Bankim's critique of reformers of his day such as Ishwarchandra Vidyasagar – his preferred genres for such critiques were essays, pamphlets, and satires – and as such an additional step which allowed him to appropriate some of the tropes and protocols of nonfictional prose. In his exchange with Vidyasagar on polygamy amongst upper-caste Hindu men, and the possible ways of restraining such practices, Bankim made two related points: first, that polygamy as a custom had lost social sanction, so much so that even men who practised it would be hard put to defend it. Vidyasagar's attempt to prove that Hindu religious texts did not approve polygamy, he maintained, was doubly redundant not only because average Bengali men hardly followed scriptural texts in the conduct of their everyday lives but more so because the social delegitimacy of polygamy had happened without critical or scriptural interventions. His second point, that to pass legislation banning polygamy would be counterproductive, was crucially dependent on his emphasis on everyday social practice which he described as evolving outside colonial interventions and developing along its own laws and customs; and this was precisely the reason for his opposition to colonial laws as an agent of social reform (II, 314–19).

In *Bishbriksha*, Bankim reformulates this question once again by using the novel as a "realistic" documentation of the social with special emphasis on the everyday. The irregularities of the form allow him to perform this crucial function. The marriage of Kunda with Taracharan in the early chapters is a case in point. The irregularity is carefully placed and commented upon in the text; even Taracharan's brief appearance in the novel is described as an anomaly: "his [Taracharan's] beauty consisted in a copper-tinted complexion and a snub nose; his heroism found exercise only in the schoolroom; and as for his love, I cannot say how much he had for Kunda Nandini, but he had some for a pet monkey."[39] The nominal marriage ending in Taracharan's death is crucial for the plot since it places Kunda as a widow in Nagendra's household. This brief episode is even more important because it allows the narrative to join two different aspects of Bankim's critique – i.e. widow marriage and polygamy – when Nagendra takes the widowed Kunda as his second wife. The critique of colonial legislation and subsequent emphasis on the social domain as an autonomous expression of shared moral codes is made possible in the text through such irregular seriality.

Bankim's reliance on ethnographic seriality was meant to accommodate both heterogeneous social and hybrid language. He first encountered this possibility in Mitra's text; in his English essay on Mitra he quoted a passage from the latter's novel to make his point:

> Baburam Babu is sitting as a Babu should. A servant is rubbing his legs. On one side are seated some pundits jabbering about shastras, maintaining that pumpkins are prohibited on one particular day and brinjals on another, that to take salt with milk is in effect to eat beef, and otherwise raising a clatter like the *dhenki*. In another direction is a party of chess-players: one of them leans his head on his hand and is lost in thought; ruin impedes [*sic*] over him, for he is about to be checkmated. On another side some musicians are tuning their instruments. The *tanpura* is giving forth its purring sound. Elsewhere accountants are writing up their books. In front stand debtor ryots and creditor shopkeepers whose debts and claims are being enquired into, and admitted or denied. The *baithakkhana* is swarming with people. (III, 111–12)[40]

[39] Ibid., 47–8.

[40] The translation here – as of other translations of his work reproduced

In Bankim's opinion, passages like these gave "some notion of the author's vigorous and natural, if sometimes rather rough and homely, style" (III, 111). What such passages also demonstrate is the narrative's ability to occupy horizontal time through copious and serial descriptions of individuals and events, a sort of "thick description" of time. In *Bishbriksha* this technique is employed to conjure a sense of everyday life that cuts across spatial boundaries and shapes the colonial subject through a range of social practices and conventions. The representation of the everyday in the novel depends on joining novelistic space with a presumed reality, the assertion of fiction with a discursive mode of representation. Two representative passages show the status of the everyday in *Bishbriksha*; the first that I will cite is taken from the first chapter, as it describes scenes on the banks during Nagendra's boat journey in the month of Joishtha (May–June):

> The river flowed smoothly on – leaped, danced, cried out, restless, unending, playful. On shore, herdsmen were grazing their oxen – one sitting under a tree singing, another smoking, some fighting, others eating. Inland, husbandmen were driving the plough, beating the oxen, lavishing abuse upon them, in which the owner shared. The wives of the husbandmen, bearing vessels of water, some carrying a torn quilt, or a dirty mat, wearing a silver amulet round the neck, a ring in the nose, bracelets of brass on the arm, with unwashed garments, their skins blacker than ink, their hair unkempt, formed a chattering crowd. Among them one beauty was rubbing her head with mud, another beating a child, a third speaking with a neighbour in abuse of some nameless person, a fourth beating clothes on a plank. Further on, ladies from respectable villages adorned the *ghats* (landing-steps) with their appearance – the elders conversing, the

---

below – though stylistically awkward or stilted in parts, is the one he had approved.

middle-aged worshiping *Siva*, the younger covering their faces and plunging into the water; the boys and girls screaming, playing with mud, stealing the flowers offered in worship, swimming, throwing water over every one, sometimes stepping up to a lady, snatching away the image of *Siva* from her, and running off with it. The Brahmans, good tranquil men, recited the praises of *Ganga* (the sacred river Ganges) and performed their worship, sometimes, as they wiped their streaming hair, casting glances at the younger women.[41]

The second is a description of Nagendra's household:

One afternoon the whole household of ladies were sitting together in the older division of the house, all occupied according to their tastes in the simple employment of village women. All ages were there, from the youngest girl to the grey-haired woman. One was binding another's hair, the other suffering it to be bound; one submitting to have her white hair extracted, another extracting them by the aid of a grain of rice; one beauty sewing together shreds of cloth into a quilt for her boy; another suckling her child; one lovely being dressing the plaits of her hair; another beating her child, who now cried aloud, now quietly sobbed, by turns. Here one is sewing carpet-work, another leaning over it in admiring examination. There one of artistic taste, thinking of someone's marriage, is drawing a design on the wooden seats to be used by the bridal pair. One learned lady is reading Dasu Rai's poetry. An old woman is delighting the ears of her neighbours with complaints of her son; a humorous young one, in a voice half bursting with laughter, relates in the ears of her companions whose husbands are absent some jocose story of her husband's, to beguile the pain of separation. Some are reproaching the *Grihini* (house-mistress), some the *Korta* (master), some the neighbours; some reciting their own praises.[42]

41 Ibid., 3.

42 Ibid., 51–2.

The everyday in such passages emerges as the result of an ethnographic realism constituted by serial descriptions. At the same time, the narrative carefully avoids any direct link between such lengthy descriptions and the plot, between for instance such minutiae relating to the women who populate Nagendra's household and what happens inside the household as part of the main plot. It would be erroneous, however, to think of this diegetic narration as external to the plot itself; in spite of the separation between the plot and such descriptive passages, the novel does not reduce this mode of narration to the level of obscure backdrop for the main events, but uses it as a vital sign of what de Certeau describes as "ordinary culture" and further deploys it as the crucial force that animates the central events in the novel.[43] Unlike the novel, the text of the anonymous and ordinary culture, it seems, exists without any explicitly assigned author, without any strict point of origin, and thus remains open to multiple possibilities. The connection between this text of ordinary culture and the democratisation of generic space, charted above in Bankim's early writings, is obvious, but the relationship needs to be fleshed out more specifically. The democratic impulse in early Bankim, as I have argued above, was closely related to notions of colonial modernity, the now-time of culture that sought to redefine available discourses of both culture and power. In its novelistic avatar, this impulse inhabits the flattened time of the novel where temporal frames unfold as the aggregate of serialised moments. This slowness of time is essential for the purpose of the everyday, for its slow unfolding in the body of the novel; the passages above testify to this temporal device of immobilising minute actions serially as they unfold in

[43] de Certeau, *The Practice of Everyday Life*, 14, and *passim.*

time. The aim of such passages is of course to create a vast canvas of human activities which produce the assurance of the quiet flow of everyday and ordinary life at different strata of the social, but the effect can only be achieved by the discrete seriality that such miniaturised representations produce. Nagendra's household in the second passage becomes a lived space through such everyday and unremarkable activities. As the novel depicts the emotional relationship between Nagendra and Kunda, which is coupled with a growing distance between Nagendra and Suryamukhi, the narrative appropriates the democratic seriality of such descriptive passages. Their relationship is staged through minute household chores and customs in a manner that uses the lived space of the household set-up through descriptions of ordinary life. Hence one observes Nagendra's growing disinterest in everyday activities in the house, Kunda's gradual immersion in the fabric of ordinary chores in Nagendra's family, and Suryamukhi's slow but sure loss of authority over the everyday life of her household. Gradually, the arrested seriality that allows minute observations of events in descriptive passages now becomes a deft mechanism of the plot; the democratic seriality that confirms the steady presence of ordinary culture also assures the plot its realistic manoeuvring.

Bankim's novelisation of ethnology, in other words, is a device to textualise the everyday and make it readable. The arrested temporal frames of horizontal time offer its flattening as a readable text that is shared by the novel and its exterior, by representation and its assumed reality. *Bishbriksha* often enacts this principle of readability quite literally. There are instances where the novel quotes liberally from letters exchanged between Nagendra and his friend Haradeb Ghoshal, or between Nagendra and his brother-in-law Shrishchandra where Nagendra debates the viability of widow marriage as proposed by Vidyasagar. The following passage from one of Nagendra's letters is a case in point:

> If anyone says that widow-marriage is contrary to religion, I will give him Vidya Sagar's essay to read. When so learned a teacher affirms that widow-marriage is approved by the Shastras, who can contradict? [. . .] You will not make the foregoing objections; you will say a double marriage is contrary to morals. Brother, how do you know that it is opposed to morality? You have learned this from the English; it was not held so in India formerly. Are the English infallible? They have taken this idea from the law of Moses; but we do not hold Moses' law to be the word of God, therefore why should we say that for a man to marry two wives is immoral?[44]

The tone of discursive prose in these letters is deliberate and unmistakable. Along with these letters – which clearly gesture towards the larger debate about reform – the text also presents Nagendra's argument as part of his conversations and interactions with other characters in the novel. The strategic dissemination of such debates through different registers is designed to textualise everyday events, to render them legible in the same way as a social document would have been. We are invited to read events and characters in the novel as participating in, and hence representing, different positions on social debates. The effortless flow of reading from documents to events, from discursivity to fictionality, is the key to our understanding of the ways the novel intervenes in the social.

It is fictionality that eventually overwhelms ordinary culture in the novel. The sudden turn of events after Nagendra's second marriage is triggered by Suryamukhi's decision to leave the house. The marriage and its consequences, however, are carefully planned

[44] Chatterjee, *The Poison Tree*, 177–8.

in the text with the help of two other characters: Debendra and Heera. Debendra is a cousin of Nagendra and the epitome of moral degeneration in the novel – he is an alcoholic, sexually promiscuous, and immoral in the conduct of his life. Heera is a domestic help in Nagendra's household, but she is ambitious and almost as equally immoral as Debendra. Together they plot several outcomes of the emotional triangle of the central characters; it is important to note here that though they are partners in crime, Debendra and Heera have very different motives for and expectations from their machinations. These different genealogies of the events in the novel alert one to the fabrications which facilitate the proliferation of fiction as a necessary resolution to the issues raised by social reform. Nagendra repents his decision to marry Kunda and ignore Suryamukhi not because he is convinced by the arguments put forward by scriptures or because the colonial government has passed certain pieces of legislation, but because of the turn of events in the fictional world that separates his first wife from him. As Suryamukhi suddenly vanishes from his house, and as he imagines various hardships for her in the world outside, he gradually realises his love for his first wife and his blunder in marrying Kunda. In related developments, Debendra and Heera also lose the plot and die; at the end of the novel, Nagendra is united with his first wife via two developments of the plot – the defeat of Debendra, and more crucially the suicide of Kunda. Both events are testimonies to the sheer power of fiction, to its reformulation of the social as a moral domain.

Let me now turn to the climactic scene of the novel and its extraordinary deployment of visuality as the final resolution of a number of issues raised within it (and also elsewhere in Bankim's writing). In this scene of Nagendra's reunion with Suryamukhi, he first enters an empty room and looks at a series of paintings that adorn the walls; the narrative tells us that Suryamukhi and Nagendra "together had chosen the subjects, and caused them to be painted by a native artist, who had been taught by an Englishman, and could draw well."[45] The paintings depict various moments of intensified conjugality and companionship from *puranic* and epic texts, and the novel engages in a lengthy digression to describe these paintings:

> One picture was taken from the Birth of Kartika: Siva, sunk in meditation, on the summit of the hill; Nandi at the door of the arbour. On the left Hembarta, finger on lip, is hushing the sounds of the garden. All is still, the bees hid among the leaves, the deer reposing. At this moment Madan (Cupid) enters to interrupt the meditation of Siva; with him comes Spring. In advance, Parvati, wreathed with flowers, has come to salute Siva. Uma's joyous face is bent in salutation, one knee resting on the earth. This is the position depicted in the painting. As she bends her head, one or two flowers escape from the wreaths fastened in her hair. In the distance Cupid, half hidden by the woods, one knee touching earth, his beauteous bow bent, is fitting to it the flower-wreathed arrow.
>
> In another picture, Ram, returning from Lanka with Janaki, both sitting in a jewelled chariot, is coursing through the sky. Ram has one hand on the shoulders of Janaki, with the other is pointing out the beauties of the earth below. Around the chariot many-coloured clouds, blue, red, and white, sail past in purple waves. Below, the broad blue ocean heaves its billows, shining like heaps of diamonds in the sun's rays. In the distance, opal-crowned Lanka, its rows of palaces like golden peaks in the sun's light; the opposite shore beautiful with tamal and palm trees. In the mid distance flocks of swans are flying.[46]

[45] Ibid., 280–1.

[46] Ibid.

The narrative continues in this mode of description for a few more passages before mentioning Nagendra again.

While the most obvious explanation for this lengthy digression is the imminent reunion of Nagendra and Suryamukhi, the very style and tone of these passages suggest several other points. The point of this unusual narrative strategy seems to be twofold – to erect a metanarrative for some of the structural manipulations in the text, and to reformulate novelistic space as it approaches contemporary history. Through the unique combination in these paintings of traditional themes and their depiction through techniques borrowed from the realistic traditions of Europe (in anticipation of an artist like Raja Ravi Varma), the novel clearly signals its own status as an artwork; it is not simply a question of legitimacy, but more importantly of reception. The logic of such intertextuality gives one the final insight into the irregularities of the form and the way the form manipulates such irregularities to intervene in the social. As evident from the passages above, and also in the ethnographic passages quoted earlier, the visual and the novelistic often overlap in the text to produce a stable space amenable to narrative administration in a way that earlier practices of storytelling were not; that is, the space lends itself as a horizontal field without spatial hierarchy. Within the text, the two-dimensional space of the painting is closely associated with the flattening of time already discussed, since it is through a complex overlapping of horizontal visual space and the spatialisation of now-time that the novel can imagine a model for the social. The visual here does not stand in for the social space the novel aims to conceive, but rather becomes a constitutive element of it. It is only by incorporating the scopic drive of the pictorial that the novel is able to imagine its own modernity, its reliance on horizontal and democratic space as the precondition for representation. This is partly why the minute description of the ordinary culture, which Bankim saw as an assurance of everyday life away from the colonial state, finds a close resonance in these paintings, depicting a mythical life with equal finesse. In this final metanarrative for the novel, significantly anchored in visuality, *Bishbriksha* attempts its eventual plea to the immediacy of the unobtrusive ordinary – a point Bankim has been trying to make through his reflections on the philology-ethnology complex. *Bishbriksha* wants to incorporate the visual immediacy of these paintings as a guarantor of its worldly being.

The Novel as a World Literary Form

As will have been evident from my discussion of Bankim's novel and other prose writings, the ethnographic realism of early novels in Bengal was not an isolated concern with form but a complex site of negotiation for colonial modernity. The hybridity of the form, its simultaneous reliance on expressive resources borrowed from different traditions of representation, and especially its premium on the political nature of representation itself, all point towards a specific way of reimagining the social that can contain a unique combination of culture and power. *Bishbriksha*'s uniqueness did not reside in its ability to formulate a counterfactual history (as in many of Bankim's historical romances), but was available in its articulation of modernity which had the potential to transform contemporary traditions and customs. In a satirical piece entitled "*Bangala sahityer ador*" (The Appreciation of Bengali Literature; 1884) Bankim cites *Bishbriksha* as an embodiment of modern Bengali literature. The text is written in the form of a dialogue between an educated Bengali babu who detests books in Bengali and his wife who is a voracious reader of Bengali fiction. Quite predictably, they have very different opinions on modern Bengali literature – the babu repeatedly describes it as immoral, obscene, derivative, often seditious; and the wife provides various arguments to refute such charges. In the course of their dialogue, the wife sets up various oppositions between contemporary English and Bengali literatures, or between the products of popular print culture like *battala* and novels like *Bishbriksha*, and argues that it is at the level of the literary that modern Bengal is most prominently visible. Interestingly enough, the final proof of the triumph of this modernity comes through the fact that the novel has been translated into English and is quite popular with its audience (II, 41–3). The argument imagines colonial modernity not as directly derivative; it is equally important that the text does not advocate any form of vulgar nativism through unqualified valorisation of the indigenous either. Instead, the logic of the modern adumbrates a reconfigured social, which remains alive to various resources but constitutes its own *bildung* through a set of codes internal to it. *Bishbriksha* is an apposite example as it indicates its modernity through a set of rules borrowed from various literary traditions, but when it works out the details of those rules, and when it engages with the contingent reality of contemporary history through those rules, it not only fashions its own representational techniques but eventually transforms those traditions as well. The fact that the novel is equally effective in its translated version only reconfirms the success of such practices.

At this point it also becomes clear that the novel form found its way into distant locations not as a portable container for local content, as Jameson and Moretti claim, but through its participation in the volatile context of cultural modernity and modern knowledge paradigms. As I have shown, in the context of Bengal, and most prominently in the stunning success of Bankim, the novel form consolidated itself by liberally drawing on contemporary developments in philology and ethnology, often mixing their codes to constitute its own narrative strategies. Within the colonial context, the novel redeployed or reformulated a number of narrative conventions external to its history, often with a self-consciousness that could have only been supported in its immediate location through its domestic tensions and debates. It is my contention that the sheer proliferation of the novel in the nineteenth century, and its astounding range of formal innovations, would not have been possible without colonial histories.

References

Bagal, Jogeshchandra, "On Novels", in idem, ed., *Bankim Rachanabali*, vol. I (Calcutta: Sahitya Samsad, 2010).

Bakhtin, M.M., *The Dialogic Imagination: Four Essays*, trans. Caryl Emerson and Michael Holquist (Austin: University of Texas Press, 1981).

Bandyopadhyay, Asitkumar, *Unabingsha shatabdir prathamardha o bangla* (Calcutta: Bookland, 1958).

Beames, John, *A Comparative Grammar of the Modern Aryan Languages of India*, 3 vols (London: Trübner, 1872–9).

———, *Grammar of the Bengali Language, Literary and Colloquial* (Oxford: Clarendon, 1894).

Benjamin, Walter, "On the Concept of History", in *Walter Benjamin: Selected Writings, Vol. 4: 1938–1940*, ed. Marcus Paul Bullock, *et al.* (Cambridge, MA: Harvard University Press, 2003).

Bhattacharya, Baidik, "On Comparatism in the Colony: Archives, Methods, and the Project of *Weltliteratur*", *Critical Inquiry*, vol. 42, no. 3 (2016).

Chakravorty, Swapan, "Purity and Print: A Note on Nineteenth-century Bengali Prose", in Swapan Chakravorty and Abhijit Gupta, ed., *Print Areas: Book History in India* (Delhi: Permanent Black, 2004).

Chatterjee, Bankim Chandra, *The Poison Tree: A Tale of Hindu Life in Bengal*, trans. Miriam S. Knight (London: T. Fisher Unwin, 1884).

Chatterjee, Partha, *Nationalist Thought and the Colonial World: A Derivative Discourse?* (London: Zed, 1986).

Chatterji, Suniti Kumar, *The Origin and Development of the Bengali Language*, 2 vols (London: George Allen and Unwin, 1923).

Chattopadhyay, Bankimchandra, *Bankim Rachanabali*, 3 vols, ed. Jogeshchandra Bagal (Calcutta: Sahitya Samsad, 2010).

Das, Sajanikanta, *Bangla gadyasahityer itihas* (Calcutta: Mitralay, 1959).

de Certeau, Michel, *The Practice of Everyday Life* (Berkeley: University of California Press, 1988).

Grierson, George Abraham, *Linguistic Survey of India*, 11 vols (Calcutta: Office of the Superintendent of Government Printing, 1903–28).

Halhed, Nathaniel Brassey, *A Grammar of the Bengali Language* (Hoogly: n.p., 1778).

Herder, Hans, "The Modern Babu and the Metropolis: Reassessing Early Bengali Narrative Prose (1821–1862)", in *India's Literary History: Essays on the Nineteenth Century*, ed. Stuart Blackburn and Vasudha Dalmia (Delhi: Permanent Black, 2004).

Jameson, Fredric, "In the Mirror of Alternate Modernities", in Karatani Kojin, ed., *Origins of Modern Japanese Literature* (Durham, NC: Duke University Press, 1993).

Kaviraj, Sudipta, *The Unhappy Consciousness: Bankimchandra Chattopadhyay and the Formation of Nationalist Discourse in India* (New Delhi: Oxford University Press, 1995).

Long, James, *Returns Relating to Publications in the Bengali Language in 1857, Selections from the Records of the Bengal Government*, vol. 23 (Calcutta, 1859).

Lukács, Georg, *The Theory of the Novel* (London: Merlin, 1971).

McKeon, Michael, *The Origins of the English Novel, 1600–1740* (Baltimore: Johns Hopkins University Press, 1987).

———, ed., *Theory of the Novel: A Historical Approach* (Baltimore: Johns Hopkins University Press, 2000).

Moretti, Franco, "Conjectures on World Literature", *New Left Review* (Jan.–Feb. 2000).

Mufti, Aamir R., "Orientalism and the Institution of World Literature", *Critical Inquiry* 36 (Spring 2010).

———, *Forget English! Orientalisms and World Literatures* (Cambridge, MA: Harvard University Press, 2016).

Murshid, Ghulam, *Kalantare bangla gadya: Auponibeshik amole gadyer rupantar* (Calcutta: Ananda, 1992).

Oswell, G.D., "Preface", *The Spoilt Child: A Tale of Hindu Domestic Life* [a translation by Oswell of *Alaler gharer dulal*] (Calcutta: Thacker, Spink and Co., 1893).

Sen, Sukumar, *Bangla sahitye gadya* (Calcutta: Ranjan Prakashalay, 1934).

Thakur, Tekchand (Pyarichand Mitra), "Preface" in *Alaler gharer dulal*, ed. Brajendranath Bandyopadhyay and Sajanikanta Das (Calcutta: Bangiya Sahitya Parishat, 1940).

Trautmann, Thomas R., *Aryans and British India* (Berkeley: University of California Press, 1997).

3

Another Genealogy of the Hindi Novel

Mallikadevi of Banaras

VASUDHA DALMIA

SOMETIMES THE STORY of an author's life, what little we have of it, becomes as significant as the novels she wrote, her own shadowy existence becoming somehow a constituent of her writing. Her story then becomes as much a part of her story-telling as the telling itself, the themes of her works poignantly throwing into relief her own precarious existence at the edge of the social order. I am speaking here of Mallika, a poet and budding novelist, attempting novel writing at a time when the language for inner feelings, personal conflict, and social setting was just being invented in Hindi. She was from Bengal, we have a photo which is quite possibly of her – a beautiful young woman with long, slightly slanting eyes, sitting in a beguiling pose alongside a supplicating Harischandra, her long tresses cascading down her shoulders. She is plainly dressed, she wears no ostentatious ornaments; she is a gentle woman, judging by her attire a *bhadra-mahila*. She seems to have brought with her a knowledge of the progressive currents in Calcutta, in her day the most culturally vibrant of the three Presidency cities of British India. The two novels she had possibly written herself have an urban setting, in one case specified, in the other case left open. The urban setting makes possible a discourse which anticipates social codes and attitudes much ahead of its time.

Mallika's early work is intimately linked to Harischandra of Banaras (1850–1885), her protector and patron, well known as a major figure in the formation of modern Hindi literature. Committed as he was to both tradition and renewal, part of the old elite yet straining out of the mores which bound it, Harischandra took a range of positions on the woman question, as I have discussed at length elsewhere.[1] But in the one novel published under his name, which later tradition ascribed to Mallika, he did allow for the anticipation of social codes more progressive than was possible in his time. Harischandra enjoyed a particularly privileged position in Banaras, belonging as he did to the city's commercial aristocracy. Like his father before him, he played a leading role in the cultural life of the city and there are accounts of the gathering of poets and of musical evenings that he organised. Mallika was not the only woman he associated with – he sorely neglected his wife – but she seems to have held a place of special importance in his life.

Harischandra collaborated with Mallika in many of his literary works. She is reputed to have been of the same age as he; she had lived under his protection since he was twenty-three, some say since he was fifteen. We know next to nothing about her early life. She was possibly a child-widow or an abandoned wife, perhaps in Banaras, perhaps in Bengal – as Ray Krishna

[1] See Dalmia, "Generic Questions".

Das (1976), famous aesthete and art critic, one of the foremost authorities on Harischandra's life – maintains;[2] the second of her two novels speaks movingly of the fate of the child-widow. She brought education, culture, and a cultivated pen with her. According to Ray Krishna Das, who has left us many biographical notes on the poet and some on Mallika, Harischandra maintained, in a letter to his younger brother Gokulchandra in 1882, that he had rightfully accepted her in his life. She wrote under the name "Chandrika" (the young moon), a derivative of the last part of his own name: the moon adorning Hari, or Vishnu/Krishna. He had changed the name of his journal – *Harischandra's Magazine* – to *Harischandrachandrika*, after her, so it can safely be assumed that she was a literary partner in this enterprise as well as in many others. There is constant play on her names in many of his literary creations. He had included in *Prem tarang* (1877), a collection of his own poems, forty-six Bengali verses composed largely by her, love poems sometimes addressed to Krishna and often including the authorial signature "Chandrika", though sometimes also Harischandra.[3] Mallika translated from the Bengali or re-created three short novels, of which *Kulin kanya athava Chandraprabha aur Purnaprakash* is published under Harischandra's name. Gopal Ray offers the most substantial information on Mallika's publications. Three works are attributed to her. The first is *Radharani*: the original (1877) is a short romance by Bankim Chandra, translated and published as "*Kisi patiprana abala*" (a helpless

[2] See Das, "Neh ke Diwane".

[3] It first appeared in Harischandra's literary journal *Kavivachansudha* on 9 April 1877, to be later published by Mallik Chandra and Company, a press Harischandra co-founded with Mallika. The text is to be found in *Granthavali* II, 177–220, where it appears in the third impression of the above press (no date is appended to this information).

woman, the life breath of her husband), in 1883.[4] The second is *Saundaryamayi*, which, according to some, is yet another translation from the Bengali, though no original has been traced, published under her own name in 1887 and printed by Amar Yantralaya in Banaras.[5] Finally, *Chandraprabha aur Purnaprakash: Upanyas*, published by the Khadagvilas Press under Harischandra's name in 1888 (not 1889, as Ray maintains), as the title page of the copy available to us clearly proclaims.[6]

In her novelistic writings Mallika seems explicitly to advocate the new domestic ideals of the middle-class mistress of the house, literate and cultivated companion and mother, the *bhadramahila* in fact of Bengali novels and short stories. Personally, she could have known none of these roles. She was probably a co-author of various articles in *Balabodhini*, Harischandra's short-lived journal for women (1870–4), and she most certainly co-wrote, if not entirely wrote, the short novel *Kulin kanya athava Chandraprabha aur Purnaprakash*. To write as progressive a literary work as she did, Mallika clearly needed the name and support of Harischandra.

Here I review two of the three novels ascribed to Mallika. I focus first on the last of her completed novelistic ventures, *Kulin kanya athava Chandraprabha aur Purnaprakash* (A girl of good family, or Purnaprakash and Chandraprabha, 1888), a love story, but also a daring social reform novel alternating between intimate

[4] Banaras: Mallik Chandra and Co.

[5] I am grateful to Francesca Orsini for procuring a copy of this work for me from the British Library.

[6] The same press brought out another edition in 1921. There is also an undated edition of the work published by the Hari Prakash Yantralaya in Banaras. According to Ray, Brajratnadas, the poet's grandson, maintained that the work was originally written in 1880, its language having been corrected and improved by the poet.

and denunciatory tones; it was, as noted above, published under Harischandra's name, and possibly a first edition was published while he was alive, that is, before 1885, though we have no record of it. I shall then discuss the second of her three novels, *Saundaryamayi*, this time a work explicitly by Mallika.[7] Both novels fiercely oppose the prevailing social norms. I begin with *Chandraprabha aur Purnaprakash* because it helps to position the rebellious tone of *Saundaryamayi*.

Kulin kanya athava Chandraprabha aur Purnaprakash appears to be no translation; it is, according to its own designation, a novel, a genre very slowly coming into vogue in modern Hindi. The creation of the novel in Hindi, begun in the 1860s, continued to be an arduous process. Most of the early ventures were written in response to the need for textbooks in the modern languages. The colonial educational authorities often offered small cash awards for such attempts. British patronage was considered prestigious and the cash incentive was most welcome.[8] The result was the strong pedagogical impetus behind such works, which by and large validated and reinforced the positions represented in journals such as *Balabodhini*. Literary histories dutifully record the titles and authors of these novels, only to dwell at greater length on the better-known novelists of the twentieth century.

However, there is another genealogy of the Hindi novel, which has largely been ignored by literary historiography, perhaps because it was authored not only by a woman but also a socially marginal figure. It seems to have come directly through Bengali,

[7] Published in Sri Harischandra samvat 3; Mallika seems to have dated the year of her publication from Harischandra's death in January 1885, which would possibly make the year of publication 1887 or even 1888.

[8] See Kalsi, "*Parikshaguru*", for a discussion of the prizes awarded, and Dalmia, "Generic Questions", for the pedagogy of the early novel in Hindi.

where under the authorship of Bankim Chandra (1838–1894) the novel had developed into a sophisticated form of entertainment as well as education. Harischandra's novel, as co-written by Mallika, was born of this lineage. It had a direct and racy style and plunged straight into the narrative, with only a short preamble. This preamble consists of an erotic description of the heroine of the piece, Chandraprabha (once again, the play on the name of one of the authors is worthy of note). The work thus also claims a classic genealogy; it is reminiscent of the opening of Sanskrit prose works such as Dandin's seventh-century ornamental prose work *Dashakumaracharita* (Narrative of the ten princes), which begins with just such a description. Our work describes the charms of Chandraprabha in conventionally sensuous terms: "the dense locks cascade down to her thighs just as a cluster [lit. garland] of clouds" (1). There is then, stylistically speaking, classic Sanskrit as well as an expressly modern parentage to the work, for on the title page it is noted as an *upanyas* (novel). The plot is clearly delineated, the character sketches are short, and the action is swiftly related. It was probably written in the early1880s, while Harischandra was still around. It was included in a posthumous anthology of Hindi works, *Bhashasar* (The essence of language; first published 1884). Though some later critics also consider it a translation, it is not offered as such and the Bengali original, if there was one, has not been traced. But it remains a work which can be considered as having been filtered: it appears under Harischandra's name, though we are told that Harischandra participated in it only to the extent that he corrected the Bengali idiom which laced Mallika's Hindi.

Later tradition has been quite clear in its verdict that this novel was primarily the work of Mallika. Most critics have agreed that it was the re-creation of a story taken from the Bengali, enriched by several minor characters of Mallika's invention, and embellished with local detail, for it is set in Hindi–Urdu-speaking Lucknow. Lucknow had been reduced to a sub-provincial town after the uprising of 1857, but it too showed signs of modernisation. The urban setting provides the frame for the presence of progressively thinking characters such as Chandraprabha's mother and maternal uncle, not to speak of the modern romantic aspirations of the young couple. The tale also refers to Canning College, a newly opened college for boys. However, beyond this sketchy information, no details of the urban setting are offered. Surely, Mallika added much that was her own to the novel; we have two fragments of novels similar in design, tone, and intent, which, though not published in her lifetime, further confirm her style and authorship.[9] They deal with romantic love, of its impossibility, and the many taboos surrounding the social interaction of young men and women.

Chandraprabha aur Purnaprakash is a boldly, self-confidently, and brightly written tale. It consists of eleven short crisply constructed chapters. They are crowned by quotations from the most venerable works, from Vaishnava scriptures, Nanddas, Tulsidas, and Brajbhasha poets of standing such as Biharilal. They endow the work with literary respectability. The narrative falters somewhat at the beginning since it is not always able to organise the information to be conveyed, and it is sometimes awkward in its introduction of characters. But once the line or two of necessary information is out of the way, the pace picks up. There is a spontaneous and easy use of language, quick exchange

[9] Another manuscript in what is believed to be her handwriting and her Bengali-inflected Hindi was found almost a century later. See Bate and Chandra, "Mallika", for further information on this work (which seems to be a compound of two unfinished works) as well as long excerpts from it, published under the title *Kumudini*, in idem.

of dialogue, and unselfconscious description of feelings which never become mawkish. The language is Sanskritic, reminiscent of Bankim Chandra, while the dialogue is in a more colloquial Hindi.[10]

The tale seems typical of its times and is quickly told. Chandraprabha is the daughter of a Kulin Kanyakubja Brahman who has married four times.[11] One wife has borne him a son and a daughter, the second wife only a daughter, and the other two have remained barren. He lives with the wife who bore the son and the daughter. The wife, Gunamañjari, with only a daughter named Chandraprabha, lives with her brother in Lucknow. Chandraprabha is of marriageable age now, but it is not easy to find a groom of her father's caste standing. She has fallen in love with a young man, Purnaprakash, who studies in Lucknow's Canning College, and he with her. The two observe each other as he goes in and out of his sister's house nextdoor. Worthy of note in this connection is the fact that the romantic union at the heart of the novel is the consequence of visual beauty and attraction. Chandraprabha sees the young hero, Purnaprakash, and falls in love: *pranay sada isi bhanti arambh darshanmatra hi se hota hai* (2; love always begins this way, just over a sighting). He responds, once again by seeing and falling in love with her. The two do not know each other more than this.

[10] On Bankim's language, see the translators' introduction to Chatterjee, *The Poison Tree*, IL.

[11] In the latter half of the nineteenth century there was intense debate around the practice of polygamy among the high-standing Kulin Brahmans of Bengal. The many young women they married – since suitable bridegrooms of the same caste were a rarity – lived a life of want and scarcity. Apart from anything else, there was always the imminent danger of early widowhood for several women at once if one such male died of illness, accident, or merely old age.

Their mode of falling in love contrasts starkly with the depictions of romantic love in British novels as they evolved from the mid-eighteenth century to the nineteenth. As Nancy Armstrong has shown in *Desire and Domestic Fiction*, from the epistolary novels of Samuel Richardson (1689–1761) through the works of Jane Austen (1775–1817) and of the Brontë sisters Charlotte (1816–1855) and Emily (1818–1848), "the novel produced a language of increasing psychological complexity for understanding human behavior" (253). It is psychological depth and moral qualities rather than surface physical beauty which account for the attractiveness of a person, the difference between male and female being their respective qualities of mind. The novels seek to depict intrinsic personal qualities and the nuances of subjectivity rather than concentrate on action of one kind or another. The moral qualities of the heroine triumph over social difference. On the other hand, over this early stage in the Hindi novel it is the social conflict of a love primarily based on physical attraction but not sanctioned by society and the ruses taken to overcome the hurdle that forms the focus of attention.

Chandraprabha's father is indifferent to her fate. This is clearly to be an ill-fated romance, since Purnaprakash is a Brahman of slightly lower-caste status. That difference alone is enough to make the union officially impossible. It is the mother who feels deeply for her daughter and guesses what preöccupies her. Whatever the gender of the possible original Bengali author of the novel, the Hindi re-creation is written almost entirely from the perspective of the women. The first chapter depicts a tender scene between mother and daughter, for it is this relationship which is key to the plot and alluded to first in the narrative. Bankim's *Radharani*, which Mallika also translated – though the translation has not survived – begins with a focus on a mother–daughter relationship, this time a dying mother tended by her devoted daughter. As the novel opens, Chandraprabha is perched on a window overlooking their neighbour's house. The mother takes the chin of her weeping daughter in her hand and says: "You'll gain nothing by worrying. Who can wipe away what the unknown has ordained for you?"

However, after initial discouragement the mother arranges to have her daughter marry the young man of her choice, and in fact she is determined that it will be so. The father was earlier asked to take a hand in the matter of finding a suitable groom but he has for long done nothing about it. Once the marriage with Purnaprakash is arranged, however, he turns up at the last minute with a prospective groom of his own choice – an elderly man of a suitable caste. The father has agreed to pay the groom a dowry. There is some hithering and thithering about the dowry, for Chandraprabha is so beautiful that at one stage the prospective groom declares himself willing to forgo it. The narrator takes some pleasure in delineating the money-conscious exchange between father and groom.

The mother, and the maternal uncle with whom she lives, support Chandraprabha entirely. The mother exchanges sharp words with her husband and shows the two men the door. Given that the father is in his wife's natal home he cannot beat her into submission – we are told he is not Western enough to forego that pleasure. So he has to resort to other means, namely to threaten and then actually proceed to fast unto death. And such is the awful force of the sin which visits those who have caused a Brahman's death that the mother is forced to give in. But while he and the elderly bridegroom wait outside the women's quarters for the marriage to be performed, inside the two young lovers are united in lawful wedlock by a ritually binding wedding ceremony. The father and the elderly groom-in-waiting – we have been told he has made it his profession to marry and that he already has eleven such Kulin wives – pronounce the most awful curses, whereupon Chandraprabha's maternal uncle, who has gone out of his way to demonstrate great emotional concern for his sister and niece, throws the two intruders out as unceremoniously as they had thrust themselves in.

Though the predicament of the mother, abandoned since early youth, and of the two lovers of unequal caste status seeking union, may seem typical of its time, the course that the tale itself takes is not typical. Chandraprabha longs for a happiness that cannot appropriately be granted her. The best way to take care of her needs would have been to have her die a tragic death of some sort. She could thus gain the reader's sympathy and provide catharsis while disturbing no norms.[12] But the dynamism and quick pace of the novel propel the narrative in another direction. The women are daring and impertinent. Their conversations and manoeuvres provide a novel perspective. They expose the wiles of the father and the elderly bridegroom mercilessly.

The mother, Gunamañjari, is the main agent of change. The reflection and action is focalised through her:

> Gunamañjari became very anxious. Her daughter's happiness was her happiness, and in her unhappiness was her unhappiness. Her worry grew as she saw her daughter grow lean. She was filled with remorse when she thought of how she had sent Purna away. Many a time she got up to write to him and then felt helpless and abandoned the attempt to communicate with him. She had sent him off once, with what face can she call him again? After three months had passed in this state, she could hold herself back no longer.

[12] I am grateful to Paula Richman for remarking upon this. Bankim's transgressive women characters are rewarded by one kind of death or another.

> She wrote a letter to Purna saying that the marriage had been fixed and all that they waited for was his arrival. Even if Chandraprabha's father was to bring a groom as good-looking as Kamadeva, as learned as Brihaspati, and even if he were of the highest *kula* [clan], Gunamañjari would give Chandraprabha's hand in marriage to him alone.
>
> Gunamañjari wrote to him thinking that if she could not make Chandraprabha happy in her own lifetime, what in fact would she have achieved in life? The compulsions of *kaulinya*, of good birth, made her live the life of a widow in spite of her husband's existence; she would not let her dear daughter suffer such torture. (9)

And this, as we have seen, is just what she does proceed to do, though hampered by all the obstacles her husband puts in her way. Throughout the narrative, in fact, there is clear resistance to the autocracy of men. When, in a heated exchange, her husband asks her what she lacks, what needs she could possibly have, living as comfortably as she does, she bursts out, "What am I unhappy about, what is lacking? My only unhappiness is that neither you nor I die" (15). Faced with such resistance, he does think of simply beating her into acquiescence, but cannot do so, the narrator points out wryly, because he finds himself in her natal home. So he has to descend to argument and ruse. And in the midst of all this he and the elderly groom bicker over the exact price of the bride. At the final moment of disclosure, when the two men discover what has taken place inside the women's quarters and break into the most vile abuse, it is the maternal uncle who censures them: "Get out of the house. You use words bigger than your mouth can hold. On such an auspicious day, you utter such inauspicious words" (23).

The work seems to have no explicit agenda, nationalist or otherwise, though obviously the theme of social reform does underlie the narrative, dealing as it does with the polygamous excesses of

Kulin Brahmans, most of whom were Bengali.[13] However, there is no rhetoric regarding the state, fallen or otherwise, of the Hindu woman. In fact, there is no mention of any of the newer institutions of authority, save on one rather telling occasion: when the prospective groom and the father discover that they have been tricked, the disgruntled bridegroom calls out to the colonial authorities, the Magistrate Sahib and Company Bahadur, for help and intervention. We may be over-interpreting if we understand this as an indictment of the colonial institutions which backed the newly reinforced patriarchal order. Yet this is the sole invocation of colonial institutional authority. Whether it sets out to propagate social reform or not, the novel remains a strong statement of women's desires, needs, bonding, and defiance, and comes from the pen of a woman who neither knew conventional domestic life nor the need to break out of it, though she may have once had to suffer the consequences of its restrictive codes.

Saundaryamayi is subtitled *Viyoganta Upanyas* – a novel with a tragic end. Told with great feeling, the narrative as much as the title leaves us in no doubt about the sorry end of child-widows. A compact tale of 65 pages and 22 short chapters, *Saundaryamayi* maintains a fast narrative pace throughout. The plot seems more developed than in *Chandraprabha aur Purnaprakash*, where the romance takes place more in the minds of the two lovers than in actual knowledge of and dialogue with each other. The tale, briefly told, is as follows.

Born in their later years to her father and mother, Saundaryamayi is a beautiful and lively child. When she reaches the age of seven, her mother begins to display anxiety about finding a

[13] The Hari Prakash Press copy does further qualify the title as *Kulin vivah sambandhi ek choti si akhyayika*, or a short tale regarding Kulin marriages, indicating that a reformatory agenda was inherent within the narrative.

suitable match for her and so it is that she is married at the tender age of eight to a boy of nine. She continues to live in her natal home and visits the village school. One day, as she comes home, she hears her mother crying inconsolably. Saundarya has become a widow. Not understanding the nature of her tragic fate, the child continues to play at home. But when she reaches the age of fourteen, she slowly begins to become a woman. Her fate is brought home to her by her friend Lavanyamayi, who tells her that had she not been married off so early, she would not now be a widow. "It happened as if in a dream. Like doll's play" (11). The bride and the groom played only a puppet-like role in their own marriage, which in some sense happened almost without their doing. The narrator takes some pains to depict the hopelessness of the situation, for in the same house has lived for sixteen years a distantly related orphan boy by the name of Hiralal. He has been raised like a son. The two become newly aware of each other as they grow into their teens.

The sixth chapter is entitled "*Asha ka sesh*" (Some hope left). The parents soon receive a visitor from Bengal who tells them of the social reform undertaken by the famous Bengali reformer and philanthropist Ishwarchandra Vidyasagar (1820–1891), who has pushed through the Widow Remarriage Act of 1856. The visitor tells the father that Vidyasagar has instituted widow remarriage in British India, so that two or three such marriages take place regularly in Bengal. But Saundarya's father is resistant. He says things such as abortion, undertaken by unfortunate widows, take place only in lowly houses. In short, that there is no danger to Saundarya succumbing to such a fate. In the next chapter, her friend Lavanyamayi discusses the sad fate reserved for Saundarya with her husband Haridas, making him cry out: "Will God make such a day come about when widow remarriage will become current in Bharat? There will [surely] be delay." Thus, this novel has a clear social reform agenda which is placed within a nationalist frame.

Inevitably, Saundarya begins to desire Hiralal. One day, she reads some verses he has penned in longing for her and thinks: "I had thought that father would marry me off under the Widow Remarriage Act. That I would receive what I want but that hope has suffered defeat . . . O Lord, cast a glance at Bharat. How many husbandless young women like me become hoarse with crying, how many commit suicide?" (25) – foreshadowing her own miserable end. Hiralal finds her reading his verses and crying and they converse. He speaks bravely. He swears he will defeat society and marry her and that he will earn his living, making use of what he has learnt. "I make God my witness that I will marry you. I will tread on society's frown and cool my heart by placing you within it" (28). She asks him to marry elsewhere; she will rejoice in his happiness. He vows with the sun god as his witness that he will marry only her. Her mother overhears them and says she will bear witness to that vow. So once again we have a sympathetic mother figure, one truly interested in her daughter's welfare. Nancy Armstrong has spoken of the "purely emotional network of relationships overseen by a woman" (4) in connection with *Jane Eyre*. In both of Mallika's novels we have a sympathetic mother, planning empathetically for her daughter's happiness, and the net of relationships is held together entirely by emotion.

But the two young people living in each other's vicinity also give rise to village gossip, which spreads everywhere. The parents ask her to stay away from Hiralal, but she is unable to leave his company. The father says, in fact, that "*pranay agni sahaj se nahim bujhati, pranayi aur pagal ek haim*" (32) – that the fire of love is not easily extinguished, that the lover and the lunatic are one. Thus, he forecasts the excessively emotional tone not only of the novel as a whole but of Saundaryamayi's words and actions in particular. She stops eating and cries all the time. And then a very uncanny thing begins to happen to her. Is it a kind of wish-fulfilment? Is desire overtaking her? Saundarya's belly begins to swell and there are other signs of pregnancy. It cannot be overlooked and people gossip incessantly. The midwife offers to rid her of her pregnancy, saying it also happens elsewhere (35), but Saundarya sends her away.

Her father regrets that he did not marry her to Hiralal. Had he done so, others would have followed suit and it would have created a *nutan samaj*, a new social order (37). This is what the narrative is pushing for. It is not the young who lack courage, it is parents who hesitate. The father now curses himself: *Kintu ham ghor murkh, ghor naraki, ghor svarthi haim, jagadishwar uska hamko dandh de rahem haim* (37-8; But we are intensely stupid, intensely hellish, intensely selfish, the lord of the world is punishing us for it). This is also the incrimination that the narrator seems to be heaping on them. Given the situation, however, the father panics: should he leave his daughter or leave society? The mother defends her daughter: it is not her fault; she is in the full bloom of her youth. She says she is not pregnant, let us wait and see. If it is truly a pregnancy, we can always reject her. However, Hiralal is asked to leave. But this is just the beginning of Saundarya's trials. She will find no respite anywhere. The signs of her pregnancy disappear after a time but the village reacts with cynicism: she must have got help from the midwife, they say. And they continue to persecute her family. Her father asks her to leave home; he will support her.

The bond with her friend Lavanya is also one of deep emotion. And it is she who comes to her rescue. Lavanya displays great social courage in inviting her friend to live with her. The narrator breaks into lavish praise for her, punctuated by many exclamation marks: *Dhanya Lavanya! Dhanya, dhanya!! Tumhare hriday mem pavitra pranay hai. Tum ramani ratna ho! Dhanya tumhara prem! Dhanya tumhari bandhuta!* (45; Praise be Lavanya! Praise, praise! There is pure love in your heart! You are a jewel of a woman! Praise be your love! Praise be your friendship!)

But social persecution is a reality even here and it is relentless. Its every cruelty is made apparent. The village does not tolerate her living with her friend. Tongues wag; Lavanya and her husband Haridas face the social ostracism that her parents did. Haridas succumbs to the pressure. Saundarya is hounded from place to place.

She has to move to an elderly relative in another village. Facing a bleak future, away from her loved ones, Saundarya begins to fade; she has no wish to live. The narrator laments at a nation such as this: "Bharat! Why does a lotus prosper on your barren heart? Mean society, devoid of morality! Who calls you knowledgeable? And you of the world! It is not proper for those to live in the world, who do not understand the sorrow of a helpless woman!"(50)

Her parents are sent for. The narrator sides with the mother when she says an innocent widow has had her happiness destroyed (54). Saundarya wants to see Hiralal and Lavanya and Haridas; it is her last wish. The mother tries to help but the father doesn't know the boy's whereabouts. The father now regrets his fear of society, which has prevented him helping his daughter: "We will die when she dies" (55). They advertise for Hiralal in a newspaper that they know he reads. Her friends and Hiralal duly appear. The parents leave her to her last meeting with Hiralal. Saundarya takes his hand; the gesture is significant, for physical touch means a kind of union, she calls him the Lord of her life's breath, says it is a happy day. And then she calls out to God: "O kindhearted Lord! Inflict no sorrow on women. May the eyes of hard, blinded society open and see the sin in the death of a helpless woman . . ." (64) Upon which she dies, a willed death, almost a suicide, the kind that she had already lamented as the fate of child-widows. The narrator's words are heartfelt: "O Benefactor of the Humble! Will you cast a gracious glance at helpless women? Who, if not you, will wipe their tears? Who aside from you will wipe out the sorrow of the unhappy, helpless widows of Bharat?" (65)

The tale does not have enough density, enough narrative complexity for a full-length novel, but the complexity has begun to be suggested. Three points are worthy of note. One, the emotional character of Saundaryamayi, which colours the whole tale. As a child-widow, her fate, one way or the other, makes for social conflict. If she is allowed to marry again by her father, she creates an exceptional situation in a social set-up that has not yet begun to accept such unions. She takes ill and with it begins her decline, but not before something grotesque happens to her. Her belly swells, in a mock pregnancy almost – is it wish-fulfilment? – making for the wider disapproval and censure her father most fears. In the end, it is as if she defies everyone after all and stages protest by an almost willed death. Second, at all crucial moments in the story both God and the fate of all such women in India are invoked, so that the particular is widened to include the national and all womankind who suffer a similar fate. Finally, then, the tragic end, already forecast in the subtitle, is used to make an example of the sorrow and ask for an end to it. This stirring end is in keeping with the rousing tone of the happy fate of the young lovers in the first novel. In this novel, we could almost say, in defeat lies victory. The tone of *Chandraprabha and Purnaprakash* helps us to recognise also in this novel the almost defiant and repeated plea to the Lord for the kind of social change that will make such deaths needless, so that we read it not only for the obvious tragedy of circumstance but also for its redress.

Did Mallika merely translate, or did she modify and embellish? Did she invent the tale? If *Saundaryamayi* is indeed a translation from the Bengali, we need to note that the setting is moved out of Bengal and the whole region cited as an example of not only progressive thinking but also action in accordance with it. That alone makes the novel, as handed down to us, a product of the North West Provinces, a region depicted as lagging behind and cruel in its handling of young women who suffer the fate of beautiful, vulnerable Saundaryamayi.

Mallika's own relatively sheltered existence was to come to some sort of an end with Harischandra's passing on the night of 3 January 1885. His close associate and cousin Radhakrishna Das – the son of his *bua* (paternal aunt), who lived in the same house as he – wrote a monthly diary for February 1885 which he used as a record of his daily transactions (*dincharya*). This diary fell into my hands during one of my many Banaras visits. Printed in Nathdwara, the great Vallabha Vaishnava pilgrimage centre in Rajasthan, it includes a copy of the letter that Gokulchandra, the poet's younger brother, wrote on the day of Harischandra's death, on 3 January 1885, as an entry made under the same date. It says that in his testament Harischandra had asked that Madhavi (another of the women under his protection) and Mallika be financially supported by the sale of property in his possession. After disposing of Madhavi's claims as superfluous, given her character – Madhavi was a courtesan and entertained other clients – Gokulchandra, the poet's brother, who had been asked for his opinion regarding Harischandra's last will and testament, devotes some lines to Mallika. He notes that Harischandra truly cared (*yatharth sneha*) for her. Harischandra wanted a provision of twenty-one rupees per month made in her favour, which wish Gokulchandra was inclined to carry out, though it would become a question of duration – for how long could the payment be maintained? But for the time being it would make possible a small house (*khsudra grha*) for her and a servant. We need to recall that Mallika had lived in relative comfort in a house south of the main house in Thatheri Bazar, in Bhikharidas Lane, a side lane, in a house connected by a bridge with Harischandra's own grand house. She was present at his deathbed and continued to live in Banaras for some years, since *Saundaryamayi* was published there in 1887 or 1888, in "Harischandra Year 3" as the title page proclaims. But after that she disappears from view and it is possible that she ceased to write. She is likely to have led the life of a widow in the years after Harischandra's passing, and she is likely to have gone to Vrindavan, another pilgrimage centre, specialising as the last refuge for abandoned and destitute widows. Her own fate possibly reflected the sorrow she had depicted as Saundaryamayi's lot.

But Mallika left behind literary efforts of enduring value. For, whatever the extent or limit of her originality, she surely deserves to be honoured as modern Hindi's first woman novelist. And as the first to write with the fate of women as her focus, their emotional being, their perspective. And as the first, perhaps, to introduce a note of defiance in the depiction of their sorry plight.

References

Armstrong, Nancy, *Desire and Domestic Fiction: A Political History of the Novel* (1987; New York and Oxford: Oxford University Press, 1989).

Bate, Krishna, and Girishchandra Chaudhari, "Mallika: Bharatendu ki Dharmagrihita", *Saptahik Hindustan*, 17 September 1989.

Brajratnadas, *Bharatendu Harischandra* (1935; Allahabad: Hindustani Akademi, 1962).

Chatterjee, Bankim Chandra, *Bankim Samagra* (Collected Novels of Bankim Chandra [Hindi]), ed. Nihal Chandra Varma (Banaras: Pracharak Granthavali Yojana, 1987).

———, *The Poison Tree: Three Novellas*. Translated by Marian Madden and S.N. Mukerjee (Delhi: Penguin Books, 1996).

Chaudhari, Girishchandra, "Bharatendu ki Preyasi", *Saptahik Hindustan*, 28 September 1986.

Dalmia, Vasudha, *The Nationalization of Hindu Tradition: Harischandra of Banaras and Nineteenth Century Banaras* (1997; Delhi: Permanent Black, 2010).

———, "Generic Questions", in *Hindu Pasts: Women, Religion, Histories* (Ranikhet: Permanent Black, 2015).

Harischandra, *Chandraprabha aur Purnaprakash: Upanyas* (1884; Patna: Khadgavilas Press, Bankipur, 1888).

———, *Bharatendu Granthavali. Dusra Bhag* (cited as *Granthavali* II), ed. Brajratnadas (1935; Banaras: Nagarapracharinisabha, 1946).

Kalsi, A.S., "*Parikshaguru* (1882): The First Hindi Novel and the Hindu Elite", *Modern Asian Studies*, 26/4, 1992.

Mallika, *Saundaryamayi*: *Viyoganta Upanyas* (translation; novel with a tragic end; Banaras: Amar Yantralaya, 1887).

———, "Kumudini", *Saptahik Hindustan*, 17 September 1989.

Ray, Gopal, *Upanyas Kosha: Khand ek, 1870–1917* (Patna: Granth Niketan, 1968).

Ray, Krishna Das, "Neh ke Diwane", *Dharmayug*, 17 October 1976.

Sahay, Shivnandan, *Harischandra* (1905; Lucknow: Hindi Samiti, Uttar Pradesh Shasan, 1975).

4

Govinda Samanta, or, Eluding Ethnography in the Colonial Novel

ROCHELLE PINTO

LAL BEHARI DAY'S *Govinda Samanta* is an archetype of early Indian novels that hold their narratives in a relationship of accountability to colonial ethnography.[1] Ethnography hovers over these novels as an epistemological limit for the representation of colonial society, and as a master narrative in relation to which the novel is an individual variation or deviation. Enumerative and detached descriptions, owned by no single persona or collective in the novel nor linked to the vision or thought or movement of any figure, is a common feature of such early novels, in which narrators describe contemporary legal and political questions in a manner more easily identifiable with journalism or a prose essay than with realist fiction.[2]

To the late Meenakshi Mukherjee I owe thanks for introducing me decades ago to *Govinda Samanta* and encouraging my work on it.

[1] Day, *Govinda Samanta.*

[2] The reliance of the novel on ethnography and other discourses is noted in Gopal, *The Indian English Novel*, 26; Mohanty, "The Epistemic Work of Literary Realism", 45–58.

Written in 1874 in English, in response to the announcement of an award by "an enlightened Bengali zamindar for the best novel, to be written either in Bengali or English, illustrating the 'Social and Domestic Life of the Rural Population and the Working Classes of Bengal'", this novel's purposiveness in rendering a *History of the Bengal Raiyat* (the subtitle of the novel) through an illustration of social categories precedes its writing.[3] It was reprinted several times, and in turn became a source for the conditions of the rural peasantry in the twentieth century.[4]

The novel begins, conventionally enough, with the birth of the eponymous protagonist, but unsurprisingly the potentially unknowable choices of the character are replaced with a stricter economy of causality that determines individual paths and directions in the narrative. Self-knowledge or self-discovery in *Govinda Samanta* is pre-empted by the norms of family and village life. The narrator delivers an already constrained individual subject to the structures that were most reified in colonial ethnography – the Indian village and caste.

In many sections of the novel, individual protagonists do not acquire distinction through the encounter between individuation and the social, but are expelled from the narrative as already identified and knowable subjects.[5] The description of the village midwife, whom Govinda Samanta's uncle has set off to fetch on the night of the hero's birth, is an instance of this. Rupa's mother's caste (Bagdi), age and height, and the fact that her teeth are

[3] Mohapatra and Nayak, "Writing Peasant Life in Colonial India".

[4] Dasgupta, "Life in a Bengal Village". See also M., "Calcutta Diary".

[5] Chapter headings, for instance, are often the names of practices or personages described as types. Day, *Govinda Samanta; or The History of a Bengal Raiyat,* 43–7.

missing, are narrated as though these details were being read off an identification document. Yet not all information about Rupa's mother is forthcoming, for customary honorifics – used to address people in place of their given names – obstruct the dredging of data: "We have used the circumlocutory phrase, Rupa's mother, instead of mentioning her own name; but the fact is, we never heard her name mentioned by anybody in the village; and though we have made laborious inquiries into the matter, our exertions have proved fruitless – everyone insisting on calling her Rupa's mother."[6] Such elisions of the empirical quest of ethnography can go unnoticed as most of the novel is framed by its logic.

So similar is this novel to the texts it cites as its sources of information that literary history could not be faulted for seeing it exclusively as an effect of bureaucratic power and the conditions of colonial rule. After all, the relationship between social judgement and narrative description in Colesworthy Grant's *Rural Life in Bengal*, from which *Govinda Samanta* draws some of its information, seems to be replicated in the novel.[7]

Containing Autonomy

The demarcation of literary from non-literary writing at the end of the nineteenth century in England has been discussed as an effect and mechanism of a regime of representation that linked the idea of truth to empirical description, facticity, notions of evidence, and causality. In colonial settings, the effect of this rationalising charge is visible in the hierarchical privileging of those discourses that rendered the colony transparent and legible to the colonial gaze.

[6] Day, *Govinda Samanta; or The History of a Bengal Raiyat*, 8.

[7] Grant, *Rural Life in Bengal;* Day, *Govinda Samanta*, 317.

In an account of how ethnography itself secured its authority in relation to colonial societies through the narrative devices of realism, Patricia Clough argues that ethnographic writing produced a concordance between the ethnographer's knowledge and the colonial subject's self-knowledge through realist narrative.[8] Realism, she states, organised subjectivity, making the "unified subject identity the linchpin of empirical science's appropriation of subjectivities for disciplinary relations and allied political economic arrangements."[9] The primary challenge that colonial societies posed to the authority of colonial knowledge is managed by allowing the subject to appear as a "statistical personation".[10] Clough suggests therefore that ethnography works to mediate the desire of the colonial subject, and, in a relay effect, the reading subject, through "an oedipal logic of realist narrativity" as it "treats the subject's struggle for self-knowledge as a struggle to obtain factual representations of empirical reality . . . Thus ethnographic realism provides sociological discourse with a kind of vision that even in the eighteenth century, Freud . . . argues, deserved to be called cinematic."[11]

Clough's development of the oedipal structure of ethnographic authority not only equips us with the mechanics through which ethnography seizes on and ventriloquises colonial society, but is most suggestive as a frame for understanding types and structures within the colonial novel. We could argue that colonial ethnography as a master narrative impeded the formation of the

[8] Clough, *The End(s) of Ethnography.*

[9] Ibid., 26.

[10] Ibid.

[11] Ibid., 26–7. See the title of ch. V of the novel, for instance: "Photographs of a Ráiyat's Cottage, and Those who Live in it". Day, *Govinda Samanta*, 27.

realist subject in the colonial novel, thwarting narrative flows that sought to normalise an indigenous subject by displacing narrative dynamism with the regularities of empirical description, classification, and types. Wielding greater authority perhaps than other Western realist literary traditions to which writers were exposed, ethnography both stands in for reality and limits the elasticity of narrative to the structure of its vision in the novel.

Authenticity and Authority

The relationship between ethnographic structures and other narrative techniques differs from novel to novel, a distinctive aspect of the genre in this period. Satya P. Mohanty addresses this in his introduction to the translation of an Oriya novel of 1897, *Three Acres and a Third* (*Chha Mana Atha Guntha*, abbreviated as *Chha Mana*) by Fakir Mohan Senapati.[12] In a comparison between *Govinda Samanta* and *Chha Mana*, it is *Chha Mana* that represents a break with the conventions of colonial representation as Mohanty notes the inversion of ethnographic authority in the Oriya novel. A local legend involving demons and their construction of the Gobindpur pond posits an inverse relationship between the pond's state of fulness and the sinfulness of Gobindpur's inhabitants, which the narrator defends: "English-educated babus, do not be too critical of our local historian, Ekadusia Chandra. If you are, half of what Marshman and Tod have written will not survive the light of scrutiny."[13] Aside from

[12] Senapati, *Six Acres and a Third.*

[13] Ibid., 20. *Six Acres and a Third* counterpoises official writing and religious authority with gossip and satire deriving from colloquial humour. It undermines colonial legal discourse, while the brutality of both colonial and indigenous power inflects its satire.

validating the moral authority of legend against the epistemic value of history, Mohanty discusses how the novel delineates new social agents such as the "touter-narrator", a combination of tout and lawyer, who "enters the modern Indian novel from the world of oral discourse" to mediate the worlds of the middle class and the downtrodden and "create a new kind of reader and a new kind of self-critical social subject".[14]

Apart from these formal innovations, the central questions about the nature and legitimacy of power in *Chha Mana* concern the economy around property, which, notes Mohanty, "in turn bring up questions about belief and action."[15] In comparison to the more recent regimes of the Mughals and the British, he suggests that medieval Oriya systems of sovereignty and land distribution are evoked as "a moral economy in which ownership might be considered a form of trusteeship."[16] The incorporation of this destabilisation of colonial and Mughal authority into the "linguistic play and self-consciously allusive style of the narrator's discourse" begets "a similar question about justification: what justifies narrative, and ultimately epistemic, authority?"[17] Both these questions constitute the ground on which formal and aesthetic conventions are reordered in novels structured around land in late-nineteenth-century India.

Mohanty, however, tends to transform this question of the correspondence between epistemic and narrative authority in both novels into one between degrees of political astuteness in realist representation. This stance is echoed in an essay by Himansu S. Mohapatra, who suggests that Fakir Mohan Senapati displays

[14] Ibid., 6–7.

[15] Ibid., 12.

[16] Ibid.

[17] Ibid.

an "analytical realism" that is truer to the unobservable realities of the social world than the realism in *Godaan* or the detached description in *Govinda Samanta* which he identifies as the timeless Orientalised village. Mohapatra and Jatin K. Nayak highlight the fact that Senapati had read Lal Behari Day's work, which they recognise as submissive to colonial intentions in comparison with Senapati's subversive text. The authors point to Day's over-compensatory disavowals of Romanticism and empiricism, which subordinates story-telling, according to them, to the demands of photographic realism.[18]

Day's metaphors, they point out, are already yoked to Hesiod, Homer, and Virgil, and the narrator often provides botanical names in Latin for village trees. Rural life in Kanchanpur, Day's novelistic village, in drawing on both eighteenth-century rationalism and nineteenth-century romanticism, "is constructed through mutually opposing paradigms as idiotic and idyllic", with praise for the "light of reason", as well as a "Rousseauistic glorification" of its lack, furnishing on the one hand mystified and ritualised Hinduism, and on the other a reworking of emotion and filial relations through notions of rationality, privacy, and individualism.[19] Critiques of colonialism embodied in the brutality of the English planter, the unfulfilled promises of Christianity, and the indifference of English law in *Govinda Samanta* still do not allow the narrative to break out of what its critics term as an "English-adorned" stance.[20]

In agreement with much of this analysis, the following sections indicate how *Govinda Samanta* authorises itself as fiction by

[18] Mohapatra and Nayak, "Writing Peasant Life in Colonial India", 30.
[19] Ibid., 29–32.
[20] Ibid., 36.

combining traditions of an Anglo-European literary canon and ethnographic writing. It attempts to reverse the pathologising of Indian society even as it confirms the protocols of ethnography as a form of knowledge production. It also positions the urban upper-caste educated as a vanguard, an authentic narrative authority, and the Hindu peasant proprietor as the sign and fount of an indigenous autonomous culture that is yet to master the art of mediating modern genres of representation; a configuration that would be reproduced in other genres.

Critical readings of the identity and positions of the author and the sources that authorise narratives about colonial society have accumulated their own history. There is no dearth of analyses on Lal Behari Day's work and life, as several accounts situate his writing within the different phases of Orientalist discourse, Christian missionary approaches to questions of reform and local knowledge, and within critiques of colonial rule. Day's selective inclusion of folktales in his *Folktales of Bengal* in 1883 said to be shaped by a search for a cultural infancy embodied in a fictive folk unspoiled by colonial contact prevented the appearance of the urban poor and those who produced legends and ghost stories in contemporary times. Day's own source of folklore, one such critique emphasises, was an indigenous Christian woman, not "Shambhu's mother", cited as the original source of folklore, whose loss is bemoaned.[21] This ambivalence over the authenticity of indigenous identity is already in evidence in the novel.

The sources for folktales collected in colonial times, Rangeet Sengupta suggests, viewed as "a murky ill-defined swarm of

[21] Sengupta, "'Spurious Additions'". This question is repeated by Shahid Amin with reference to the glossaries and reports on peasant life produced by colonial officials, discussed below.

balladists and rural bards", differed from the sources for Sanskrit texts studied by Max Müller and became the object of administrative record and description.[22] Sengupta notes that Richard Temple, one of the prominent collectors of the period, used "images that would blur the boundaries between his role as an administrator and his vocation as a scholar."[23] The development of such a cross-disciplinary location for cultural and literary production in the colony was further mediated, as Sengupta emphasises, by *munshis* who were often the initial translators:

> Chaina Mal's proficiency in both Punjabi and English seems to be a matter of speculation. He stands as the mysterious middleman in this entire colonial game. This intricate linguistic exchange was hence pervaded by . . . an incessant latent fear of slippage and chaos. This in many ways reflects the pervasive ambivalence in anthropological narratives born out of colonial encounters.[24]

By situating Day's "Scottish Reformist viewpoint" amidst the Brahmo Samaj, the Gaudiya Samaj, and the approach of Vidyasagar, Sengupta indicates the available complexity of positions on cultural and economic questions. The significance of this is evident in representations of the indigo revolts, already embedded in patterns of representation, many of which served to inaugurate the political role of the urban elite – as an early essay has pointed out.[25] While Day may have been a member of the Calcutta Missionary Conference that opposed the abuse of labour in the extraction of indigo, as an indigenous Christian his participation was controlled by metropolitan missionaries.

[22] Ibid.

[23] Ibid.

[24] Ibid.

[25] Guha, "Neel-Darpan".

This helps contextualise the variety of narrative sources that compete and combine in Day's novel with varying degrees of self-referentiality regarding their provenance and instrumental use; a compelling reason to view this novel, in particular, in continuum with other genres of writing, much like the multiple forms of authority embodied in the administrator-scholar (as Sengupta terms Richard Temple). While the initial sections of the following analysis examine structures of time and space within the text, the latter sections read the text in the context of contemporary ethnographies to suggest how social actors and counter-narratives are culled from them.

Failing Romance, or, the Bengali does not Court at all

Narrative movement in *Govinda Samanta* is horizontal, tacking between prior texts that speak more authoritatively of society, or literary texts that provided equally definitive aesthetic templates through which to represent experience. While intertextuality as a critical method works as a disclaimer to the promise that language is the vehicle of unmediated experience, the ethnographic novel presents an inverted problematic; it claims to represent the real but is in fact hindered from engaging in the play of structure or meaning by a prior authorised version of reality. Thus the novel slides from one authorised representational regime to another, occasionally qualifying ethnographic typologies or marking difference from European literary schema. The volume and precision of information that precede the novel seem to exhaust the possibilities of narrative. The village and the market are mapped spatially, and their animate and inanimate contents described and categorised; houses are classified into types and their structure and fabric and process of construction described in detail.[26]

Mohapatra and Nayak's critique, which points to the combination of rationalism and romanticism, resonates with histories of European realism. Michael McKeon for instance, or J.M. Bernstein, would examine how the realist aesthetic was achieved through the synthesis of representational structures that were potentially opposed to each other.[27] Day presents those aspects of contemporary rural life as they would be objectified within European empiricist knowledge production or as they would appear within the categories of romance, only to suggest how Indian rural life successfully fulfilled those expectations or failed them, particularly those that envisioned romance, individuality, and the unpredictability of human will as inherent to the condition of being human:

> I think I hear my English reader exclaim – "What a fool of a writer this novelist is! An orthodox novel generally ends in a marriage, but this fellow talks of . . . a wedding, before he has well begun his story." Well, my defence against this grave charge is, that I cannot help it. Malati must now get married, whether I wish it or not. The customs of the country require it.[28]

Positing social custom is a tautological device (it calls on an orientalist stereotype as a reality) that offers a civilisational absence of structures of individuation as a cause of emotive and literary impoverishment: "the reader will please remember that nothing

[26] The village of Kanchanpur, we are told, "has a population of about fifteen hundred souls, belonging to most of the thirty-six castes into which the Hindus of Bengal are generally divided . . ." Day, *Govinda Samanta*, 10.

[27] McKeon, *The Origins of the English Novel, 1600–1740*, 267.

[28] Day, *Govinda Samanta*, ch. XIII, 81.

very striking does, in point of fact, ever occur in the history of . . . a Bengali peasant boy."[29]

An earlier discussion of the place of literature in colonial India noted that it was thrust into being a subset of knowledge without clear boundaries and "launched as a terrain of social history, law making *et al.*, from within a conception of colonial utility."[30] The writer of this observation, Kumkum Sangari, argued that "the specialized meaning of literature as creative emerges as a polarization between imagination and *colonial* utility."[31] The novel typically maps the division between fiction and non-fiction onto this division, acknowledging the readers' likely exasperation, and arresting explorations of subjectivity with the repeated assertion: "the Bengali does not court at all." The reader is instead promised "a plain and unvarnished tale of a plain peasant, living in this plain country of Bengal . . . told in a plain manner."[32]

Such puritanical eschewing of adventure and "gorgeous metaphor" in favour of literary verisimilitude is complemented by the rejection of familiar Indian texts, "Válmiki, Vyás and the compilers of the Puránas", as well as of Swift and Rabelais.[33] English and European literary epigraphs precede and punctuate chapters, not necessarily by providing an ironic counterpoint that brings the failures of colonial society into relief, but as a prior framing of experience to which it can be aligned. Such literary citations are another cultural authority with which the novel is compliant; but

[29] Ibid., 186.

[30] Sangari, "Relating Histories", 62; Dharwadker, "Orientalism and the Study of Indian Literature".

[31] Sangari, "Relating Histories", 64.

[32] Day, *Govinda Samanta*, 3–4.

[33] Ibid., 2.

these lend themselves more easily to the task of weaving a narrative than the colonial report.

The Ethnographic Pastoral

Day's use of allusions and quotes from canonical texts does not trace any single literary tradition but combines these to form an amorphous continuous literary trope of romantic pastoralism. These serve as an opposing pole to the narrator's empiricist account of the village, as though to secure the novel's literariness despite the labour of following the protocols of ethnographic and scientific enquiry. The account of the village draws on botanical, literary, and geographical references: "The third curiosity of the vegetable kingdom at Kanchanpur is a magnificent *vata* tree (Ficus Indica) which grows near the hát to the south-west of the village . . . Milton must have had one of these trees in his mind's eye when he sang of the big tree which, 'In Malabar or Deccan spreads her arms/ Branching so broad and long, that in the ground/ The bended twigs take root, and daughters grow/ About the mother-tree . . .'"[34]

The botanical terms that structure small sections of the text devolve from a wider genre of orientalist romanticism in which botanical features were figurative of the life of the colony.[35] David Arnold details how Romanticism as a literary form was a resource for Orientalist botanists such as Joseph Hooker who, "in emulation of the earlier scientific travels of Darwin and . . . Humboldt . . . deployed the language and imagery of

[34] Ibid., 15. The quote from Milton is from Book IX of *Paradise Lost*.

[35] Arnold, "Deathscapes", in idem, *The Tropics and the Traveling Gaze*.

Romanticism to elicit the 'effects of association' and to enhance his botanical narrative."[36]

Early novels aligned themselves with such cross-referenced norms of representation by reauthorising their metaphors. If Milton's or Southey's orientalist invocations of an unseen land found their way into early botanical works, absorbing the landscapes and flora and fauna of India into those metaphors, the ethnographic novel in India authorised itself as fiction by associating itself with orientalist literature, and reproduced botanical figures as both literary trope and knowledge.

The weight of comparative representation is never so visible as in the section that immediately follows Milton's verse about the banyan tree, which cited Henry Maine's widely distributed, *Village-Communities in the East and West.* Within Maine's synthesis of the ancient Teutonic village with contemporary Indian ones, Kanchanpur lacked one element – the wastelands.[37] As though to salvage its own literariness from Maine's enumerated structure, the narrative slides towards pastoralist description and shows how, in the absence of wastelands, cattle graze on "land situated near pools of water which ever and anon relieve the eye amid the infinite expanse of never-ending paddy."[38] At other points this Burdwan

[36] Ibid., 346. Romanticism, he suggests, was "less an ideology of escapism or a means of rejecting convention than a doctrine of colonial appropriation." He also refers to studies that trace how, conversely, India featured in the literary texts of European Romanticism. Ibid., 344, 113–14.

[37] Rich, *Race and Empire in British Politics*, 16. Rich suggests that "the comparative method was dominated by . . . Maine who established the essential terms of debate among both legal historians and scholars of comparative institutions." Maine, *Village-Communities in the East and West.*

[38] Day, *Govinda Samanta*, 16.

pastoral erases difference by universalising the Bengal plough, an object that is not "too low to be described, especially when we remember that it exercised in antiquity the genius of two such poets as Hesiod and Virgil."[39]

A single sentence bears the compounded referential weight of classical epics, contemporary Bengali, the Burdwan inflection, and botanical classification in Latin: "For the ilex oak of the Theban bard, and the elm of the Mantuan, the Bengali husbandman substitutes the *bábul*, or rather *bábla*, as the Vardhamana peasant calls it – the *Acacia Arabica* of botanists."[40] This equalisation through botany is further stabilised with a question: "What, then, is a Bengal plough?" The answer, "The Bengal plough is very much the same as the Greek and the Roman one . . ." seems ironically simple.[41] Peasant life as the sign of the origin of civilisation is static.

The pastoral also invokes the opposition between country and city in Bengal, whose provinces provide a corrective to the snobbishness of the newly formed "Calcutta cockney, who glories in the Mahratta Ditch, despises the scenery of the country, and plumes himself upon the fact of his having never seen in his life the rice-plant . . ."[42] Day's usage leans on the tongue-in-cheek colonial urban idiolect to further disparage the city in favour of the village.[43]

[39] Ibid., 17.

[40] Ibid., 18.

[41] Ibid.

[42] Ibid.

[43] Yule and Burnell, *Hobson-Jobson*, 329. The Maratha Ditch was constructed in the eighteenth century in anticipation of a Maratha invasion. The compilation states of the Calcutta dwellers: ". . . its inhabitants are often styled Ditchers, as the citizens of London are called Cockneys." "Bengal as it is", *Calcutta Review*, 207. "Anglo-Indians are not so happy in the coinage

Closing off the Present

Each time *Govinda Samanta* ruefully closes off the present by portraying all volition as pre-empted by tradition, temporal movement is minimised and the only axis along which the narrative can move is the accumulation of detail, and by becoming in itself a store of information. Some of the categories are predictable enough, such as superstition, which stands in for any belief that drew links between the supernatural and the course of human life. Various characters in the novel who adhere to superstition delay and impede movement, leading to destructive life decisions and interfering with a rational allocation of the household economy.[44] In missionary accounts critical of Hinduism in the first half of the century, colonial intervention is often portrayed as the only impetus for change.[45] However, while superstition impoverishes its practitioners, the existence of ritual, as discussed later, ensures the peasant a place in caste Hindu society because it signals separation from the primitive.

Some of the labour of the novel is expended towards countering

---

of words to meet the exigencies of the occasion as their brethren of the United States; consequently, they have no better terms to describe the self-sufficient, prejudiced, narrow-minded, arrogant, and ignorant Ditcher, than that of 'Calcutta cockney.'" "The Mofussil and the Ditch", *Asiatic Journal and Monthly Register*, 36.

[44] All of ch. 7 is devoted to a description of the Putreshti *yagya* and the legend of Sashti. Day, *Govinda Samanta*, 373; ibid., 6–9.

[45] Arnold, *The Tropics*; Day, *Govinda Samanta*, ch. XVIII, 122. "This was the last time when the *satí* rite was performed at Kánchanpur, for in a few months after this event, Lord William Bentinck, one of the most beneficent of rulers that ever wielded the destinies of an empire, had the moral courage to enact, on 4th December, 1829, that law which for ever put a stop to that murderous practice."

pejorative stereotypes, as when evidential detail demonstrates superior civic and bodily hygiene: "[O]ur Mofussil villages are better supplied in regard to sanitary arrangements than Europeans might suspect", or "[c]onsidering that Bengali Hindu peasants bathe every day . . . we have no hesitation in saying that they are about the cleanest peasantry in the world."[46] In defiance of the idea that widows were underfed or starved, the narrator suggests, in a somewhat unusual analogy, "that most widows are sleek and stout"; and that like the widows "many of the strong and able-bodied peasants of the North Western Provinces, and the Hindu Sepoys in the Bengal army, take only one meal in twenty-four hours."[47] The novel's descriptive potential is diminished as the narrative moves back and forth between the truisms of colonial typologies and instances that potentially contradict them.

Thus the typology of the hero's friends serves to prove the absence of rank among them, held up in comparison to English society where cross-class interactions are said to be unlikely.[48] In the novel this not only serves to dilute the notion that caste barriers create absolute divisions but also provides an opportunity to salvage male friendship from analogies with homoerotic and homosexual same-sex friendships in classical Greece.[49]

On occasion, the English language itself debars cultural particularity, neutralising any efforts the author may make to overcome

[46] Day, *Govinda Samanta*, 31–2 and 141.

[47] Ibid., 134.

[48] Ibid., 150.

[49] The novel refers to the friendships "of Damon and Pythias, the half-legendary tale of Harmodios and Aristogeiton", and to the suspicion that there was something "morally rotten in those outwardly graceful friendships, and that a Hellenic erastes was not always a virtuous friend." Day, *Govinda Samanta*, 149–50.

it: "Gentle reader . . . [Y]ou perceive that Badan and Alanga speak better English than most uneducated English peasants . . . But how could I have avoided this defect in my history? If I had translated their talk into the Somersetshire or the Yorkshire dialect, I should have turned them into English, and not Bengali, peasants."[50]

Terms and Names, Companionate Genres

In a monograph about Ram Gharib Chaube, the unacknowledged assistant to what would become significant ethno-linguistic projects at the end of the nineteenth century, Shahid Amin recovers the story of "the *dobashi* native insider" from the scribe's handwritten jottings in the notes he sent in the 1890s to the "collector-ethnographer" William Crooke, and to the "collector-linguist" George Grierson.[51]

Like Rangeet Sengupta, Amin reveals how the enterprise of language learning, ethnography, and translation was linked through the figure of Chaube, whose official notes were published by Crooke as an attempt to access ethnographic information "beyond the missionary, the planter and the collector".[52] Reading against Chaube's own professed political distance "from subalterns and the new nationalist elites alike", and against the

[50] Ibid., 61. In another instance: "When narrating the conversation he had with Badan, we found it impossible to represent his nasal intonation in the English language, though it would have been quite easy in Bengali. In uttering the words, 'how do you do?' Ráma Rúpa would say 'hnow dno ynou dno?'" Day, *Govinda Samanta*, 75.

[51] Amin, "The Marginal Jotter", 6.

[52] Ibid., 5.

colonial ethnographer's desire for immutable indigenous objects and subjects, Amin notes, "Indian informants never missed the opportunity to harp on the theme of 'progress'"; they sought evidence of "change" in the everyday life of their countrymen.[53] The configuration of late-nineteenth-century colonial knowledge producers, ethnographers, missionaries, planters, collectors, and linguists had generated counterparts among the indigenous elite, such as the enlightened zamindar Joy Krishna Mukherjee, who had offered a prize for the novel *Govinda Samanta*, and the pastor and English teacher Lal Behari Day himself, who enjoyed greater recognition than Chaube could hope for, but is evidence that the native informant often reauthorised the master ethnographer.

Just as the figure of Chaube suggests the links between ethnography, administration, and linguistics, the novel is discursively linked to the genres of the glossary, gazette, and memoir of the time.[54] Classification laid bare the detail of colonial life as a perusable object, states Amin, by fragmenting it into categories. He

[53] Amin, *A Concise Encyclopaedia*, 34.

[54] The contemporary publications of Radhakanta Deva Bahadur, quoted by Lal Behari Day in the novel, seem to illustrate the simultaneous interest in literature and administration and the shared structures across the genres of horticulture, grammar, and administration that were a feature of colonial knowledge production. Radhakanta Deva Bahadur, whose works were quoted in *Govinda Samanta*, was Justice of the Peace and honorary magistrate, and vice president of the Agricultural and Horticultural Society; he published the first Bengali spelling book or reader, the *Nitikatha* in 1820, as well as an English translation of a Persian work on horticulture, and a Sanskrit Encyclopaedic Lexicon, the *Sabdakalpadruma*. *A Rapid Sketch of the Life of Raja Radhakanta Deva Bahadur, with Some Notices of His Ancestors and Testimonials of His Character and Learning by the Editors of the Raja's Sabdakalpadruma*, 20–1. Deva, "An Account of the Agriculture of the 24-Purgunnas".

cites the linguist Ashok Kelkar's account of how words shift from being names to terms that in the context of colonial ethnography generate a "master language . . . credited with possessing 'terms'", while "the indigenous languages are seen as having only 'names'."[55] The two parts of the title *Govinda Samanta, or the Life of a Bengal Raiyat*, are a sign that the fictional subjectivity promised in the name is precluded by the terms of the master language, where it becomes an illustration of a category.

Govinda Samanta revels in its relentlessly awkward instantiation of Indian names to match European terms, sometimes intended – though not always succeeding, as comic relief ("In Ireland Paddy makes riots, in Bengal, *raiyats* make paddy").[56] While the relation of most names to terms (Lakshmi, the Indian Demeter; Puri, a vast Golgotha; Yama, the Indian Rhadamanthus) defers to the Anglo-European tradition as the norm, the transition of the word peasant from word to term in colonial usage, and its equation with *raiyat*, is an instance of how the relation between terms and names was transacted through multiple genres.[57]

Perhaps narrative pleasure is elicited despite the ethnographic habitus through the plenitude of enumeration, for instance, as with lists of local produce that appear in the novel. Narrative pleasure potentially lies not only in the wealth of a hundred and nineteen varieties of rice in the twenty-four Parganas, but in the opportunity to turn their descriptions into a savouring of their particularities, as with the Randhuni-Pagal: "(Rándhuni-Págal,

[55] Amin, *A Concise Encyclopaedia*, 37.

[56] Day, *Govinda Samanta*, 200.

[57] Ibid., 73, 226, 245. A body of writing about peasant history debates the legal, economic, and political connotations of the terms "peasant" and "raiyat" and the consequences of the unreflexive usage of these terms in Indian economic history.

that is, cook-maddening) is so fine and fragrant that, while boiling it, the cook becomes mad with joy."[58]

From Buchanan's travel writings at the beginning of the nineteenth century, to 1842 when the East India Company's Court of Directors commissioned the compilation of an administrative glossary, the task of extracting intelligence about land relations and its associated practices moved from the hands of individual officials to becoming company policy.[59] If *Govinda Samanta* differs from these reports, it is because it shifts the work of reliable and benevolent representation away from the colonial official to the indigenous urban intelligentsia.[60]

The Vanguard

An essay discussing the conflicted relationship of the Bengali urban intelligentsia to peasant unrest counts Joy Krishna Mukherjee, the patron for the novel *Govinda Samanta*, among the conservative

[58] Ibid., 201–2. Likewise, ghosts are divided between Hindu and Muslim ghosts, and caste-specific ones – such as the spirits of departed Brahmins and friends – are classified into *mitra, bandhu*, perhaps indicating the plenitude in cultural particularities. Ibid., 105, 149.

[59] Amin, *A Concise Encyclopaedia*, 27. Works such as John Crawfurd's, *A Descriptive Dictionary of the Indian Islands & Adjacent Countries* (1856) or George Grierson's *Bihar Peasant Life* (1885), are coterminous with the emergence of a wide range of classificatory studies such as the census on caste and race.

[60] It swerves away from mentioning the 1857 revolt, and, despite replicating the problematic structures of ethnography, it does not eventually dismiss all of Hindu society as alien. Along with detailing ritual and festivals, it suggests that the bracketing of significant events within ritual revealed the reverence with which daily lives was conducted, and was proof of the meaningfulness of events and action for peasants.

elites who were unsympathetic to calls for reforms that would benefit *raiyats*, and were unified with the liberal intelligentsia in the condemnation of peasant violence.[61] Yet, as the essayist Kalyan Kumar Sen Gupta points out, it was Mukherjee's patronage that created the widely popular sympathetic account of the contemporary *raiyat*. The novel distributes these contradictions more manageably across the figures of both oppressive and benevolent zamindars, maharajas, indigo planters, and colonial officials, and contributes to the cautious criticism offered of powerful figures in the rural economy.[62] The most explicit critique of state is offered through the individuated figure of the planter, against whom the narrator unleashes a Christian moral charge to reveal the brutality accompanying his overt works of charity and religious practice. Badly conceived legislation that preceded the reforms of the Rent Act (Act X of 1859, or the Bengal Rent Act) also receives its share of attention for having caused peasant distress.[63]

Sen Gupta's discussion alone, in contrast to other discussions of the novel, notes that the publication of *Govinda Samanta* was preceded by Mir Musharaff Hussain's *Jamindar Darpan* (*A Mirror for the Zamindar*, 1873) and the anonymous novel *Asha Marichika*, published from Pabna, both critiques of zamindar families.[64] This essay is singular for neither fetishising the language in which *Govinda Samanta* is written, nor requiring its historiographic separation from texts in other languages, allowing for the novel to be juxtaposed with preceding works. In contrast with other anti-zamindar texts, it is not Day's deference to the colonial state that

[61] Gupta, "Bengali Intelligentsia and the Politics of Rent".

[62] Dakua, "The Novelistic Discourse in the Early Indian Novel in English".

[63] Day, *Govinda Samanta*, 361.

[64] Gupta, "Bengali Intelligentsia and the Politics of Rent", 30.

stands out, but rather his advocacy of the benevolent zamindar and maharaja.

The social subgroup that the narrative inaugurates, to complement the peasant/*raiyat* as a moral and political vanguard of colonial society, is the author's own: the urban upper-caste indigenous intelligentsia educated in English, whose newsprint and actions are invoked in the novel as signs of progress, enabling a critique of the state and of local oppression.[65] The causal logic of the novel gestures at the reformist capacity of the state and the new intelligentsia, while framing the dénouement and the leeching of life from the *raiyat* within the immediate priorities of vicious overlords, a process that is enabled, or at least unhindered, by indifferent colonial policy and fate.

Counter-ethnography

And yet the text does attempt a counter-ethnography that occasionally exceeds a refutation of colonial critiques to extricate an alternative conception of rural hierarchies in peasant mispronunciations or diminutives of formal terms:

> As the raiyats of Bengal find it difficult to pronounce English names aright, they generally lengthen and widen them agreeably to the genius of their mother-tongue, and make them correspond to some Bengali names or sounds . . . Campbell is turned into *Kambal* (a blanket); . . . Mr. Murray, the planter, was called *Mâri*, which in Bengali means either flogging or the plague. And, truly, when we consider the relation in which Mr. Murray stood to hundreds of the peasantry in the neighbouring villages, we think he merited the cognomen . . .[66]

[65] Day, *Govinda Samanta*, 312–15.

[66] Ibid., 301.

Despite the conflicted relation to critiques of colonial rule, stray comparisons suggest that peasant unrest, even violence, was not illegitimate: "Were Bengal peasants like Irish cottiers, Orangemen, Ribbonmen, and the rest, zamindari oppression would be impossible."[67] A righteous zamindar in the novel attempts to protect the *raiyats* from the wrath of the planter by sending his own armed support, and, while the violence that results is not initiated by the peasants, the possibility of violence is not shunned, as is evident in the discussion of the *dharmaghat* (collective strike action) by a group of friends when the local *pattanidar* seeks to extract a fee to finance his son's wedding from Govinda Samanta.[68] The narrator delimits the possibilities of the *dharmaghat* from inception, by reproducing familiar racial epithets to suggest that the docility innate to the Bengali peasant, and the divisions inherent in caste solidarities, would divide the Sadgopa caste from the Aguri, both cultivating groups.

Raiyat, Peasant, Caste

The family in the novel is said to be Aguri, though the majority of the other peasants are of the Sadgopa caste.[69] In personalising the story of dispossession of a peasant family, Day chose a group that had not been marginalised within the social hierarchy and was more centrally assimilated within the devotional and caste economy than the recently pastoralist Sadgopa.

[67] Ibid., 280.

[68] Ibid., 266. *Pattanidar*: land-holding rank found mainly in western Bengal, created by the Raja of Burdwan.

[69] Dalton's *Descriptive Ethnology of Bengal* (1872), focused largely on the tribes of eastern India, has an entry on a pastoral tribe, the Gopas. Other studies indicate the higher status enjoyed by Sadgopas with the rejection of pastoralism. Dalton, *Descriptive Ethnology of Bengal*; Sanyal, "Continuities of Social Mobility".

The figure of the oppressed agriculturist was the focus of liberal critiques of land laws.[70] As the hindered heroes of a novel, the Aguri acquired personhood in the name *Govinda Samanta* and were universalised with the European peasant, which endowed them with the distinction of having enjoyed possession of their land, though they had just lost it to the zamindar. Fit subjects of their own story from the perspective of the urban liberal intelligentsia, the Aguri perhaps suitably represented caste-entrenched indigenousness. Religious rituals are detailed and deprecated because of the expense incurred in performing them, but eventually become a sign that the peasant, though not upper caste, is not primitive.[71] Sudras, the broader caste category to which the Aguri in the novel belong, are distinct from and enjoy a higher social position than the strongmen, the poorest labourers, and the Buná coolie or "natives of Chota Nagpore and Sonthal Pergunahs" who feature only briefly as victims of the indigo planter. If we were to examine contemporary ethnographic reports of the region, we would find them substantially occupied with the Santals and other tribal groups.[72]

As is well known, despite protestations that nothing usually happened in the lives of *raiyats*, the Aguri, *raiyat*, peasant, and zamindar were dynamic entities in the nineteenth century and provided narrative possibilities as they featured in reports on unrest, in economic treatises, and in articles criticising colonial

[70] The idea of the autonomous village republic in decline complemented that of the independent peasant and was prominent in the writings of the Henry Maine and Baden-Powell. Maine, *Village-Communities in the East and West*.

[71] For Day, the nineteenth-century pastor, this also constituted proof that he had not descended from a monkey.

[72] Ibid., 298–300. See, for instance, Hunter, *Annals of Rural Bengal*.

policy.[73] The links between ethnography and administration meant that groups such as Raiyat and Aguri cumulatively acquired historical, moral, and political dimensions, particularly after political crises and rebellions.

Economic histories have emphasised that the Permanent Settlement of 1793, intended by the colonial state to remedy the apparent absence of private property, did not in fact bestow outright proprietorship on the zamindar, and that property relations in different parts of India comprised interests and claims, and occasionally absolute ownership of land, rather than a uniform system of private property.[74] However, the contemporary valorisation in economic theory of private property as the guarantee of independence, and the notion of the dispossessed peasant, were complemented by narratives such as Day's that hinted at economic self-sufficiency as an intrinsic property of the small peasant.[75] Conceptions such as these became personal and caste attributes of the family and the individual in the novel.

Similarly, utilitarianism informs the critique of education, with the Brahmin-run *pathshala* expressly criticised for embodying

[73] Guha, "Neel-Darpan".

[74] "Through Bengal's Permanent Settlement of 1793, the East India Company government, under Lord Cornwallis, had granted zamindars (the revenue-collecting gentry of the Mughal empire) exclusive proprietorship over their estates, fixing their revenue obligations to the state in perpetuity, and thereby reconstituting them as landlords with private ownership of the rental value of those estates, a revenue that they would therefore have an incentive to increase through improvements." See Sartori, "A Liberal Discourse of Custom in Colonial Bengal", 165. Relief was provided by the Rent Act of 1859. A seminal text elaborating the philosophical context for the emergence of the Permanent Settlement is Guha, *A Rule of Property for Bengal.*

[75] Sartori, "A Liberal Discourse of Custom in Colonial Bengal", 170.

a high culture without contemporary utility, while the skills imparted in the Kayastha instructor's class are seen as more empowering. This contradiction, which echoed similar critiques in England, found the elite urban Bengali ill equipped with skills for new trades while suggesting they had mastered the signs of social distinction through colonial education.[76]

The Missionary Text

Missionary preaching in the novel intersects the question of education but has an ambivalent place for it appears both as an articulation of daily suffering and oppression, as well as a claim to a superior knowledge that is countered by the village schoolmaster. The account of missionary preaching reproduced a stock image of the preacher under a tree that dots narratives of Christianity in India. The narrator in *Govinda Samanta* asks: "But, lo! who is that European gentleman who has just entered the *hat*, and is standing in the shade of that big *vata* tree to which I have so often alluded, with a Babu-looking person beside him, and a coolie with a bag under his arm?"[77] These descriptions form a pattern visible in documents of the Church Missionary Society.[78]

It is likely that, as in the sixteenth and seventeenth centuries, the reports of missionaries developed schematic representations of encounters with the unfamiliar so that the story of the success

[76] Day, *Govinda Samanta, or the History of a Bengal Ráiyat*, 70–5.

[77] Day, *Govinda Samanta*, 170–1.

[78] Bhabha, "Signs Taken for Wonders". Extracts from the documents of the Society are reproduced in Bhabha's essay. Some overlaps in the area of missionary work discussed by Bhabha and Day are possible, as Bhabha mentions the Burdwan education plan of 1818, the district to which Day returned to preach and where his novels and other books are based.

of the missions could be anticipated and absorbed irrespective of the differences in colonial cultures.[79] A recurrent feature of the scene of the missionary and his texts is, as Homi Bhabha points out, the exhibition of desire for the book: "At the sight of the Saheb a number of people leave off bargaining and rush towards him. The Babu opens a book which he has with him, and begins to read. Govinda and scores of other people listen attentively."[80] There is a desire for both the message and the material text, as at the end of the preaching, when "*Satya A'sraya* (The True Refuge)" or "Christian tracts written in Bengali" are distributed, and the listeners "showed such eagerness to obtain them that they trod upon one another's toes, and nearly threw the missionary and his catechist off their legs."[81]

The missionary's message is often both affective and learned, attributes attached to both the written and spoken word. A sentence about labour and suffering leaves the listening crowd "greatly affected", while the preacher's "earnestness and fluency" leads them to remark, "[A]ll that the Padre Saheb is saying is quite true!"[82] Missionary teaching is depicted in contest with other belief systems, where what is at stake is not the truth of the doctrine but the mastery of rhetoric and argument exhibited by the speaker. The village schoolteacher's reputation for sagacity, valorised over

[79] Hofmeyr, *The Portable Bunyan*; Županov, *Disputed Mission.*

[80] Day, *Govinda Samanta*, 171.

[81] *Satya asraya. The True Refuge.* A Christian Tract (13th edition), 24pp, 12mo. (Cuttack, 1869); *Satya asraya. The True Refuge*, pp. 30pp (Midnapur, 1870), British Museum Dept of Oriental Printed Books and Manuscripts; and James Fuller Blumhardt, *Catalogue of the Marathi, Gujarati, Bengali, Assamese, Oriya, Pishtu, and Sindhi Manuscripts in the Library of the British Museum* (British Museum, 1905); Day, *Govinda Samanta*, 173.

[82] Day, *Govinda Samanta*, 171–3.

brahmanic instruction, is also confirmed in a comparison with the missionary:

> But Rama Rupa was not only mathematical, he was eminently logical. Though he had not read the *Sútras* of Gotama, he was an acute reasoner. Whenever the Christian missionary of Vardhamana came to the village . . . he did not fail to pay a visit to the lame schoolmaster, who had many a tough argument with him; and the villagers always thought that the missionary was invariably worsted.[83]

There is also ambiguity about accepting the entirety of the message, where it seemed to pose concepts entirely different or opposed to those of prevailing beliefs, as also seen in the Bhabha essay extract. In *Govinda Samanta* the narrator states: "When, however, he touched on the last clause of the text and spoke of the eternal rest as the gift of the Saviour, he did not seem to carry along with him the sympathy of his audience."[84]

Perhaps in missionary accounts such ambiguity over the acceptance of parts of Christian doctrine helped explain the disproportion between the enthusiasm to possess the written or printed tract (for which there are multiple reasons, as book history has indicated) and the number of those eventually converted.[85]

[83] Ibid., 76.

[84] Ibid. Discussions follow between Brahmins and Kayasths, states the narrator, but refrains from reproducing these arguments.

[85] Bhabha's reading of the indigenous Christian Anund Messeh's encounter with people reading the Bible under a grove of trees aligns it with colonial imaginings of native desire for the coloniser's book and suggests how mimicry and "sly civility" elide that claim to determine and decipher its reception. A recent reading of Bhabha argues for a less passive reception of the Bible and Christianity in India, embedding his account in book history and a history of possible inter-religious hermeneutics. Gupta, "What Really Happened under a Tree Outside Delhi, May 1817"; Bhabha, "Signs Taken for Wonders", 145.

A Story to Tell

Midway through the novel the narrator appeases the reader, promising that despite appearances to the contrary he has a story to tell. In the individual struggle of the *raiyat* against the local *pattanidar* and the indigo planter in the latter part of the novel, the enumerative pattern of the text is punctuated with conflict and violent events that befall the family.

It is only in an instance of personally catastrophic rebellion against the zamindar's extraction of a tribute that Govinda Samanta's individual emotions and political being find articulation. From the time he finds himself unable to obey the zamindar's demand, Govinda Samanta and his family lose everything in their direct and tragic confrontation with the local *pattanidar* – called zamindar in the novel for reasons of terminological familiarity – and with the English planter John Murray who exploits the local *raiyat* to supply the East India indigo concern with product.[86]

The account of the brutal death of Govinda's brother-in-law in a conflict against the indigo planter followed the well-known play *Neeldarpan*, as well as other representations against the conditions of indigo cultivation. Labour conditions worsened after 1847, and from the 1850s the periodical press began to voice concerns over the cause of the *raiyats*. Following the submissions of the Indigo Commission in 1860, all print genres represented the conflict over indigo.[87]

[86] The novel carries occasional critiques of colonial policy, in one instance mentioning the availability of alcohol: "swallowing country spirits, which, thanks to the considerate and Christian kindness of the British Government, are now available in almost every village, though in the rude and uncivilised days of our forefathers they could hardly be had anywhere, either for love or for money." Day, *Govinda Samanta*, 188.

[87] Guha, "Neel-Darpan".

Realist time when it surfaces in the novel is ordered by the legislation of the colonial state and policy in the face of man-made disasters portrayed as natural ones. Thus an epidemic of 1870 reveals the inadequacy of ancient Hindu medicine, and the famine of 1873 allows the energy and effectiveness of colonial officials to be demonstrated.[88] While the hero loses his grandmother to the epidemic, his aunt escapes domestic widowhood in apparent submission to a summons to be a companion to a Vairagi (an ascetic mendicant group whose sexual behaviour was a cause for concern for the colonial state) – a summons that her mother-in-law is unable to challenge.[89]

Colonial records can be more emotive than this novel with their occasionally emphatic statements of differences with policy or the appearance of a petition appealing for fairness and justice, often within the terms of colonial legality, but with more impassioned representation than is permitted to Day's Bengal *raiyat*.

It is the historically referenced legislation transforming land relations in Bengal and other areas between 1793 and 1859 that is the agent of change in the structure of the *raiyat*'s life, and the enabler of the individual *raiyat*'s agency in the novel. The Permanent Settlement of 1793, in seeking to distil and fix revenue relations to assure the zamindar autonomy from the state, is said to have, however unintentionally, threatened and erased many of the customary rights of the *raiyat*. The regulations of the early-nineteenth century, the *haptam* of 1799 and *pancham* of 1812, which endowed the landlord with rights to seize property to ensure payment of revenue, are said to have caused much suffering to those lower down the hierarchy of agrarian production by eroding

[88] Day, *Govinda Samanta*, 374–6. Chapter LX titled "The Epidemic" details the ravages of an epidemic fever in Kanchanpur.

[89] Ibid., ch. XXXIV, 231.

the customary negotiating power *raiyats* may have enjoyed.[90] Against these measures the Bengal Rent Act of 1859 – called the *raiyat's* Magna Charta in the novel, and which sought to curtail the powers of the landlord and define tenures that secured the rights of *raiyats* – is said to have arrived too late to save Govinda Samanta, whose fortunes had gone into free fall as home and land were assailed initially by the violence of the zamindar's protectors and then by disease and famine.[91]

Particular figures in the system of land relations gained visibility in studies of legislation and economy, as the embodiment of principles of property, liberty, labour, and individuation, drawing attention to how the same figures appear or are modified within the structure of relations in the novel. While the ideas of custom and of individual proprietorship informed colonial theories of property, in the novel liberty and constraint are personified through the distinction between the self-sufficient peasant and the dependent wage labourer.[92] In fact, the differentiation of entities constituting positions within the hierarchy of land relations has been the subject of dispute, with some emphasising that the individual proprietor was initially conceived of in abstraction, then realised in law, and the relative incompatibility with the contemporary transitions of hierarchy in India was viewed as a sign of chaos.[93] Jon E. Wilson's *The Domination of Strangers*, for instance, emphasises how the political relations between zamindars, talukdars, and *raiyats*, and their tactical manoeuvrings,

[90] Wilson, *The Domination of Strangers*, 120–2.

[91] Day, *Govinda Samanta*, 364.

[92] Sartori, "A Liberal Discourse of Custom in Colonial Bengal".

[93] Wilson, "'A Thousand Countries to Go to': Peasants and Rulers in Late Eighteenth-Century Bengal"; Ray and Ray, "Zamindars and Jotedars: A Study of Rural Politics in Bengal".

went unrecognised in the technologies of knowledge that called instinctively on categories used in land governance in England and Scotland: "the landed proprietor was a phantom figure who existed nowhere but in ledgers and accounts housed in the Company's revenue offices."[94]

In a chapter titled "The Ráiyat's Magna Charta" the narrator states, "Anyone that has paid attention to the subject of the tenure of land in Bengal can hardly deny that that tenure is based on the right of labour. He who clears the land of jungle becomes its owner."[95] The claim of the original settler over land converged with the idea of the tradition-bound peasant, making the *raiyat* the repository of an original sovereignty that was recognised by all rulers: "It is true he pays a certain share of his profits to Government, or to the zamindar, who is usually a collector of tax appointed by Government; nevertheless the right of ownership lies with the clearer of the jungle and the occupant of the soil. This theory underlies all legislation on land in this country."[96]

Govinda's decline into the status of a day-labourer, a fall from independence that he does not survive, ends a section of the narrative that had begun with the stirring of dissent and defiance in the peasant, when he perceived the landlord's levy of a fee to finance his son's wedding as illegitimate and unaffordable.[97] The *raiyat* tends to be the illustrative example or effect of policy, as repressive land laws seed the conditions for predictable tragedies

[94] Wilson, *The Domination of Strangers*, 123.

[95] Day, *Govinda Samanta*, 364.

[96] Ibid.

[97] "He had never in his life hired himself out as a day-labourer. He had always tilled his paternal acres, and lived upon their produce. But now, in mature life, he had to stoop to the degradation of becoming a coolie. This thought dried up his life's blood." Ibid., 376.

to unfold in a novel within which the most active persona are colonial officials who rescue, govern, oppress or reform their subjects.

References

A Rapid Sketch of the Life of Raja Radhakanta Deva Bahadur, with Some Notices of His Ancestors and Testimonials of His Character and Learning by the Editors of the Raja's Sabdakalpadruma (Gaumisse, 1859).

Amin, Shahid, *A Concise Encyclopaedia of North Indian Peasant Life: South Asian Colonial Archive I: Being a Compilation from the Writings of William Crooke, J.R. Reid, G.A. Grierson* (Manohar Publishers and Distributors, 2005).

———, "The Marginal Jotter: Scribe Chaube and the Making of the Great Linguistic Survey of India c. 1890–1920", IIC Occasional Publication No. 27, 2011.

Arnold, David, "Deathscapes: India in an Age of Romanticism and Empire, 1800–1856", *Nineteenth-Century Contexts* 26, no. 4 (December 1, 2004), 339–53, https://doi.org/10.1080/0890549051233l329349.

——, *The Tropics and the Traveling Gaze: India, Landscape, and Science, 1800–1856* (Seattle: University of Washington Press, 2011).

Asiatic Journal and Monthly Register for British and Foreign India, China, and Australia, The (London: Parbury, Allen, and Company, 1839).

Bhabha, Homi K., "Signs Taken for Wonders: Questions of Ambivalence and Authority under a Tree Outside Delhi, May 1817", *Critical Inquiry* 12, no. 1 (1 October 1985), 144–65; https://doi.org/10.1086/448325.

Calcutta Review, The, University of Calcutta (1845).

Clough, Patricia Ticineto, *The End(s) of Ethnography: From Realism to Social Criticism* (New York: Peter Lang International Academic Publishers, 1998).

Crawfurd, John, *A Descriptive Dictionary of the Indian Islands & Adjacent Countries* [Electronic Resource] (London: Bradbury & Evans, 1856).

Dakua, Rajendra, "The Novelistic Discourse in the Early Indian Novel in English: A Study through the Fictional Texts of Bankim Chandra, Lal Behari Day and Krupaḅai Satthianadhan", *University,*

31 December 2014. http://shodhganga.inflibnet.ac.in:8080/jspui/handle/10603/119663.

Dalton, Edward Tuite, *Descriptive Ethnology of Bengal* (Kolkata: Office Superintendent of Government, 1872).

Dasgupta, Samir, "Life in a Bengal Village", *Economic Development and Cultural Change* 13, no. 1, Part 1 (October 1964), 115–17.

Day, Lal Behari, *Govinda Samanta; or, The History of a Bengal Raiyat* (London: Macmillan, 1874).

Deva, Radhakanta, "An Account of the Agriculture of the 24-Purgunnas and On the Agriculture of Silhut, Rajshahee, and Dinajpoor", in *Transactions of the Agricultural and Horticultural Society of India* (Serampore: Baptist Mission Press, 1838).

Dharwadker, Vinay, "Orientalism and the Study of Indian Literature", in *Orientalism and the Postcolonial Predicament: Perspectives on South Asia*, ed. Carol A. Breckenridge and Peter van der Veer (New Delhi: Oxford University Press, 1994).

Gopal, Priyamvada, *The Indian English Novel: Nation, History, and Narration* (Oxford: Oxford University Press, 2009).

Grant, Colesworthy, *Rural Life in Bengal: Illustrative of Anglo-Indian Suburban Life, the Habits of the Rural Classes, the Varied Produce of the Soil and Seasons, and the Culture and Manufacture of Indigo: Letters from an Artist in India to His Sisters in England* (London: W. Thacker, 1866).

Grierson, George Abraham, *Bihar Peasant Life, Being a Discursive Catalogue of the Surroundings of the People of That Province* (Calcutta: Bengal Secretariat Press, 1885).

Guha, Ranajit, "Neel-Darpan: The Image of a Peasant Revolt in a Liberal Mirror", *Journal of Peasant Studies*, vol. 2, no. 1 (October 1974), 1–46.

Gupta, Abhijit, "What Really Happened under a Tree Outside Delhi, May 1817", in *Founts of Knowledge*, ed. Swapan Chakravorty and Abhijit Gupta (Hyderabad: Orient Blackswan, 2015).

Gupta, Kalyan Kumar Sen, "Bengali Intelligentsia and the Politics of Rent, 1873–1885", *Social Scientist* 3, no. 2 (1974), 27–34. https://doi.org/10.2307/3516249.

Hofmeyr, Isabel, *The Portable Bunyan: A Transnational History of the Pilgrim's Progress* (Princeton, NJ: Princeton University Press, 2004).

Hunter, W.W., *Annals of Rural Bengal* (1868).

M., A., "Calcutta Diary", *Economic and Political Weekly*, 10, no. 22, 31 May 1975, 846–8.

Maine, Henry Sumner, *Village-Communities in the East and West. Six Lectures Delivered at Oxford* (London: J. Murray, 1871).

McKeon, Michael, *The Origins of the English Novel, 1600–1740* (Baltimore: Johns Hopkins University Press, 2002).

Mohanty, Satya P., "The Epistemic Work of Literary Realism: Two Novels from Colonial India", in *A History of the Indian Novel in English*, ed. Ulka Anjaria (Cambridge: Cambridge University Press, 2015).

Mohapatra, Himansu S., and J.K. Nayak, "Writing Peasant Life in Colonial India", *Toronto Review of Contemporary Writing Abroad*, Spring 1996, 29–40.

Ray, Ratna, and Rajat Ray, "Zamindars and Jotedars: A Study of Rural Politics in Bengal", *Modern Asian Studies* 9, no. 1 (1975), 81–102.

Rich, Paul B., *Race and Empire in British Politics* (Cambridge: Cambridge University Press Archive, 1990).

Sangari, Kumkum, "Relating Histories: Definitions of Literacy, Literature, Gender in Early Nineteenth Century Calcutta and England", in *Rethinking English: Essays in Literature, Language, History*, ed. Svati Joshi (New Delhi: Oxford University Press, 1994).

Sanyal, Hitesranjan, "Continuities of Social Mobility in Traditional and Modern Society in India: Two Case Studies of Caste Mobility in Bengal", *The Journal of Asian Studies* 30, no. 2 (1971), 315–39. https://doi.org/10.2307/2942917.

Sartori, Andrew, "A Liberal Discourse of Custom in Colonial Bengal", *Past & Present*, no. 212 (2011), 163–97.

Senapati, Fakir Mohan, *Six Acres and a Third*, trans. Rabi Shankar Mishra, Satya P. Mohanty, and Jatindra K. Nayak (Berkeley: University of California Press, 2005).

Sengupta, Rangeet, "'Spurious Additions': Lal Behari Day and the Discovery of the Genuine Folk", *Bengali Folktales in English Translation*, June 2007. http://www.literature-study-online.com/essays/bengali-folktales.html.

Wilson, Jon E., "'A Thousand Countries to Go to': Peasants and Rulers in Late Eighteenth-Century Bengal", *Past & Present*, no. 189 (2005), 81–109.

———, *The Domination of Strangers: Modern Governance in Eastern India, 1780–1835* (London: Palgrave Macmillan, 2008).

Yule, Henry, and Arthur Coke Burnell, *Hobson-Jobson: The Anglo-Indian Dictionary* (London: Wordsworth Editions, 1996).

Županov, Ines G., *Disputed Mission: Jesuit Experiments and Brahmanical Knowledge in Seventeenth-Century India* (Oxford: Oxford University Press, 2001).

5

Novel Social Form

Gulvadi Venkatrao's *Indirabai* (1899)

M. MADHAVA PRASAD

HISTORIES OF THE early novel in India deal with a variety of prose narratives by writers who were introduced to the European novel over the colonial encounter. Of these I find the "social novel" particularly interesting as a site for the investigation of the ideology of form. Unlike historical romances, such as those inspired by the example of Walter Scott or Alexander Dumas, for instance, the social novel, it seems to me, could not be transposed onto Indian soil without at the same time committing the writer, whether consciously or otherwise, to a socially transformative purpose. I am mainly interested in exploring this compulsion imposed by a form and the consequences that it entails in terms of actual narratives produced and worlds imagined. In this essay I will examine in detail the formal characteristics and historical context of a Kannada novel, Gulvadi Venkatrao's *Indirabai* (1899), and end with a few reflections on the theoretical issues that arise.

What we know as modern Indian literature – whether we see it as a complex unity or as a collection of separate developments – is now commonly acknowledged to be a product of the colonial encounter. In various genres – the novel, lyric poetry, drama, the prose essay – English or European works served as the first models for emulation, and literary historiography subsequently charted the growth and maturity of these forms, their eventual breaking free of foreign influence and re-grounding in Indian soil. Alongside, and often pre-dating this, has been the rediscovery of indigenous literary traditions which made their own contribution to the further development of modern literatures. Such histories have a way of treating the earliest works with indulgence, as the stammerings of a toddler that would pave the way for more accomplished works to come – which would not matter if, in addition, the relationship of the early works to their socio-political context had also been taken into consideration. A more complex periodisation of cultural history, which takes into account social and political temporalities, enables precisely such a break from quasi-biographical linearity so that the works of a specific historical moment – their aesthetic qualities as well as their political significance – may be read in relation to their context.[1] Thus it will turn out below that the "hybrid prose" of early novels like *Indirabai* not only indicates immaturity and lack of skill but mirrors social realities indirectly – a point entirely missed within considerations that look exclusively at maturity of form.

Such in any case is the approach I take in this study of *Indirabai* (1899), regarded as the first published "social novel" in the language. This distinction between "the first novel ever written or published" and the first "social novel" is made by literary historians themselves: there is no doubt that the second advent,

[1] Film history has seen such a productive turn away from conventional historiography, as in the work of Tom Gunning.

within the larger historical movement inaugurated by the first, is considered to be of cardinal importance by the tradition, though this has never been explicitly theorised. Why should this be so?

On encountering the novel form, one of the first reactions was to assimilate it to the Indian tradition of prose narrative. But this resolution was not entirely satisfactory, as the thoughts of one early practitioner of the art of the novel in Kannada (Gubbi Murugaradhya, author of *Sringarachaturyollasini*), indicate:

> I first had the idea of taking a "novel" from English and translating it into Kannada. But I had to abandon that plan when, after close consideration of a few such "kavyas" they were found to be at variance with the Hindu social customs. Next I thought of selecting a well-known "itihasa" in verse from our own tradition and rendering it in prose but this entailed abandoning the social characteristics of the "English novel" which was not acceptable. Hence I decided to write an altogether new story retaining Hindu social content while adopting the method/style of the "English novel".[2]

Murugaradhya here distinguishes style and content, but at the same time he finds that the content, though indigenous, must be new, because social in nature. Abstracted from the European context, the English novel style nevertheless demands a new content. V.N. Inamdar's historical essay, published as an introduction to another early novel, Kerur Vasudevacharya's *Indira*, is worth going into in some detail for it is not only an informative account of the novel form's early history in Kannada but also reflects the state of critical appreciation of this genre at the time.

Noting that the Kannada novel's prolific and independent development gets going only in the 1930s, Inamdar places

[2] Cited in Inamdar, "Prasthavane", 20. See also Padikkal, "Inventing Modernity", p. 227.

Kerur – and along with him Galaganatha, M.S. Puttanna, and Gulvadi – in the infancy period of the Kannada novel. Inamdar's backward glance at the history of the Kannada novel is informed by his conviction that "the novel must afford a realistic portrayal of life". Elaborating on this, he appreciates Kannada novelists for having made it socially oriented in content and realistic in form and style.[3]

In dialogue with Srinivasa Havanur's earlier account of the history of the Kannada novel, Inamdar reports that Kempu Narayana's *Mudramanjusha* and Yadava's *Kalaavatiparinaya* (for which the date given is 1815) are contenders for the honour of first Kannada novel, the latter being Havanur's choice. Early novels are classified as (1) romances and mythologicals (*adbhuta-ramya, pauranika*); (2) historical (*aitihaasika*); and (3) social (*saamaajika*). *Kalaavatiparinaya* is identified as a romance, *Mudramanjusha* as a historical, and Gulvadi Venkatrao's *Indirabai* as the first social. In addition there are translations from Marathi and other sources, such as that of *Robinson Crusoe* by Krishnaswami Iyangar in 1854, and the historical romances of Hari Narayan Apte. (Havanur attributes an autobiography to Iyangar of which Inamdar disputes the date and opts for 1854. The Basel Mission also published a novel by Padamanji called *Yamunaparyatana.* Inamdar mentions a translation of *Pilgrim's Progress* by G. Weigle of the Basel Mission in 1847, which Havanur considers not a novel because of its allegorical [*anyaarthapratipadane*] form.)

Here Inamdar makes a couple of interesting moves. "If we examine the history of any nation with a long literary tradition," he asserts, "we see that in its early phase the prose form called 'kadambari' invariably adopts the romance style." As examples

[3] Inamdar, "Prasthavane", 9.

from the Indian subcontinent he cites Bana's *Kadambari*, of course, but also Dandin's *Dasakumaracarita*, and other works like *Vasavadatta* and *Avantisundarikathe*. A combination of entertainment and moral instruction (*ranjane, nitibodhe*) is characteristic of these romance narratives. In Kannada he cites works from Gubbi Murugaradhya's *Sringarachaturyollasini* (1896) and the works of Galaganatha to the canonical *Madiddunno maraya* (M.S. Puttanna, 1915), suggesting a long career for the *adbhuta-ramya* in Kannada prose narrative. Describing the nineteenth century as a period of historic transition, he sees it dominated by romance narratives which gradually yield pre-eminence to the social novel in the twentieth century.

Inamdar has done two things in this passage: first of all, taking advantage of the fact that the term *kadambari* designates the novel in Kannada, he positions the social novel in a long tradition of prose narratives going all the way back to Bana. In doing so, he seems to endorse an approach to the novel which seeks to minimise its novelty. When we examine the reception of the novel form in different language cultures of India, we see that some of them attempt to simply add the European novel form to the list of already existing prose narrative forms, while others register the unexpected shock of its novelty in various ways, one of which is to retain the English name "novel" with appropriate phonetic modifications (e.g. *navala* in Telugu, *naaval* in Tamil). Kannada appears to have followed the lead of Marathi in this matter.[4] It may not be far-fetched to see in this choice a certain nationalistic gesture which believes in absorbing the best of European culture into Indian tradition, domesticating it, and giving it a place in an existing canon, as against seeing the incursion of Europe/the

[4] See Mukherjee, *Realism and Reality*, 11–13.

novel as a rupture, a break with the past and a new beginning. The latter approach would appear to involve a greater degree of coping with the alien as well as an acknowledgement of the irreversibility of the rupture of colonialism.

At the same time, Inamdar is quite confident in his assertion that the social novel marks the maturity of the *kadambari*. In other words, while subsuming the novel under a prose narrative tradition going back several centuries, Inamdar retains an appreciation of the novelty of the latest addition insofar as it has turned to society to capture it in realistic style. The novelty of the novel is thus both denied and asserted. The Indian literary tradition, in this rendering, rejoins world history as it moves towards a new social awareness, the rise of democracy, the entry of the masses into history.

Bankim in Bengal, Hari Narayan Apte in Marathi, and Galaganatha in Kannada are among the first writers of historical novels and romances. Bankim, emulating Walter Scott, himself becomes a model for Galaganatha to follow. Many writers like Galaganatha achieve quick success in this sub-genre which shows a degree of continuity with indigenous prose narrative traditions. The social novel, on the other hand, poses new challenges, initially of an almost insurmountable kind. It is of course the requirement of contemporaneity and by extension that of social realism that is the source of this difficulty. The genre apparatus comes with its own demands, as it were, requiring of the social substance a certain concrete type of distribution and relations. The nature of this demand is interpreted in many ways, but we may characterise it, based on Ranciere's recent argument, as having to do with an aesthetic regime which flattens the representational stratifications and hierarchical relations in society so as to present them on a horizontal plane, within the novel's own autonomous aesthetic space, freed from the burden of mirroring in its own structure and language the differences of status and rank in society at large.[5] It is thus the objectifying realist strategy that, above all, defines the novelty of the social novel.

For the social novel, the historical condition of possibility is a social segment which has internalised the modern ideals of parity between the sexes, and a moral or symbolic if not actual equality between all human beings. While social reform does occasionally extend into the larger question of caste divisions, it is primarily in the reform of gender relations, and in the relations between communities and religious authorities, that much of the social content is derived. This gives us the first defining characteristic of the writers of social novels: they are (unlike the first writer of Kannada historical novels, Galaganatha) all English-educated men who have some professional and/or social position in colonial society. Inamdar provides details for several of them. This context will help shape the principal characters of such novels, imbued as they often are with precisely those ideals that are absent in the larger social context and which the novel introduces through them into a traditional and orthodox milieu, thereby setting off the conflicts necessary for narrative movement. The difference that these "snatched bodies" introduce into the scene enables a quasi-ethnographic/realist representation of the dominant social reality. The difference is sharp because idealised. The protagonists of the new morality are uncompromising in their adherence to their ideals, although some, especially the women, may suffer silently rather than revolt or protest against their oppressors. Thus, such novels often seem to be staging an experiment rather than depicting a state of affairs. But while the social reality as depicted

[5] Ranciere, *The Politics of Aesthetics*, ch. 1.

may appear to be distorted by an impossible idealism, the scenario in its totality nevertheless reflects real conflicts that have begun to agitate traditional Indian society, even as the novel itself often appears to be playing a partisan role. The conflicts that typically erupt in these novels are not so much internal to a society as between two segments of it opposed to each other, which renders them all allegorical, some more so than the others.

Indirabai is, in my reading, a novel of this kind. In it a morally corrupt traditional society serves as the setting for the emergence of a new moral and social order. I will examine the narrative strategies by which this change is effected and discuss what I see as an insight stemming from the novel's unconscious.

Secondly, such an experiment – of staging an encounter between two inimical social orders – located as it is in a concrete cultural context, also presents us very often with a stylistically hybrid text. Some of these stylistic peculiarities have to do with the initial difficulties posed by the in-built objectivist epistemological character of novelistic prose. By the time the novel form reaches India, it has acquired a more or less stable form in which the authorial signature has been relegated to the paratextual domain. Henry Fielding's first-person interpolations are a thing of the past – indeed, for Watt they were already, in their own time, a failing. But the hybrid character of the social field in which the social novel is reborn is reflected in the stylistic hybridity of the text itself. This can take many forms. I will give a couple of examples: in an early Hindi novel, *Bhagyavathi*, by Shradha Ram Phillauri,[6] a man arrives at the king's court and narrates to the king and courtiers what he has just witnessed on his way. The content of his account provides the beginnings of a social novel, but the narrative retains a conventional feature of classical narrative

[6] I thank Mohinder Singh for bringing this text to my notice.

whereby the narrator and the context of narration are always specified. The novel soon cuts loose from this initial narratorial setting, but retains idealisations of character that render it closer to the *adbhuta-ramya* genre. Another symptomatic feature present in *Indirabai*, and which is also frequently encountered in Bankim's novels, is the authorial interjection. From recent literary theory we have learnt that first person "authorial" interpolations are to be regarded as immanent in the textual field, producing authorial presence as a literary effect rather than as comments by the actual author of the novel. The purpose of this theoretical move is to deny any space within the novel to a metanarrative discourse of the kind that provides the fiction with a running commentary. But the interjections of Gulavadi and Bankim are, to my mind, resistant to such immanentisation because they often express a difficulty faced by the actual author, who presents himself in his role as writer of a new kind of fiction and sometimes seeks his reader's indulgence or excuses himself for his shortcomings.

Here is an instance: "Meanwhile let the readers figure out for themselves how the *santashiromani* spent a sleepless night in the room, or let them find out in the next chapter when the *santashiromani* himself relates it. Because I fear that it would be sinful on my part to describe his tribulations."[7] We can, of course, read such interpolations as immanent in the fictional text, but in doing so we would be ignoring the distinct feeling that is conveyed by them of a writer grappling with a new form, a writer who shares with his readers this sense of novelty. "I am trying my best," they sometimes seem to be saying to their readers, "be patient with me."[8]

[7] Venkatrao, *Indirabai*, 184.

[8] An example from Bankim's English-language novel *Rajmohan's Wife*: "The reader need not be informed that with much of the subject of this interesting

The social setting of *Indirabai* is a traditional Brahmin community in the throes of change in the latter half of the nineteenth century, subject to disruptions and attractions introduced by colonial rule. The author, a police officer in the colonial service, is a social convert and writes from the position of a reformer. The novel is unapologetically and often fiercely partisan and so falls somewhat beside the theoretically elaborated standard type of the novel in peripheral modernity, even though the readings of the Brazilian postcolonial novel by Roberto Schwarz and Franco Moretti's theoretical project are quite useful in understanding what is going on here, in a corner of British India. Thus the encounter between global and local forms is quite vividly present – in the form of a struggle between habituation to a representationalist textuality and attraction to an epistemologically oriented one. These are two styles belonging, if one wants to put it that way, to two different social orders, and thus the spatialising tendency of the Schwarz-Moretti model is seen to be set adrift in, as it were, the rapids of history. Thus, as we have just seen, there is acute self-consciousness about textuality and the simultaneity of narrating activity to the emergence of the narrative itself, which is characteristic of pre-modern prose narratives. In the novel, however, the text-consciousness is more often manifested in repeated references to the act of narration itself (e.g. "as I have said in the previous chapter"; "the reader will understand why I cannot describe what happened next"; etc.) which border on coyness. This is of course a feature of Bankim's novels as well, and

---

dialogue, he is already acquainted . . . The concluding part of this conversation we shall, with the reader's leave, place before him for his gratification" (70). Rochelle Pinto cites narratorial utterances in her essay on *Gobinda Samanta* in the present volume which strike me as being of the same type.

there is evidence here that Bengali novels had some influence on early Kannada novelists. Traditionally, narratives always included references to the occasion of the narration, so that a narrator and one or more listeners were always explicitly indicated.

Sudipta Kaviraj, writing about Bankim's novels, refers to the persistence of the ornate prose of classical narrative, especially hyperbolic elaborations on feminine and natural beauty, which clash with the prose of novelistic fiction, something we will later discuss as the problem of survivor forms. In *Indirabai*, however, there are two types of hybridity, only one of which corresponds to this type. Thus the opening paragraph of the novel is reminiscent of the openings of traditional narratives such as the Panchatantra tales:

> In the southern region of Vindhyachala, on the banks of the river Rohini is an expansive city by the name of Kamalapura. This historic city of ancient renown is filled with numerable mansions, temples, agraharas, forts, courts, flower and fruit gardens, broad thoroughfares, bridges and other adornments. People of all the four varnas, Brahmin, Kshatriya, Vysya, and Shudra lived in different parts of the city and followed their professions.

This conventional opening can be seen as an instance of the interference of survivor forms. By the end of the novel, however, the prose has undergone complete transformation and the narrative ends on a quiet note in plain prose. The rule of immanence prevails at the end.

A more intriguing example of such hybridity is the presentation of conversations between or with servants and other characters of low social rank in Tulu/Konkani,[9] with Kannada translations

[9] Amur, "Prasthavane", xi.

provided alongside. In the text available, which is said to be based on a copy of the original 1899 publication, these passages are printed in double column. Here again a certain ambiguity prevails as to the historical/aesthetic status of this practice. On the one hand it seems to hark back to the representational regime of Sanskrit drama where a similar distinction of language is maintained between masters and servants, thus suggesting a continuity with classical representational conventions. On the other hand it acquires, within the novel's "eco-system" a certain ethnographic significance.[10]

At the same time the desire to achieve epistemological distance, to narrate from a position of invisibility, haunts the novel. At the head of the novel is placed this caveat:

> What is written in this book is the life story of a woman called Indirabai. It is not in order to show himself to be a master of language, a poetic genius or in any way talented that the author has written this. He has none of these virtues. Hence if there are any errors in this, discriminating readers should not deny me their forgiveness.
>
> So what is the purpose of this book, readers may well ask. As for that: truth and purity of heart are the two virtues that serve us well in this world and the next. In their absence, all efforts are in vain. It is the purpose of this book to illustrate this truth. To what extent this purpose has been achieved in this book is for the readers to decide.

One thing that sets this novel apart from others of its kind and time is that unlike, say, Chandu Menon's *Indulekha,* where the plot is the product of the author's imagination, *Indirabai* makes reference to actual events that shook the Saraswat Brahmin community of South Kanara over some three decades preceding its publication. Shivarama Karantha, in his foreword written in

[10] For the role of ethnography in the prose of the early Indian novel, see Rochelle Pinto's essay in the present volume.

the 1960s, reports memories of having read an English translation done by a district collector by the name of Coachman. We learn from this that Venkatrao was in the colonial police service and that what he depicted in *Indirabai* was based on "incidents that took place at that time" in the Saraswat Brahmin society to which he himself belonged. "Making use of incidents that took place at that time, he has shown the unrest that gripped Saraswata Brahmin society when it was undergoing modern social revolution."[11] Govinda Pai repeats Karantha's view that the novel is based on true events: "It was a time when society was moving from traditional frames into English-inspired modern culture. The author has used details from that moment to put his story together."[12]

A descendant of the novelist Santosh Kumar Gulvadi provides a brief biography. Born in Kundapura in 1844, the youngest among four sons and two daughters and initially educated in Mangalore, he went to Madras University for his BA before joining the police. Initial efforts at reform of the Saraswat community were countered by traditionalists who expelled the reformists from membership of the community's *matha* (spiritual institution), boycotted them, and proscribed interdining with them within the community. Reacting to these measures, in 1870 Ullal Raghunathayya and Rao Bahadur Kudmal Rangarao (Swami Eeswarananda) joined the Brahma Samaj. Interdining events with Dalits were organised, leading to their being declared outcastes by community elders. This was in 1896, three years before the publication of *Indirabai*. Gulvadi was enraged by this development, writes Santosh Kumar.[13]

[11] Venkatrao, *Indirabai*, vi.

[12] Ibid., vii.

[13] Ibid., viii–xii.

Indirabai begins, as seen above, in a conventional style familiar to readers of Sanskrit prose narratives. Kamalapura, the fictional setting, may be modelled on the coastal city of Mangalore – as the prominent literary critic G.S. Amur has suggested.[14] Hampe Bhimaraya, father of Indirabai, is introduced in a breathless paragraph which refers to his family's roots in Bijapur, his migration to Kamalapura in a penurious state, education, employment as a village accountant, marriage, prosperity, plans to give up employment and go into business discouraged by his wife and lucky mascot, Ambabai, a Lady Macbeth-like figure. By the time we meet him and his family, this accountant, entrusted with the management of a factory by his employer, has acquired considerable wealth which he spends on organising frequent *yakshagana* performances and other entertainments, pujas and receptions for holy men, and lavish meals for Brahmins and others according to custom. Lack of children remains a source of worry.

The next chapter introduces the second important family, Sundarayya and his wife Susheela along with their five-year-old son Bhaskara. Hailing from a family of accountants, the unemployed Sundarayya renders services to Bhimaraya in the hope of securing employment. Bhimaraya, however, on his wife's orders, kills him, thus leaving the widowed Susheela alone with her child. The episode of the murder of Sundarayya, prompted by Ambabai (who fears that he knows and will reveal the secret of her affair with Bhimaraya's employer) follows the murder scene and aftermath from *Macbeth* closely. Bhimaraya's guilt is publicly exposed when, at a banquet, he sees the dead Sundarayya and addresses him. There is also an echo of Draupadi's vow of revenge in the passage where Ambabai orders Sundarayya's death.

[14] Amur, "Prasthavane", ix.

As part of a cover-up, Bhimaraya himself feigns illness, relatives are summoned, and a comic episode ensues in which traditional Brahmins' incomprehension with English medical treatment and technology is highlighted in the way they speak about things like the alarm clock. Here the writing appeals to the superior knowledge of the reader and shares the joke with him/her, thus distancing these traditional people from their own social class. Their condemnation of Western practices and objects as "the Englishman's weapons for destroying caste" exposes their ignorance.

As a police investigation begins, the cowardly Bhimaraya exposes himself to further suspicion with his inept attempts at cover-up, such as bribing the constables who are on watch outside his home. The novel now incorporates police procedure as part of its plotting. Higher police officials are introduced who begin interrogating neighbours, gathering evidence. Post-mortem analysis is ordered. Though the investigation itself is hardly of any significance in furthering the plot, it is an occasion for the author, himself a police officer, to introduce a lot of technical vocabulary from the discourse. The constables confess to receiving a bribe right at the start of the inquiry. Increasingly jittery, Bhimaraya utters the dead man's name and is rescued from immediate arrest by his wife. The inquiry continues with a search of Bhimaraya's house, interrogation of a servant and of Devaki, the woman who supplied the poison. Though the search is compromised by bribed policemen, Devaki confesses in the police station and subsequently so does Bhimaraya. Inexplicably, he is released and told to make himself available when summoned.

With this the plot turns towards a court trial. On his way home from the police station, Bhimaraya meets a lawyer, Attura Surappayya. Seeing an opportunity for gain, Surappayya pretends that confession need not be irreversible and, by repeatedly looking into a book he happens to be holding, convinces Bhimaraya that he is the man to trust, wangles some advance payment, and goes off to plot his own game to deceive Bhimaraya. Eventually he and Devaki are arrested, his employer returns and hires a big lawyer (along with Surappayya) to defend him. The defence fails and the lawyers are fined for contempt of court for challenging the judgment. In a higher court, the case is dismissed for lack of evidence, leading to release and a celebration featuring a *yakshagana*.

Surappayya tries to extort more money, as does Devaki. At a grand dinner organised by Bhimaraya, the large gathering includes a number of BAs and FAs whose conversation in English is, like that of the lower-status speakers of Konkani, accompanied by Kannada translations. The chapter includes a satirical description of Brahmin rituals followed by a mockery of Anglicised young men.[15] The evening ends with fireworks and a performance by dancing girls.

Hitherto, the novel has entertained us with a series of episodes of conversation that are enjoyable in themselves as vignettes of social life in a changing Hindu society: educated young men with their English dialogue, traditional Brahmins with their ignorance of modern medicine and technology, and glimpses of an already corrupt legal system which is manipulated at will by lawyers who dupe ignorant people, rich and poor, effortlessly. These apart, in terms of storyline we have a tale of magic, witchcraft, poisoning,

[15] Some of these entertaining aspects of the novel are strikingly similar to those Sambudha Sen discusses in his essay on *Hootum Pyanchar Naksha* in the present volume. The relations between English and the vernaculars seems to be of central concern to many writers in the nineteenth century. A survey and critical reading of more such instances from across the subcontinent would be highly rewarding.

and a woman's thirst for revenge reminiscent of epic narrative. In other words up to now we have *scenes* rendered in a novelistic style depicting social mores, with a novel-like character construction in the form of the wily lawyer Surappayya combining with a temporally indistinct tale of revenge and punishment. Surappayya differs from the rest of the characters so far introduced by being the only one with a split self, a secret interior self that plots deceptions in pursuit of gain and an outward mask of knowledge and sincerity.

Chapter 17 introduces a break in the narrative. From the flourishing manager of a wealthy landlord's estate he now becomes what the author calls a *dharmavicharaka*, someone who will enquire into the state of the religious community and report back to its spiritual centre, the *matha*, and its head. This is a narrative shift whose primary purpose is to refocus the narrative on the theme of religion and modern education/social conduct. In this transitional moment, Ambabai gives birth to a girl, Indira, the principal protagonist of our story.

Indira's future husband Bhaskara has already been introduced as the son of the murdered Sundarayya. Bhaskara manages to enter into the lawyer Amritaraya's service. Later, like the author himself, Bhaskara goes to Madras to study for his BA. He now has a friend, a fellow student, Sanjeeva Rao. Returning home for the vacations, Bhaskara finds himself torn between his filial affection for his mother and his loyalty to his benefactor Amritaraya, which is further complicated by the maternal interest Amritaraya's childless wife Jalajakshi takes in him.

Bhaskara, in conformity with traditional society's stereotype ("It's like that, as soon as they go to Madras, they give up all caste practices, cut their hair . . . join Brahma Samadhi or whatever it is called"[16]), becomes a modern educated young man, prompting

[16] Venkatrao, *Indirabai*, 78.

complaining letters from Bhimaraya to the Guru. The latter's own daughter, Indira, now eight years old, is to be married off early and to a husband as unlike Bhaskara as possible. A lavish wedding overflowing with gold and precious stones, dancing girls, and other entertainments is described in great detail.

There follows a period during which Bhaskara goes away to London for further studies and disappears from the novel during the time of Indira's marriage to a profligate who, within a couple of years, drinks himself to death in the company of dancing girls. This is followed by a long episode of the head of the *matha* and a retinue of monks arriving at Bhimaraya's house in order to inspect the religious state of affairs and wean Indira away from the books she is reading (*Stridharmaniti*; Aesop's Fables; Panchatantra; *Satyavati Charitre*) towards a more "normal" Hindu widowhood (reading Radhavilasa, Krishnaleele, etc.). These two episodes are an unrelenting exercise in black humour. Indira's mother disapproves of her reading "*mleccha*" books such as *Stridharmaniti* and instead recommends books about Krishna's exploits with Radha and the *gopis*, because in doing so she will be repeating the name of Krishna, a sure way to gain *punya*. As her husband lies dying in bed, Indira tries in vain to have a medical doctor brought in to attend to him. Both sets of parents are determined to go with the *vaidya*. The go-between is busy discussing his commission with the *vaidya* and the two dancing girls who have been entertaining the dying man until the end are busy trying to get something for themselves before he kicks the bucket. The entire episode beginning with the first intimation of the husband's illness to his death is a masterfully orchestrated, action-packed segment showing Venkatrao's satirical skills at their sharpest. The debauchery of the monks who arrive with their Guru at Bhimaraya's house is another shocking episode told with similar biting humour. Girls from all the families are brought in to "serve" the monks and only Indira refuses, defying her parents' orders. When finally she is trapped in a room with a lecherous monk, she escapes by tricking him and leaving home, literally migrating to the space of modernity and virtue.

The episode of the monks' debauchery culminates in a hapless Indira seeking refuge with the lawyer Amritaraya. In her new home Indira discovers how good modern people live. Women do not veil themselves and are allowed to enter a room where a man is present. Learning English, mathematics, and history is allowed. She is asked for her opinion on topical matters such as women's education. The public revelation of Indira's hiding in Amritaraya's house is brought about by means of a riverside conversation between servant maids (in yet another resort to traditional narrative devices). Bhimaraya comes to reclaim his daughter but Amritaraya threatens him with a court case and refuses to let her go. Instead he sends her to Satara, where a Pandita Anandibai (obviously modelled on Pandita Ramabai) runs a Saraswati Mandira where young widows are taught English, Sanskrit, and other languages, mathematics, history, *stridharma*, morality, etc. By the time she returns after completing her education, Bhaskara too is scheduled to return from London.

The telegram bearing the news is deployed by the couple to play a game upon Indira. They place it on a table, along with Bhaskara's photograph, and retreat to another room from where they can see the table unobserved. This is how the scene is narrated:

> Indirabai comes straight to the table, stands, finds the telegram. She picks it up and reads it, and as she is looking around to see who is there, finds the photograph, picks it up with the other hand, and begins to look now at the telegram now at the photo five or six times, putting them back on the desk fearing that she might be

> being watched, picking them up again to look at them, stopping to think, wondering if she is asleep or awake and placing her palm over the burning flame of the lamp to test it, withdrawing it with a cry and rubbing it, looking as if she had concluded that she was awake, rubbing her eyes, sitting in the chair, thinking for a minute or two, getting up again, looking at the picture again and smiling, then again after a minute crying, then as if she had figured out that all this had been done to test her, smiling at the thought, and saying aloud "I will call father", as she starts to step out, Amritaraya and Jalaja emerge from their room laughing and accost her.[17]

This passage marks an important moment in the clarification of style that is an ongoing process in the novel. The rudimentary construction of articulated space introduces a division of space into a place of performance and a place of viewing in order to elicit from the performer a secret, the truth of her desire. Though the results coincide with the viewing couple's own plans, rendering the episode somewhat redundant, or rather perhaps because of this very redundancy, the scene's experimental status as a contrivance for the staging of desire is foregrounded. The epistemological dimension of novelistic discourse is also at work here, the language stripped of all ornament, piling on observations of actions as evidence of a hidden desire.

The marriage of Bhaskara and Indira is followed by a fresh attempt at social boycott of the foreign-returned, but, as more and more young men go abroad, the Guru's boycott order has little impact. Venkatrao shows through a conversation how people have responded to the *matha*'s orders: they seek forgiveness of the Guru and then go back to their old ways. Here are two "BAs" in conversation (the italicised words are in English in the original):

[17] Ibid., 220.

Well, do you want caste?

I do, what is the *price*?

It's a *trifle. Dead cheap*.

How much did you pay for it?

I paid three rupees. Now it's come down a bit.

What is it now?

Just two rupees.

Why the *fluctuation?*

What else? It's a *market*, keeps going up and down. Sometimes it reaches as high as 25.

Is that so? But I am not in need of forgiveness now. My son Sundara's upanayanam is next year, its ok if I get it then. Maybe the price will have gone down further by then?

There you are mistaken my friend. If it becomes known that an upanayanam is due, the price may even hit 50. Be warned.

In that case I'll go tomorrow and get the forgiveness paper. Just two rupees? No other accompaniments?

A coconut, seven bananas and three sacred threads. That's it.[18]

The conversation proceeds in this vein, explaining the selfish motives behind the *matha*'s opposition to widow remarriage. The latter portion of the novel is full of such conversations which go from cynical denunciation of the religious order to a more conciliatory expression of hope for future reconstruction of community. The marriage of Bhaskara and Indira having been performed, a perfunctory reconciliation with Bhimaraya and Ambabai is reported in conclusion.

G.S. Amur, in his prefatory essay, discusses some negative critical responses, notably those of D.R. Nagaraj and the novelist Shantinath Desai. He refutes Nagaraj's comment that Indira is a "totally passive" character by pointing to her independence of

[18] Ibid., 251.

mind, reflected in her sharp and thoughtful remarks in exchanges with her mother and intellectual conversations with her husband and adoptive parents. Desai comments sarcastically that District Collector Coachman's interest in translating the novel into English was prompted by the positive image of British rule that it gives and the celebration of English education and westernisation. In his response, Amur refers to several passages where the novel satirises the Anglicised youth of the time, arguing that Coachman's interest (as evidenced by his foreword to the translation) was based on the realistic portrayal of Saraswat life and the mockery of caste prejudices by an insider of the community. While Amur makes a good case for the achievements of the novel, the severity of the critical tone of the novel appears to have been a cause of unease among many readers.

In conclusion, let me turn to another aspect of the novel's spatial organisation – the spatial distribution of the novel's characters and events. As we have noted, the historical condition of possibility of the social novel is a social segment which has adopted modern ideals of equality between the sexes and symbolic equality between all human beings. In Tagore's *Gora*, a Brahmo family becomes the enabling factor. Similarly, Venkatrao introduces the household of the lawyer Amritaraya as a space apart which stands for the reformist section of Saraswat society. The key spatial dislocations which enable the novel to continue with its dramatisation of the conflict over social reform are those of Bhaskara first and then Indira. As Amritaraya and Jalajakshi adopt Bhaskara, he finds himself with two mothers. The novel mentions but minimises the conflict of passions that this gives rise to. That is not where its interest lies. Indira in her turn ends up in the lawyer's household by a compulsion that the novel does not even try to justify adequately, as if it knows that such an attempt could hardly succeed.

What is striking about this dualistic/agonistic organisation of social space into two sectors is the way that it seems to foretell the very structure of "Indian society" as it has come to be. For the society we inhabit today is similarly divided. There are any number of prior divisions within the social orders that prevail in the various regions of India. Within each of these there are caste, religious, and other divisions which have remained quite stable. But there has arisen alongside them a new space which I would describe as a "society by representation", drawing from all the regions and communities, though in this space some enjoy a disproportionately high presence whereas others continue to struggle for inclusion. One might say that what was under colonial power a society by recruitment has, in independent India, turned (though not without resistance) into a society by representation. In asserting its right to existence, this class may bear superficial resemblances to the European revolutionary bourgeoisie, but in reality its bid for social dominance was short-lived, and in the time of the national movement that was to follow its project went underground, as it were. Thus, even today aspirants to modern subjectivity must repeat that emigration undertaken by Indira in her moment of distress, running away from caste and community oppression towards spaces defined by other norms. The spatial logic of Venkatrao's narrative thus proves, in hindsight, to be a prescient foretelling of the Indian present.

I now turn to a consideration of some theoretical issues arising from this reading of *Indirabai* which are of interest to novel studies.

The origins of the Indian novel in the unusual conditions of "an exposure to Western literature" brought about by colonisation notwithstanding, certain aspects of the dialectic of form noted in the Western history of the novel remain relevant to this specific context.[19] Thus it was Michael McKeon who, expanding upon and revising the work of Ian Watt and Mikhail Bakhtin, took up for consideration the congenital and apparently incurable impurity or generic hybridity of the novel form, the problem of "a dense layering of precursor and survivor forms" in the dialectic of genre formation.[20] In the Indian novel, judging by Meenakshi Mukherjee's survey, there are "survivor forms" that impinge on the new form, though not, for obvious reasons, anything that might be designated as precursor. The oft-noted survivor forms include the conventions of Sanskrit literature, in particular the "sonorous passages of nature description and evocations of feminine beauty" found in Bankim, or the conventions of oral recitation of the puranas, as at the end of Chandu Menon's *Indulekha*.[21] The first of these is an example of that "linguistic ornateness" that in Watt's account precedes the advent of novelistic prose, for which literary achievement consists in "the extrinsic beauties which could be bestowed upon description and action by the use of rhetoric;"[22] while the second relates to the communal nature of traditional story-telling which has its Western parallel in the non-individualised character types of the communal romance form that, along with other such residual features, abound in the novels of Henry Fielding.[23] It would seem then that when considered as a question of the history of literary forms, there is much in common between the situations that prevailed in the period of emergence of the novel in Europe and in India.

But of course there are differences. These have all to do with the shock of colonisation, that break in temporal flow which brought

[19] Mukherjee, *Realism and Reality*, 3.

[20] McKeon, *The Origins of the English Novel*, 12; Watt, *The Rise of the Novel.*

[21] Mukherjee, *Realism and Reality*, 15.

[22] Watt, *The Rise of the Novel*, 28–30.

[23] Ibid., 20.

with it many novelties across all dimensions of social existence. Exposure to the novel form itself was enabled, as is well known, by the introduction of English education which led to the creation, as envisaged by Macaulay, of a new class of Indians who would henceforth mediate the relations between the coloniser and the vast majority of Indian subjects.[24] Thus, McKeon's analogy between "the rise of the novel and the rise of the middle class" would seem to hold good here too.[25] But there remains a difference of historical experience, related to what McKeon describes, following Marx's methodological reflections in the *Grundrisse,* as the emergence of the novel as a "simple abstraction" after a long period of "novelistic usage", during which older names continued in use.[26] This period of organic growth of the form in some sort of alignment with the ongoing social transformations is replaced in the Indian instance by a period of accommodation to a new reality and the cultural forms that accompany the emergence of the new state of affairs. Mukherjee notes that the first novels began to appear a generation after the introduction of English education, from which we may infer that the education in question inculcated an aspirational or developmental disposition towards the culture of the coloniser. On the other hand, the emergence of a properly *social* novel, which is after all the primary focus of the histories of the novel we have been drawing from, takes a lot longer and, as in the European case, requires the emergence of new subjectivities.[27] Initially, the novel appears to have been received primarily as a species of prose fiction and placed alongside well-known indigenous equivalents. Stylistic distinction, or, following Watt, the paring down of style in the service of the new genre's epistemological function as well as its

[24] Mukherjee, *Realism and Reality*, 3.

[25] McKeon, *The Origins of the English Novel*, 15.

[26] Ibid., 20.

[27] Mukherjee, *Realism and Reality*, 3.

stakes in authenticity, will take time to register, and even today, this type of amalgamation relativising the novel's claim to distinction is much favoured. Such a preference may itself be related to the colonial turn and the perversion of the social field to which it gives rise by prejudicially colouring the aspirational relationship to the new culture. In other societies, the encounter with Western ideas led initially to feelings of shame or deficiency which fuelled efforts towards subjective inhabitation of the modern discourse and the associated project of transforming the social substance. In India too, such a potentially productive moment of self-recognition and shame did occur, but a variety of factors prevented it from giving rise to a larger movement, not the least of these being the presence of the coloniser himself. This is how colonisation warps a subject population's relation to the acknowledged superiority of the post-revolutionary culture of Europe. The coloniser is eager to claim it as his own in order to buttress his claim to superiority, thus adding to the aspirational quest of the subject people the taint of servility to an oppressor's ideas. The shame of a benighted existence recognised in the mirror of enlightenment thought, which was a spur to self-transformative action, is soon replaced by the shame of adopting the ways of the master and a concomitant search for evidence of cultural superiority in the pre-colonial past. This latter shame, which makes it shameful to feel the former kind of shame, was to become a decisive and fateful element in shaping the struggle for freedom. It was an ideological victory against the project of social reform for an elite fearful of the effects of such change on its own future.[28]

The social conditions under which experiments in the social novel are conducted in India are thus unique, and any idea of a

[28] For a nuanced discussion of these issues from which I have drawn, see Padikkal, "Inventing Modernity", esp. 223–4.

dialectic of genre must take into account the particular logjam of virtual and actual subjectivities involved, for sorting out which a model like the theory of dominant, residual, and emergent does not suffice. The modern and the "traditional" are emergent or dominant or residual, depending upon one's political perspective, and this ambivalence has played a crucial role in our history. The powerful retrospective effect of "national consensus" on the priority of political freedom over social transformation obscures from view the specificity and distinction of a time prior to such an emergence.[29]

It is in this context that it pays to see the early Indian novel as an important site of ideological struggle within "native society". At this stage, which lasts through the nineteenth century and into the early decades of the twentieth, instead of the "simple abstraction" signalling the ascent of a genre to supremacy in relation to a transformed society, what we have is the sudden introduction of a form through a variety of the available examples of it, leading to a period that we might designate, following McKeon, as one of "novelistic usage". This is justified because though the name of the novel is prevalent, the relation to prevailing "survivor" forms of prose fiction remains to be sorted out and the process of clarification proceeds alongside the development of a social class.

Thus to the social (the middle class) and the formal (the novel genre), the two terms of McKeon's genre dialectic must be added a third – the political – which stymies the dialectic or renders it

[29] A recurring theme in Indian political discourse, this question of priority between social reform and political freedom is impossible to answer if posed in the form of two alternatives presented in the abstract. It is only in its dialectical aspect that it begins to make sense: the escalation of the movement for political freedom constitutes a response to and the negation of the thrust for social reform.

complex. That the social novel finds both its practitioners and its readers in the social class brought into being by colonial policy is clear. In most of these novels the narratives are concerned with the conflict between the desires and aspirations and values of this class and the larger social context within which it is enmeshed. This is usually treated as a conflict between tradition and modernity, thus restricting the dialectic to the realm of ideas and assuming an allegorical correspondence of the two terms to the two sides of the colonial game of power. Such a reading, however, eliminates from the scene the very middle ground of the colonial order, the small but growing society of modern Indians who are now engaged in exploring their own place in the world. Far from serving as a neutral ground from which to observe and record some raging tension between tradition and modernity, this society is concerned with its own existential questions. To be sure, issues of old and new, and traditional and modern, are the ideational form taken by this existential quest, but the larger question is of their own destiny. And the ideological resolution consists in bracketing out or underplaying the political antagonism in order to make space for the social to come into view. Alternatively, we can see assertion of the reality of colonial *society* as the political project that is undertaken in the early social novel.

The point can be clarified with the help of a scene from Tagore's *Gora*. In the middle of this novel Tagore stages a confrontation in which what is precisely at issue is the question of the difference between the political and social logics of coexistence. A mixed social gathering of Indians and English people is the occasion at which the Indians, including some of the main characters of the novel, are to perform a play, which to Gora seems like an act of self-abjection. A lot of drama ensues and the performance is eventually aborted. To Gora's eyes, the occasion is simply an extension of political subjugation into the social domain, a performance of servility, in short a humiliation that he is determined to oppose at all costs. Gora sees Indo-British relations along a vertical axis of political power relations where there is no scope for an extension along the horizontal axis of social coexistence. The novel's entrapment of Gora proceeds by giving his political animus full play before the final revelation that destroys his illusions and makes him accept a place in the emerging society which he previously related to as a dissenting outsider.

Here a clarification is in order regarding my usage of the terms social and political. What I mean to convey thereby is that there is a politics involved in choosing to regard colonial India in its social dimension or, on the contrary, in its strictly political character. The latter choice is predicated on a disavowal of the existence of colonial *society* in the name of an agonistic model of colonial rule which is a retrospective construction. In *Gora* Tagore is presenting, in its protagonist, that idea in its early construction which would soon dominate Indian ideology and promote the picture of an all-round antagonism, apart from rendering suspect liberals like Tagore and social reformers like Ambedkar who emphasised the necessity of social reform as a necessary condition for political freedom. The kind of shame that lies behind each of these political options is also, accordingly, different.[30]

What is implicit in Tagore is given theoretical form by a novel published some twenty years later in which this scene is re-staged as part of a different narrative in order to draw out its implications not only for modern Indian society, but also for the novel form.[31] *Ananya* by Achintyakumar Sengupta is a rather simple novel about the special bond between a father and his daughter whom he

[30] For a more detailed discussion of these issues, see Prasad, "The Struggle to Represent and Sartorial Modernity".

[31] I must thank here my old landlady Mrs Mazumdar of Lake Gardens, Kolkata, in whose library I found this interesting novel quite by chance.

brings up as a modern girl, leading to conflicts within the family and community of the usual tradition–modernity variety. The restaging of the scene from *Gora* (the girl in question is to dance in front of a mixed gathering of white people and Indians) allows the author to make explicit a social rationale that overrides the political (here rendered as traditional) objection. Expressed by the father as a justification of his decision to allow his daughter to perform, the argument is clinched by an analogy with the society of novel readers itself. "Those who read novels," the father says, "may criticise this or that particular novel, but not novel-reading itself."

This rule of immanence joins the world of novel writing and reading to modern society as a site of existence. Along the horizontal axis of society, new rules of sociability apply. Like the readers of novels, members of modern society can be critical of certain aspects of the new society in which they live, but they cannot both be modern and be critical of the very idea of a modern society. This is the rule of immanence that Sengupta proposes and which captures very well the contradiction between the political and social in colonial society, which is both the subject matter of the social novel at this moment and the target of its critique. There is an irreducible element of idealism, of the experimental construction of possible worlds, in many of these novels, bearing witness to the aspirational ideologies of a distinctive class in the throes of forging its own identity. In the great novels of the twentieth century, by contrast, a more stable realism aided by ethnographic distance and representational logic is very much in evidence as class aspirations get recruited into the expanding project of imagining, mapping, and building a new nation. If then, in the late nineteenth century, when *Indirabai* was published, the novel form still bears traces of a discursive hybridity characteristic of a period of "novelistic usage", it is as much the sign of a social struggle for self-fashioning as it is a process of formal clarification. *Indirabai* is, in this respect, a unique instance of experimentation on many levels.

Acknowledgements

This essay had its beginnings in a study group on the early Kannada novel that met for several sessions in 2011. Many thanks to all the participants at these valuable sessions and in particular V.B. Tharakeshwar, Shivarama Padikkal, Jaisrinivas Rao, Nikhila H. Raghvendra, Ravi Kumbar. The essay has since evolved through discussions with the editors Baidik and Sambudha, as well as Rochelle Pinto and Shefali Jha, all of whom I thank for their extremely useful suggestions and probing questions.

References

Amur, G.S., "Prasthavane", in Gulvadi Venkatrao, *Indirabai athava saddharma vijayavu* (Bengaluru: Vasantha Prakashana, 2013).

Gunning, Tom, "The Cinema of Attractions: Early Film, Its Spectator and the Avant-Garde", *Wide Angle*, vol. 8, nos 3 & 4, Fall 1986.

Inamdar, V.M., "Munnudi" (foreword), in Kerur Vasudevacharya, *Indira* (n.p., n.d.), 9–32.

McKeon, Michael, *The Origins of the English Novel: 1600 to 1740* (Baltimore: Johns Hopkins University Press, 2002).

Mukherjee, Meenakshi, *Realism and Reality: The Novel and Society in India* (New Delhi: Oxford University Press, 1985).

Padikkal, Shivarama, "Inventing Modernity: The Emergence of the Novel in India", in Tejaswini Niranjana, P. Sudhir, and Vivek Dhareshwar, ed., *Interrogating Modernity* (Kolkata: Seagull, 1993).

Prasad, Madhava M., "The Struggle to Represent and Sartorial Modernity: On a Visual Dimension of Indian Nationalist Politics", *Inter-Asia Cultural Studies*, 15.4 (2014), 572–88.

Ranciere, Jacques, *The Politics of Aesthetics* (London: Continuum, 2004).

Venkatrao, Gulvadi, *Indirabai* (Mangaluru: Prapancha Prakashana, 1962).

Watt, Ian, *The Rise of the Novel: Studies in Defoe, Richardson and Fielding* (London: Chatto and Windus, 1967).

6

Sovereignty, Allegory, and Political Affect

K. Narayana Kurukkal's Novels

UDAYA KUMAR

HISTORIES OF THE NOVEL in Malayalam place the initial efflorescence of the genre in the last decade of the nineteenth century. Appu Nedungadi's *Kundalata* (1887), O. Chandu Menon's *Indulekha* (1890), Cheruvalathu Chathu Nair's *Meenakshi* (1890), C.V. Raman Pillai's *Martandavarma* (1891), Komattil Padu Menon's *Lakshmikesavam* (1892), Kizhakkeppatt Ramankutty Menon's *Parangodi Parinayam* (1892), Potheri Kunjambu's *Saraswathivijayam* (1892), Kochuthomman Appothikkiri's *Parishkarappathi* (1892), C. Anthappayi's *Naluperiloruthan* (1893), and Joseph Mooliyil's *Sukumari* (1897) were all published within the span of a decade and have been, to various degrees, vital to discussions of features the novel form acquired when adapted to the local conditions of Kerala. However, the decade that immediately succeeded this fertile period seems to have elicited little scholarly attention. After the novels of the late-nineteenth century, discussions of the Malayalam novel often move on to *Dharmaraja* (1913), written by the renowned historical novelist from Travancore, C.V. Raman Pillai, who broke with this novel his twenty-year-long silence after the publication of *Martandavarma*.

This essay examines a new form of the novel that emerged in Malayalam in this interregnum – the political novel. The first decade of the twentieth century saw the publication of two multi-volume novels by K. Narayana Kurukkal – *Parappuram* (The Rockface) and *Udayabhanu* (The Rising Sun) – that sought to engage with contemporary politics in the princely state of Travancore. They show a political-aesthetic configuration of affect that distinguishes them from novels of romantic love, social reform, religious conversion, and historical recall which have dominated accounts of the early novel. This distinction is evident in the plot structures, techniques of characterisation, and discursive resources used in Kurukkal's political fiction.

However, the absence of these texts in discussions of the early novel is not a result of their marginal status in their own day. As we shall see, they were widely read, appreciated, and debated when they appeared. Their lack of prominence is rather the effect of the normative frames that came to define the genre in later years. The realist thrust of the English novel and poetic conventions of the Sanskrit *kavya* and its *bhasha* counterparts are often cited as the principal contexts within which the novel shaped its aesthetics in Indian languages. Kurukkal's novels refer more prominently to forms of contemporary public and popular writing. The trope of romantic love and its consummation, which serves as narrative spine for several early novels, undergoes major modifications in these political novels. Characters are portrayed here less through an elaboration of inner emotions and reflection than through techniques of external manifestation. If we are to view the genre of the novel as constitutively connected with modernity, Kurukkal's novels seem to offer a different perspective on this link by training their lens on the experience of the political and the public at a moment of historical change.

The emergence of the political novel in Travancore was closely linked to public discussions around the politics of the court, especially contests for royal favour and positions of power within the palace and the government. This makes it necessary to understand its form in relation to the shape of new political discourses and expressions that came into circulation at the end of the nineteenth century. The genre of the political novel therefore demands an understanding that exceeds aesthetic framing; however, it also resists a solely extra-literary reading, since the use of the novelistic apparatus seeks to achieve ends not obtained in the same measure or manner through non-fictional means.

A contemporary reading of Kurukkal's novels faces two challenges. Firstly, as noted, normative conceptions of the novel established in later years make us regard these works as aesthetically imperfect. It is important, however, to recall that many of the early novels have been judged as defective in retrospect: derivativeness of plot, implausibility in turns of event or characterisation, incoherence in narration, and unwieldy description deriving from native poetic tradition – these have all been described as signs of the novel's infancy, since they work against the impulse towards realism.[1] Even Chandu Menon's *Indulekha*, which has received near-unanimous approbation as the first modern novel, has been judged as defective on account of its long "eighteenth chapter". This suddenly appears towards the novel's end to discuss science, religion, and nationalism, deferring the final resolution of the plot and the eagerly longed-for reunion of the protagonists after

[1] Irumbayam, *Malayalanovel*.

their distraught separation.[2] Chandu Menon, however, appears to have thought of this chapter as important enough for him to order books specially to aid its composition, and even to delay the novel's completion and publication on that account.[3] By the middle of the twentieth century, as the Malayalam novel acquired a clearer relationship to realism, literary critics began assessing older novels in the light of more recent aesthetic norms. Features which novelists and readers accepted and enjoyed at the turn of the nineteenth century were seen in retrospect as signs of incomplete development. This evolutionary view of the novel stands in the way of our reading Kurukkal's novels on their own terms.

Secondly, the reception of these novels now is impeded by changes in the configuration of the political domain. Novels such as *Parappuram* and *Udayabhanu* are deeply embedded in a phase of Travancore politics which was overtaken by the emergence of electoral democracy and caste mobilisation on political lines in the 1930s.[4] These later developments – in which a conception of the "people" as a mobilisable political entity was central – interfere with our appreciation of fiction embedded in that idiom of public intervention which drew on an older grammar of ritual subjection, petitioning, customary entitlements, and community relationships. The concerns of politics around the Travancore court from the first decade of the twentieth century may seem parochial against the background of the relatively expansive idioms of political justice in more recent times.

Earlier languages of political expression – especially in their "vernacular" form – were vital for the making of early political

[2] See, for example, ibid., 70–1; Paul, *Novelsahityam*, 170–1.

[3] Menon, *Indulekha*, 14–15.

[4] For accounts of these changes, see Jeffrey, *The Decline of Nayar Dominance*; Ouwerkerk, *No Elephants for the Maharaja*.

novels in Travancore. The last decade of the nineteenth century saw the rise of mass petitions in Travancore, spearheaded by an emergent caste and community consciousness. This led to the development of new forms of political publicity where interventions in newspapers, petition-related campaigns, and resolutions and speeches in public meetings were most prominent. The Malayali Memorial, a mass petition with more than ten thousand signatures from the Nayar, Christian, and Ezhava communities, was submitted to the Maharaja of Travancore in 1891, and this was followed by the Ezhava Memorial of 1893 endorsed by more than 13,000 signatories. Both petitions highlighted inequalities in the access of different communities to the state's resources and demanded the redressal of grievances over government employment and education. Several articles on similar themes were published in the vernacular press as well as in English newspapers from Madras.[5] These petitions and newspaper writings usually made a distinction between on the one hand the maharaja as the sovereign who elicited ritual obeisance, respect, and worship from his subjects, and on the other the diwan, the administrative head, who was often accused of misinforming and wrongly advising the king, thus harming what were characterised as long-standing ties of loyalty and compassionate protection between the king and his subjects.[6] As the public legitimacy of princely sovereignty declined, these writings increasingly used the diwan, their primary target, as a thin rhetorical screen for accusations that involved the king but could not be made directly against him. The political discourse of the time saw the paradoxical convergence of enhanced ritualistic acclamations of sovereignty

[5] Jeffrey, *The Decline of Nair Dominance*, esp. 142–60.

[6] For a discussion of the mode of petition writing in Travancore, see Kumar, "Dr. Palpu's Petition Writings".

with an implied criticism of the decline in the king's effective autonomy and power.

Criticism directed at Travancore diwans had regional and caste dimensions as well, since most of the diwans of this period were non-native Brahmins. Prominent members of a newly formed Nayar organisation, the Malayali Sabha, such as G.P. Pillai and C.V. Raman Pillai, mounted an attack on the dominance of Brahmins from outside Travancore in the bureaucracy, which they saw as a major cause for the denial of government employment to Nayars and other "native" caste communities.[7] Raman Pillai wrote a series of articles on the diwans of Travancore under the title *Videshiyamedhavitvam* (Foreign Domination), where *videshi* referred not to British colonial power but to non-Malayali Brahmins. K. Ramakrishna Pillai (1878–1916), in print the most prominent critic of the government, wrote a series of articles in *Keralan*, *Swadeshabhimani*, and other newspapers edited by him, fiercely criticising diwans such as P. Rajagopalachari and important palace officials.[8] The corruption and immorality of high officials in the bureaucracy and the stranglehold they had on the administration and the king were recurrent themes in these writings.

The attenuation of sovereign power, however, possessed a further historical dimension in the case of Travancore. Following the defeat of Tipu Sultan by the British in 1792, the Travancore state was forced in 1795 into a treaty with the English East India Company which compelled the state to bear the substantial

[7] Jeffrey, *The Decline of Nair Dominance*, 144–50.

[8] For a biography of Ramakrishna Pillai, see K. Bhaskara Pillai, *Swadeshabhimani*. Many of Pillai's editorials have been compiled in K. Ramakrishna Pillai, *Bhayakautilya Lobhangalkkethire!*

annual cost of maintaining a standing army. The unsuccessful rebellion of the Travancore minister Veluthampi Dalawa against the Company in 1807 led to a tightening of Company control over governance in Travancore. Colonel John Munroe, Resident of the East India Company, also assumed the position of Diwan of Travancore from 1811 to 1814, signalling direct control by the Company. By the end of the nineteenth century the British Resident's approval was required for most policy decisions and key appointments, including that of the diwan. In his political essays, C.V. Raman Pillai argued that under Diwan Sir T. Madhava Rao, the moderniser who ruled Travancore between 1857 and 1872, practices of direct consultation between the king and prominent householders were replaced by impersonal procedures of petitioning before a bureaucracy.[9] The palace was rendered an inaccessible fortress for his subjects (*praja*), the secretariat and the police station becoming the new sites for the presentation of grievances. On account of their effective control over king and government, the British Resident and the imperial government began to appear as the indirect and more important addressees of the mass petitions of the late-nineteenth century, even though these were formally addressed to the maharaja. Translations of these petitions were published in the English-language press in Madras, in newspapers such as the *Madras Standard* and *Madras Herald*.

The connections between these new discourses and the novel are perhaps most prominently visible in the career of C.V. Raman Pillai. In addition to his crucial role in drafting the Malayali Memorial and in campaigns against "foreign" Brahmin domination, C.V. Raman Pillai also authored novels that engaged

[9] C.V. Raman Pillai, *Videshiya Medhavitvam*, 1.

profoundly with questions of sovereign power. His trilogy of historical fiction – *Martandavarma* (1891), *Dharmaraja* (1913), and *Ramaraja Bahadur* (1918–19) – had as their theme the consolidation of the Travancore state in the eighteenth century during the reigns of the princes Martandavarma (r. 1729–58) and Ramavarma (r. 1758–98). However, at the core of this fictional project lay a deeply ambivalent estimation of sovereignty. Martandavarma's dominance was achieved through the destruction of an older configuration of power where local Nayar chiefs possessed not only the control of local governance but also armed militia and the power to carry out punishments. The acclamatory tone of Raman Pillai's novels reveals, on a closer reading, the inlay of a strain of mourning anchored not only in the legends of Nayar heroes who sacrificed their lives for the king, but also in the repeated sprouting of rebellions against the royal house. The celebratory plot line of these novels works as a screen beneath which the royal destruction of an earlier universe of community relations and power is invoked and mourned. Interestingly, Raman Pillai is believed to have planned – but not written – two novels that directly thematised the tragic destruction of an older Nayar sovereignty. One of them supposedly centred on the life and rebellion of Veluthampi Dalawa, who killed himself when the British forces were about to capture him, and whose body was brought to Trivandrum and displayed on a gibbet in a grotesque demonstration of the destruction of native sovereignty.[10]

These manoeuvres in Raman Pillai's historical fiction may be seen as an affective supplement to his initiatives in the political domain. They brought with them specific discursive challenges. The forging of a new, extraordinary register of solemnity was, for

[10] For a detailed discussion, see Kumar, *Writing the First Person*, ch. 5.

Raman Pillai, important towards producing political affects of veneration and nostalgia. He devised a narrative machinery with a high-sounding, seemingly Sanskritised narrative style and a diversity of caste and regional dialectal variations in conversations. His sonorous narrative style, often mistaken for a classical gesture, may more accurately be described as an instance of vernacular literary innovation. Well-known classicists such as Keralavarma Valiyakoyil Thampuran faulted Pillai's style in *Martandavarma* for its lack of adherence to Sanskrit grammatical rules.[11] It has also come to light that some of the difficult, elevated, and Sanskrit-sounding passages in *Ramaraja Bahadur* were first composed in English and then translated.[12]

Interestingly, the true embodiments of sovereignty in Raman Pillai's novels – the king and to a large extent the minister – did not speak in this high-sounding register. Their speech in its restraint and elegance differed from both the novel's elevated diegetic style and the regional and caste-based dialects in which most characters – from various strata of Travancore society – spoke. Pillai's fashioning of the king's speech in a language unmarked by region and caste implicitly drew on modern idioms of public address that were beginning to make their appearance in Malayalam. These were visible in the language of newspaper journalism, campaign writing, printed pamphlets, and speeches delivered in meetings of community organisations.

The narrative style of the political novels of K. Narayana Kurukkal was closer to these new idioms of public address. It did not resort to the acclamatory register of Raman Pillai's fiction, except on rare occasions. In trying to produce a form of fictional

[11] Nair, *C.V. Raman Pillai*, 166.

[12] E.V. Krishna Pillai, *Jeevitasmaranakal*, 708.

narration that engaged with issues of sovereign power, Kurukkal may be seen as a successor of C.V. Raman Pillai. There are self-conscious allusions to moments in Raman Pillai's *Martandavarma* within Kurukkal's novels. However, Kurukkal's aim was to produce a form of novelistic narration that used a thinly veiled allegorical mode to intervene in the domain of contemporary politics. The aesthetic and political challenges he faced were, as a result, different from those engaged by Raman Pillai in his historical fiction.

II

K. Narayana Kurukkal (1861–1948), after obtaining his BA degree, worked from 1886 to 1893 as a teacher in an English high school in Trivandrum. In his literary history of Kerala, Ulloor S. Parameswara Aiyer notes that *Parappuram* was written during this period.[13] Subsequently, Kurukkal served as a school inspector and as headmaster of various high schools in the Travancore government's service. The first part of *Udayabhanu* appeared in serial form anonymously in ME 1079 (1903–4) in *Keralan*. The first two parts of the novel were published in book form by K. Ramakrishna Pillai in 1911, and the third and fourth parts appear to have been published several years later, in 1925.[14] The novel seems to have incurred the displeasure of

[13] Aiyer, *Kerala Sahitya Charitram*, vol. 5, 327.

[14] Aiyer notes that the first part of *Udayabhanu* was published as a book by K. Ramakrishna Pillai in 1905–6 followed by the second part two years later. This however seems to be incorrect, as the Introduction to the first edition of Part 2 of the novel reprinted in subsequent editions is dated 3 October 1911, and it refers to the first part as having come out two months earlier. A.M. Vasudevan Pillai also places the date of publication of the first and second parts of the novel in August and October 1911. *Novelum Rashtriyavum*, 112.

the government and led to Kurukkal's dismissal from service in 1905–6. His second novel, *Parappuram* – probably written earlier than *Udayabhanu* – was published anonymously in the guise of a chapter from a recently discovered text under the title "Manorajyam" in the third issue of *Keralan*.[15] The text's criticism of corruption in the Travancore court provoked interest as well as the apprehension that its publication would lead to prosecution. Publication was also delayed by the costs involved in printing this long novel in two volumes. The first volume, comprising the first two parts of the novel, was published by Ramakrishna Pillai in 1906, without the author's name. This was followed eleven months later by a second volume which had the third and final part.[16] *Parappuram* created much interest and uproar even before it came out. Posters announcing the novel appeared in prominent streets of Trivandrum but were quickly removed, very likely by the police. It is said that the keepers of shops that displayed the announcement were summoned to the police station.[17]

Parappuram also received approbation from established literary circles. *Rasikaranjini*, a prominent literary monthly published from Kodungallur and edited by the renowned poet Kunjikkuttan Thampuran, was the first to publish a laudatory review. "We felt that there are very few authors [*kavikal*] who have grasped with such nuance the diversities of human nature and thus revealed the fundamental truths about life [*jeevitatatvajnanam*]," the review said.[18] It went on to comment on the anonymity of the author:

[15] K. Bhaskara Pillai, *Swadeshabhimani*, 138.

[16] Ramakrishna Pillai's Preface to the second volume, dated ME 1083, Chingam 3 (19 August 1907), mentions the first volume as published eleven months earlier. See K. Ramakrishna Pillai, "Preface to the First Edition", iv.

[17] Ibid.

[18] "Pusthakabhiprayam: Parappuram", 110.

> It is stated that even the publisher K. Ramakrishna Pillai does not know who the author of this book is. The story's author may have hesitated to publish his name perhaps because he feels that he has not yet proved his mettle in the tournaments of prose and verse [*gadyapadyakkalari*] or has not reached the levels of accomplishment he considers necessary for his project. However, we think that his name should not only be included in the list of commendable authors but that it be inserted not at the bottom of the list but as a correction in one of the higher positions.[19]

Keralavarma Valiyakoyil Thampuran, arguably the most prominent figure in Travancore literary circles, sent his observations on *Parappuram* to the publisher, who subsequently printed them in issues of *Swadeshabhimani*.[20]

Kurukkal also authored books of metaphysical or spiritual orientation such as *Ente Gita* and *Jyotishmati*, as well as *Satyagrahi*, a novel that dealt with nationalist politics. In his preface to *Maunachandrika athava Vijayamangalam*, he classified his books using the concept of "*tapatrayam*" – the three fundamental human cravings – as a point of departure. He suggested that *Udayabhanu* and *Parappuram* dealt with the level of the physical (*adhibhautikam*), *Ente Gita* and *Jyotishmati* with the spiritual plane (*adhyatmikam*), and *Satyagrahi* and *Vijayamangalam* with that of the mental (*adhidaivikam*).[21] Traces of Kurukkal's spiritual–metaphysical ideas appear as an idealistic strand in his political novels. These become more pronounced in the third and fourth parts of *Udayabhanu*, which were published two decades after the first two. The novel ends, as we shall see below, with images

[19] Ibid.

[20] "Prasthavana", *Udayabhanu*, pt 1, iv–v.

[21] A.M. Vasudevan Pillai, *Novelum Rashtriyavum*, 127. See also 89 and 96.

of new nationalism clustered around the "new Indian nation" (*rashtriya navyabharatam*). The protagonists of both *Udayabhanu* and *Parappuram* were portrayed in idealistic terms as model figures. While reprinting *Udayabhanu* soon after Independence, the publishers noted: "Bhaskaran – the hero of *Parappuram* – and Udayabhanu – the hero of *Udayabhanu* – serve as two excellent models for political leaders to develop the progressive aspirations of the people of this land [*nattukar*] and thus uplift the land's freedoms – political, social and spiritual."[22] The novels were regarded by their original publisher Ramakrishna Pillai not only as texts on politics, but also as precious guidebooks on ethics. While he was being arrested for expulsion from Travancore, when the police commissioner enquired about the copies of *Parappuram* stocked in the press, Pillai is said to have replied that the book was his "Holy Bible".[23]

Both *Udayabhanu* and *Parappuram* are set in imaginary countries: the events of the former take place in Dharmarajyam (The Land of Dharma) and Dwaraka, a self-conscious allusion to the Mahabharata. *Parappuram* is set in Manorajyam (Dream Land), in a region called Mazhanadu (Rain Land). The Malayalam novel was not unfamiliar with imaginary geographies: early novels such as *Kundalata* and *Indumatiswayamvaram* were set in regions distant from territories familiar to their readers. Even when these novels used the names of real cities and regions, they often functioned like imaginary entities. Appu Nedungadi, the author of *Kundalata*, took care to mention in his introduction that the place-names used in his novel, such as Kalingam, should

[22] "Prasthavana", *Udayabhanu*, pt 1, x–xi.

[23] Kurukkal, "Author's Introduction", *Parappuram*, pt 3, iv. A.M. Vasudevan Pillai, *Novelum Rashtriyavum*, 101.

not make readers mistake them for places with those names in the contemporary world, thus pre-empting criticisms of lack of verisimilitude.[24] Invented place-names in early novels and short stories often invoked toponymic practices familiar to readers from the *kavya* tradition. Characters too had names similar to those found in Sanskrit literature or in Malayalam narrative poems which followed this practice. In some of the early novels, these names coexisted with elements from contemporary life: *Indumatiswayamvaram*, for instance, refers to trains and British rule.[25]

Narayana Kurukkal's novels, however, seem to introduce a set of important innovations in these toponymic practices. Here, place-names do not invoke a poetic geography familiar from *kavya*; instead, they seem to have been chosen for their literal meaning, as in Mazhanadu or Manorajyam. This gives an allegorical dimension to names, which has also been part of poetic tradition, but which sits ill with the commitment of the novel to realism and the use of names as performing a designative rather than denotative function.[26] In Kurukkal's novels, the significatory status of names is made more complex by a mix of the exotic with the familiar and the ordinary. The name of the country where the action of *Parappuram* takes place may be Manorajyam, but households have ordinary Malayalam names like Kalpakassery or Parappuram.

[24] Nedungadi, "Preface", *Kundalata*, v.

[25] Raja, *Indumatiswayamvaram*.

[26] Allegorical naming of characters was not unfamiliar to the early novel in Malayalam. This is particularly evident in novels that deal with lower-caste conversion to Christianity such as Joseph Mooliyil's *Sukumari*. Christian missionary literature, including translations of John Bunyan's *Pilgrim's Progress*, was a source for the introduction of allegorical place names into Malayalam prose narration.

Characters too have names commonly used in contemporary Kerala, such as Kesava Pillai, Krishna Pillai, Gomathi, Aandi, and Bhaskaran.

In *Udayabhanu* the situation is different: the country is called Dharamakshetram – an allusion to the opening lines of the Gita, which confers an allegorical dimension to the novel as recounting a battle between the forces of *dharma* and *adharma*.[27] Names from the Mahabharata such as Dhrtarashtrar, Duryodhanan, Sakuni, and Gandhari cohabit in the novel's pages with Udayabhanu, Chuppu Annavi, Ponnamma, and other common names. The mixture we see in names is a sign of the melange of temporal schemas: the epic schema of the Mahabharata is made to mix with an ordinary, non-elevated plane of representation where characters perform actions that do not evoke awe or admiration.[28]

We are familiar with such deflationary mixtures in the mock-heroic mode. What distinguishes Kurukkal's technique in *Udayabhanu* is the sense of asymmetry and incongruity prominent in its application of the epic schema to contemporary times. The time of the novel is described as that of a second Mahabharata war, but the war is not between the Pandavas and the Kauravas, as in the epic; both these parties are on the same side in the new, second war, and their antagonists are the Bhishmakas – the followers of Bhishma – a group that the epic does not refer to. Kurukkal's re-orchestration of the warring parties obliquely

[27] Travancore was referred to in royalist discourse as "*dharmarajyam*" in the late-nineteenth century, provoking its ironic use in the title of Samuel Mateer's *Land of Charity*. This strand of ironic invocation continues in the language of political criticism in Travancore in the twentieth century. See, for instance, Palpu, "Dharma vs Organized Pefidy"; Basheer, *Dharmarajyam*.

[28] For a discussion of the mode of the epic as involving elevation and distancing from contemporary times, see Bakhtin, "Epic and Novel".

refers to the configuration of forces in the contemporary political arena of Travancore. The Pandavas and Kauravas of the novel's times are sections of the native elite of Travancore, impotent or corrupt, allying with each other in spite of their mutual hostility to safeguard their own interests. The Bhishmakas appear to stand for non-native powers that seek to plunder the wealth of the state.

It may however be incorrect to see the use of epic names in Kurukkal's novels as aimed at enabling a sustained comparison to illuminate contemporary politics. The purpose is rather to mobilise certain associations that cluster around individual characters and make the reader guess who in the contemporary political world each figure could refer to. Kurukkal's allegorical techniques do not rely on an overall structure of meaning; they work in isolation as masks that label the characters concealed under them. The technique is similar to the one used by cartoonists who recast contemporary public figures in the shape of animals or objects or mythological or historical figures. Kurukkal's primary aim does not seem to be a general deflation of the contemporary via an implicit elevation of the epic; it is rather to transfigure the contemporary political arena into an object for political judgement.

Parappuram does not use an epic frame but the allegorical mode is indicated with sufficient clarity. The setting is Mahishapuram, the capital town of the imaginary country Manorajyam, which is located in the fictitious geographical region of Mazhanadu, prompting identification with the Kerala coast known for abundant rains thanks to twin monsoons. Power is configured not through large state structures but more locally. Instead of the king's palace in Travancore's capital, it is Palottu Matam, the Brahmin household of Atheri, a wealthy landowning Brahmin, that offers a miniature model of sovereign power. Atheri is portrayed as a man of weak moral fibre, supported in his evil deeds as well as subjected to exploitation by his Tamil manager Aandi and corrupt Nayar employee Kesava Pillai. State power appears in the form of the police force, which has an ambivalent status in the novel's world. In return for bribes, the police arrests and tortures innocents at the behest of Aandi and his minions; the police though is not officially under the control of Atheri, and refers to structures of governance which lie beyond local power. At the end of the novel, the new police commissioner to the town intervenes decisively at the right moment to prevent the murder of the heroine. He is revealed to be an important character who had disappeared from the novel after the early chapters; while his return closes the circle of injustice through a just private act, the intervention of the police also points to an authority that does not yield to Atheri and Aandi's control. Through these characters *Parappuram* maps the three key players on the Travancore political stage: an effete and somewhat passively evil king, evil-minded Tamil officials, and a corrupt and nepotistic Nayar coterie. Alongside these, the novel sketches its hope of redemption through virtuous figures – especially the protagonists Bhasi and Gomathi – and an eventual intervention from superior powers. Towards the end of the novel we finally encounter the king, who is a repository of moral virtue and sound judgement. Normative ideals of kingship are projected on to this figure, while criticisms of the current sovereign of Travancore are deflected from the figure of the king and embodied in the lower figure of local power, Atheri.

The mode of political allegory used in Kurukkal's novels is best seen in relationship to certain forms of political and journalistic writing that became prominent at the time. As mentioned earlier, public criticism of the diwan and palace officials during Sree Mulam Tirunal's reign (1885–1924) was most vociferously made by Kurukkal's friend and publisher K. Ramakrishna Pillai. I have elsewhere argued that Ramakrishna Pillai's work as a journalist and literary critic relied on an innovative deployment of forms of address.[29] One of his powerful weapons was the mode of scandal journalism which highlighted the corrupt and sexually promiscuous practices of the elite. However, on account of the risk of libel, Pillai relied for a time on techniques that insinuate without fully revealing the identity of the powerful people he criticised. He often used suggestive phrasing that provoked interest and curiosity in his readers and made them recognise the identity of the persons obliquely referred to. As in the case of gossip, his journalistic writing interpellated its readers to a circuit of clandestine political criticism through a carefully crafted mechanism of address. The form of political allegory used in Kurukkal's novels has striking similarities with this method of risky assertions of the truth under the protective veil of imprecise referencing. While in journalistic writing this took the form of a tactical reluctance to offer names and details, in Kurukkal's novels fictional detail and fictional names often prompted a search for parallels with the real world. Allegorical place names in both *Parappuram* and *Udayabhanu* as well as names of characters from the Mahabharata in the latter novel acted as triggers for such a reading.

An aesthetic characterisation of the status of fictional writing and a disavowal of any direct connection between fiction and the real world formed a part of this strategy of political criticism. In his Preface to the second volume of *Parappuram* in 1907, Ramakrishna Pillai wrote:

> What we see in novels are not matters that have never taken place in the world. Therefore, we cannot regard a novelist's characters as solely his creation. However, we cannot say with certainty that they denote

[29] Kumar, "The Public, the State and New Domains of Writing"; idem, "Ambivalences of Publicity".

> specific persons. When an author creates various characters with his imagination by bringing together diverse experiences, why should one insist that they are referring to such-and-such individuals? Is it not sufficient to determine if the story accords with the way the world behaves [*lokagati*]? Because of some defect in the integrative powers of their childish minds, some people with charming intelligence have misunderstood the approximate resemblance between the ways of some characters in this book and their own ways, like a thief who mistakes everyone he sees to be a constable of police. I hope my readers will excuse me if I smile in compassion at their pathetic foolishness in revealing their own roguish deeds by glowering at this book, gnashing their teeth and readying their hands for attack.[30]

Scandal journalism and political allegorical fiction seek to level accusations obliquely, without having to prove them. They aim to shame without naming particular individuals who will nonetheless be identified by the larger public. Even those who are not sure about the veracity of the accusations cannot ignore the address of such texts, as the scandalous nature of the events described puts at risk the assumption of dignity that underlies the very conception of a public sphere. The reader is expected to feel outraged and disgusted even when unsure about the culpability of the targeted. Moral outrage and a more visceral sense of disgust were thus mobilised as important affects of political criticism in Ramakrishna Pillai's journalism. We find them performing a similar role in the early political novels of Narayana Kurukkal.

III

Although allegorical parallels between fictional and real entities offer a frame for the novel's composition, they cannot be seen as explaining these novels in their entirety. A challenge faced by

30 K. Ramakrishna Pillai, "Preface", iii. Translation slightly amended.

the novelist concerned the work of detailing that the form of the novel demanded: how does one produce a fictional world sustained through narration, portrayal of an array of characters, description of situations, and representation of conversations? In many early novels, a teleologically structured plot line also offered in its unravelling room for the presentation of fictional entities loosely connected to it. This enabled novels to present descriptions of marvellous objects or dramatic incidents as narrative vignettes. Kurukkal adopted this method with a pronounced variation in texture and tone. The serial form in which some chapters of his novels were initially published probably encouraged such episodic orientation, where some sensational events or elements of mystery could be offered in each chapter. However, instead of the pleasures of the marvellous, Kurukkal's novels were dominated by affects such as disgust, fear, anger, and contempt. Unlike novels of romantic love which foreground the inner emotions of characters, the affects generated in Kurukkal's political novels often have a pronounced public character. The reader is invited to experience and respond to situations in the novel as if she were placed in a space with others, and not in a private area of solitary contemplation. In this, too, political novels share similarities with forms of political journalism that deal with sensational or scandalous events. We shall explore these connections later in the essay.

Parappuram opens on a scene where mysterious events take place, triggering narrative curiosity and leaving it unsatisfied. In this Kurukkal's immediate predecessor was, as noted, C.V. Raman Pillai, whose celebrated historical novel *Martandavarma* opens on the dark and threatening landscape of a jungle to focus on the wounded, blood-covered, yet resplendent body of a young man who is later carried away by a group of unknown people wearing foreign clothes. The reader will later recognise this youth as Anandapadmanabhan, the protagonist of the novel, who appears in disguise at crucial moments without being recognised and performs feats of extraordinary valour and martial virtuosity. In a similar vein, the opening chapter of Kurukkal's *Parappuram* sketches a mysterious moment that eventually proves to be crucial for the subsequent development of the plot. On a dark night of torrential rain, a baby is found abandoned at the door of a childless couple. The orphan, brought up by this virtuous couple, develops as the protagonist of the novel. The opening scene is invoked towards the end of the novel, and the mystery of the child's parentage resolved. The abandoning and subsequent emergence of an orphan as the novel's protagonist – with all the anxieties of class origin and miscegenation that they provoke – were tropes familiar to readers of English novels such as *Tom Jones* (1749).[31] In the context of Travancore, the trope of unknown parentage, closely linked to doubts about caste and religion, served to mobilise anxieties of ritual pollution. O. Chandu Menon's incomplete novel *Sarada* worked with a variant of this trope: it is not a foundling but a child born outside the region from the unauthorised marriage of a woman of an elite Nayar family, with its consequences for matrilineal inheritance, that triggers the development of the central plot of Menon's novel.[32] *Parappuram*'s beginning seems to resonate with these familiar uses of an opening mystery as a device of narrative consequence.

However, this proper opening of the story is offered to the reader only in the second chapter. The first chapter contains another narrative vignette. Manorajyam is introduced as a land

[31] The connection with *Tom Jones* is seen also in Bhasi being sentenced to death and then exonerated and freed at the last moment.

[32] Menon, *Sarada*.

of prosperity and happiness, the centre of which is occupied by a famous Sree Krishna temple. Although the Puranas celebrate Krishna as the "object of love of sixteen thousand women", rules forbid the entry of women in the inner courtyard of the temple despite the popular belief that childless women are sure to conceive if they perform ritual austerities of devotion and sleep in the outer hall assigned for such devotees. A legend surrounding the origins of this strange and intriguing injunction, the narrator claims, is found in a text of regional mythology (*sthalapuranam*), of which he offers a summary translation.

The legend recounted in this text is about a beautiful and chaste young woman whose husband disappeared or died (*maranju poyi*) on the day of their wedding. All attempts to unravel the cause of his death proved fruitless. The disconsolate woman, to protect her chastity and get back her spouse, stayed in the temple and passionately undertook devotional austerities. Idioms of devotion merge into those of erotic desire: "every night, before going to bed, she would read with devotion songs on Sree Krishna's love play, chant Sree Krishna's name, and pray that the Lord who satisfied the erotic desires of the gopikas fulfil her erotic craving by marrying her and uniting her with her lost lover."[33] Soon another young woman of resplendent beauty arrives and begins performing the devotional routine, explaining that she was married and her prayers were for a child. The two women soon become friends and begin sharing descriptions of their respective lovers. The first woman expresses some disbelief at her friend's ecstatic accounts of her lover; the latter responds by offering to make him appear before them. After some hesitation, the first woman is persuaded to agree. The narrative now takes a surprising turn: the second

[33] Kurukkal, *Parappuram*, vol. 1, 5.

woman transforms into the lover whose appearance she promised, assumes male as well as female forms, and begins erotic play with the first woman devotee. After a night of passionate love, before disappearing, the lover reveals his true form as Sree Krishna to the first woman devotee. The latter, upset at being tricked out of her chastity, curses the deity – "Those who worship you lose their chastity. Let no woman ever enter your temple!" – and drowns herself in the temple pond. The legend ends with onlookers witnessing the divine form of Sree Krishna emerge from the pond carrying the woman devotee and ascend to the heavens.[34] After summarising this legend, the narrator moves on to introduce a prominent Nayar *taravad* named Kalpakassery and its inhabitants. The reader here enters the domain of the story proper.

It is difficult to figure out the status of this legend in relation to the narrative that ensues. The legend does not aid the reader in interpreting the story of the novel. Rather than a coherent message or a meaning, the predominant effect of this brief narrative is the violation it performs on distinctions between devotion and erotic play, chastity and immoral love, devotion and desire, and the granting of boons and sexual predation. Sanctioned affects of devotion and bliss merge with those of disgust and shame. The reader remains confused as to the nature of the agent who performs the actions that result in the death of the devotee: was it really a Sree Krishna, or was it a male predator who initially masqueraded as a woman and then as a male god, or was the deity of this fictional land an epitome of corruption and promiscuity?

Even as the legend does not have any direct narrative relevance for the development of the novel's plot, it introduces an affective ambivalence in relation to the perception and presentation

[34] Ibid., 9.

of virtue in the novel. It contains an initial articulation of a form of sovereign power as commanding obedience and worship, and at the same time as untrustworthy and immoral. The mixture of contradictory affects mobilised here prepares the reader for the novel's ambivalent and critical portrayal of figures of sovereign power, of which Atheri forms the most vivid and direct example.

Atheri is presented as a weak and decadent specimen of inherited sovereign power. His interests, instead of being identified with those of the land and the people over whom he has effective control, are confined to his own self-gratification, and more narrowly to the fulfilment of his sexual desires with their constantly shifting objects. These, in the novel's idiom, turn him into a figure of slavery rather than mastery or sovereignty: he is afraid of his mistresses, his procurers, and most of all his manager Aandi. His portrayal produces contempt and disgust. This occurs in a series of situations presented not so much as moments in a process of evolution of action than as set pieces or tableaux, illustrating the qualities of characters and the configurations of relations it aims to visibilise. Atheri is repeatedly shown in conversation with his principal assistants and procurers – Aandi and Kesava Pillai – or his mistresses, trying to appease their greed and disgruntlement. Interspersed with these are moments when Atheri orders cruel and outrageous deeds prompted by his sexual desire or by the advice of his assistants. Such decisions are often taken hastily to avoid inconvenience, and are marked by a moral indifference which appears explained by the shrinking of his self-interest in sexual gratification.

One might say that the political novels of Kurukkal work with a moral compass whose poles are self-interest and an orientation towards the other. While villainous characters appear propelled by selfishness and a destructive hatred for those who stand in their way, against them are pitched the two children Bhasi and Gomathi, who grow into adults in the course of the novel. These virtuous figures are defined through their love and compassion for others and their mutual devotion. Bhasi's constant care for Gomathi is presented as a virtue in itself, and his beauty, good manners, and speech appear as an object of universal adulation from good, ordinary people in the novel. The novel is not invested in demonstrating the virtues of characters through idioms of interiority. Adulation for Bhasi is often portrayed as a matter of immediate attraction and of being moved to happiness by his mere appearance and beauty. Even the evil character Bhageerathi, the wife of Kesava Pillai and later one of the mistresses of Atheri, is touched by the beauty of Bhasi's appearance and demeanour.[35]

Kurukkal's political novels use characterisation as a means of moral differentiation. Moral subjects are not developed here through inner conflict, deliberation, and conscious choice, nor through the articulation of affective experience and unconscious energies. This needs to be seen against the backdrop of the somewhat complex relationship of early Malayalam novels with issues of interiority. Novels that deal with romantic relationships sought to develop a new language for the portrayal of inner emotions and their expression in situations of affective intensity. Alongside these idioms of interiority, the external appearance of characters possesses semiological significance in many novels. Such signs were to be read at times with the help of traditional taxonomies of bodily features and inner qualities and at other times as indicating characters' cultural orientation or inner states. The superimposition of these schemata has the potential to make the reading of characters complex and create effects of depth or

[35] Ibid., 145–6.

mystery.[36] Kurukkal's method is different: characters appear in his novels as transparent discursive entities. Their speech does not conceal its meaning from others or from themselves. Even where deliberate deception is involved, acts of dissimulation are presented on the surface of discourse. This is evident in the compositional structure of both *Parappuram* and *Udayabhanu*. Both texts are predominantly written in the form of dialogues, with intervening diegetic passages that serve to fill in additional information, present sensational vignettes, or move the action forward. The thoughts and emotions of characters are often presented directly in conversations and on a few occasions as inner reflections expressed in a form that resembles soliloquies.

The use of insufficiently integrated narrative vignettes ought to be seen in relation to the revised conception of plot in these political novels. While the story's overall orientation contributes in large measure to its ethical and political impact, the plot also serves to create a space where various discursive entities, not necessarily dovetailed with one another, can be exhibited. For instance, an elderly policeman, moved by Bhasi's good manners and flattering attention, offers him a description of the police's torture methods. In response to Bhasi's questions about the objects scattered in the police's shed, the policeman, boasting about the successful interrogations he conducted in his youth, gives a commentary on each object in the shed and its use in torturing the accused after arrest:

> First, his hands will be tied tightly behind the back with *this* rope. One can then hear the bones in the chest break. If you press a coconut into that rope and hit him with the fist, his liver will melt and dissolve. If you pierce his groins with a sharp coconut needle,

[36] A more detailed discussion may be found in Kumar, "Seeing and Reading".

will he just speak the truth? He will say even more. *These* chillies, if you make a paste with them and put them in his eyes, he will start spinning right there . . . If he starts howling, *this* cloth will be pushed into his mouth.[37]

The policeman's boasts about his past are a pretext for the enumeration of the cruel torture methods and a demonstration of the falseness of the confessions they procure. In fact, his statements are not addressed to Bhasi but rather to the reader, or to a public of readers. The policeman serves primarily as a discursive token to produce an inventory of tools and methods of torture. Instead of fear, they create a sense of odium which is at times attenuated by the contrived and somewhat comic nature of the powerless policeman's performance of bravado.

This discursive segment is succeeded by Bhasi's reflections in one of the rare moments where the reader is offered access to inner thoughts. The narrator tells us:

> I believe you will find a part of Bhaskaran's inner thoughts to your taste: Laws which were thoughtfully introduced for peace and welfare among subjects have turned into means for violating peace and oppressing defenceless people [*sadhukkal*]. There is nothing in this world that does not have some admixture of the bad or cannot be employed for evil ends . . . Officials [*karyasthanmar*] serve as slaves to the prostitute called Wealth. O insect called woman [*sthree-keedam*], desiring your slave-work, what do people not do? They oppress others and perform inhuman deeds solely on account of this desire. Women-insects, like spiders, spread their web and with their heads outstretched wait for some worm to fall into the trap. They do menial acts in conflict with truth and honour. This is all because of their desire for you, O Wealth! Your power is indeed amazing.[38]

[37] Kurukkal, *Parappuram*, vol. 1, 90. Italics added.

[38] Ibid., 91.

Within the novel's discursive economy, Bhasi's inner thoughts do not work as the representation of what a character experiences in a situation where a close friend is in grave danger of unjust execution. Inner reflection is merely a discursive form for the presentation of a public moral critique of wealth, corruption, and sexual immorality. Like the detailing of torture methods, these reflections are not anchored in a realistic economy of inner reflections and conversations between characters. They are regulated by a logic of public presentation.

The technique of deploying characters and situations as tools for the production of public discourses within a fictional space extends to the portrayal of the goings-on in spaces of power. Aandi speaks mostly in Tamil and refuses to use Malayalam as it does not possess sufficient gravitas (*gauravam*).[39] This alludes to the preponderance of Tamil Brahmins in Travancore's bureaucracy, and to the use of Tamil for file notes by these officials till the early decades of the twentieth century. Discussions between Kesava Pillai, Bhageerathi, and Nangeli often display their evil and greedy intentions with shameless transparency. These passages are primarily addressed to the public and cannot be adequately understood within the logic of the fictional universe presented in the novel. Their function is to present characters in a state of total exposure before readers.

The features we identified in *Parappuram* are also found in *Udayabhanu*, in a slightly different configuration. We saw that *Udayabhanu* employs parallels with the Mahabharata in a piecemeal rather than comprehensive manner. A consequence of this, we noted, was to prompt the reader to look for the specific individuals obliquely referred to through the epic characters. Another result of the partial and local invocation of epic names

[39] Ibid., vol. 1, 44.

is to pedestrianise the epic world. Since Duryodhanan, Dhrtarashtrar, Dharmaputrar, and others speak about everyday matters, expressing ordinary sentiments in contemporary Malayalam, the elevation and distancing that the mode of the epic is predicated on are made unavailable. This is not a matter of dragging the epic into contemporary times, or of interpreting the contemporary through the lens of the epic. Instead, the epic is treated as a repertoire of characters and situations, some of which may be adapted, distorted, and used as nicknames or labels of verbal caricature. We do not find subtle judgements based on the actions or attitudes of specific figures. The labels invoke and refer to the public criticisms and accusations surrounding prominent figures. It is important to note that epic naming is applied only to the negative or evil characters who stand for political figures and forces against whom the novel's criticism is directed.

IV

The two prominent figures in the Travancore court during Sree Mulam Thirunal's reign – who appear as the primary objects of derision and criticism in Kurukkal's novels and in Ramakrishna Pillai's writings – were Ananda Narayana Iyer (*c.* 1857–1920), popularly known as Saravanai, who rose from the position of a cook to become Fauzdar Commissioner, and T. Sankaran Thampi (*c.* 1857–1930), the palace manager. The influence of these officers over the king was widely known. Robin Jeffrey cites a note by Resident Hannyngton from 1888, in which the latter calls Saravanai "a most mischievous man" and mentions that "his favour is sought and paid for by persons desiring appointments or advancement in the State service."[40] The emergence of Thampi

[40] Jeffrey, 102.

as a royal favourite in 1900 is believed to have limited Saravanai's influence. Thampi was married to a Nayar lady from the Kaippally family, and had a son in 1898. Sree Mulam Thirunal married this lady the following year and had a son with her in 1901. The king's marriage to Thampi's wife and the latter's rise in influence in the government became matters of public gossip. Bureaucratic corruption, it was insinuated, possessed a scandalous sexual dimension involving the king himself. In 1906, bribes paid to Thampi surfaced in a court case, but this did not result in a reduction of his influence.[41] These two officials were prominent objects of attack in Ramakrishna Pillai's editorials as well as in his political novel *Narakathil Ninnu* (1914).

Saravanai and Sankaran Thampi figure as the principal evil figures in Kurukkal's novels. The former is the hardly concealed reference for Aandi in *Parappuram*. Like Saravanai, Aandi is presented as someone who grew up in the palace kitchen and gradually gained enormous influence over Atheri. A homosexual dimension to Aandi's relationship with Atheri is mildly insinuated, reinforcing other tropes of attenuated masculinity and sovereignty. Kesava Pillai is presented as a representation of Thampi, and the parallels are developed through scandals about the exchange of sexual favours: Pillai's rise in Palottu Matam is directly linked to his procuring women, including his own wife, for Atheri. In *Udayabhanu*, Mulam Thirunal is present in the portrayal of Dhrtarashtrar, the ineffective king, who is under the influence of Duryodhanan, an allegorical replica of Thampi. The figure

[41] See K. Ramakrishna Pillai's editorials on the Travancore High Court's judgment on the Vadassery Ganapathy Kovil case in *Swadeshabhimani*, 28 February and 7 March 1906. These and the text of the judgment are reprinted in K. Ramakrishna Pillai, *Bhayakaudilya Lobhangal*, 111–27. See also Jeffrey, 374.

of Dharmaputrar serves as an oblique presentation of Saravanai Ananda Narayana Iyer. Gandhari, the wife of Dhrtarashtrar, and her daughter stand in for the mother and daughter of the Kaippally house. Vasudevan Pillai suggests that the deranged behaviour of Gandhari towards the end of the novel might be an allusion to the "abnormal characteristics" of Sree Mulam Thirunal's wife.[42]

The inscription of political corruption as sexual corruption is a key element in Narayana Kurukkal's political satire in both novels. In *Udayabhanu*, Duryodhanan's daughter Kushiki, who has no counterpart in the Mahabharata, is shown as sexually promiscuous, involved in liaisons with her own father and grandfather. Udayabhanu, initially welcomed and courted by many prominent figures in the city, finds his fortunes change when he declines the proposal for marriage with Kushiki and speaks his mind about the luxurious, corrupt life of the elite, leading to his forced exit from the country at the end of the second part of the novel. This part was published in 1911, a year after the expulsion of Ramakrishna Pillai from Travancore, and the parallels with Udayabhanu's fate are evident. Active virtue in *Udayabhanu* assumes the form of political journalism. It is not accidental that Udayabhanu's ally in Dharmakshetram is a newspaper editor. In the novel, it is the vocation of the journalist that serves as the paradigmatic instance of truth telling.

The portrayal of political and moral evil has a pronounced sexual character in Kurukkal's novels. While *Udayabhanu* is replete with references to the decadent life and sexual indulgence of the elite, *Parappuram* has more references to active sexual predation and manipulation. In both works the darkest moment in the story takes the form of an attempted assault on the chastity of the

[42] A.M. Vasudevan Pillai, *Novelum Rashtriyavum*, 119.

heroine. In *Parappuram*, Atheri, prompted by Kesava Pillai and Aandi, approaches a sleeping Gomathi, prevents her escape from the room by grabbing her hair, only to be prevented and sent out of the room by Bhasi who suddenly appears in the room.[43] This is a reworking of a similar moment in *Martandavarma* where Pappu Thampi, the Travancore king's son, attempts to assault the chastity of Parukkutty, the heroine of the novel, and is thwarted by the unexpected appearance of her lover Ananda Padmanabhan in disguise.[44] In *Udayabhanu*, the protection of virtue from libertine assault is given a supernatural dimension. While on a pilgrimage, the chastity of Devi, the heroine of the novel, is threatened by a zamindar with the aid of Devi's villainous Tamil Brahmin manager; Devi rebuffs the zamindar's erotic advances with a sharp reprimanding look which makes him collapse on the floor and lose his speech.[45]

Against sexual promiscuity and predation, Kurukkal's political novels appear to pitch an affective universe of virtue uncontaminated by manifestations of sexual desire. This distinguishes them from other novels that deal with sexual relations, especially novels of romantic love. The relationship between Bhasi and Gomathi is presented as childhood devotion in the beginning of the story, and this does not really undergo any major transformation in the direction of acquiring characteristics of romantic attraction. Not only novels where romantic love occupies the central place, such as *Indulekha* and *Lakshmikesavam*, but also C.V. Raman Pillai's historical novels, such as *Martandavarma* and *Ramaraja Bahadur*, sketch the inner experience of romantic engagement as a mode

[43] Kurukkal, *Parappuram*, vol. 1, 233–8.

[44] C.V. Raman Pillai, *Martandavarma*, 157.

[45] Kurukkal, *Udayabhanu*, vol. 3, 41–3.

of access to character subjects and their affective lives. Kurukkal's novels by contrast stay away from the erotic and do not attempt to sketch a morally positive deployment of sexuality. There are striking instances of this in both novels. In *Parappuram*, soon after preventing Atheri's assault on Gomathi, Bhasi lays her down on the bed, places her head on his lap, and puts her to sleep, and then overcome by feeling places a kiss on her forehead. However, this moment of togetherness plunges him into misery:

> "What I did was outrageous [*akramam*]. What is Gomathi's status? And mine? Who am I? What I did was unjust. Not at all correct," thinking thus, Bhasi placed his head on the bed. "My Gomathi, forgive my outlandish act. Forgive me!" Praying thus again and again, he lifted both her arms and kissed her hands. Again, uttering "What have I done" contemptuously to himself, he rose from the bed. "Let me utter Gomathi! My Gomathi! to my heart's content. How will Gomathi suffer this? . . . My mother, please forgive the wrong I committed." Having said this, he touched her feet with his lips, opened the door on the west, and went out. He came in again, and uttered "Forgive all my sins" and covered both her feet with his hands. Then went out through the door. After some time, he returned. "Please forgive the wrong I did to Gomathi and [our] mother!" Saying this, he touched her feet with his head, and left the room and walked out of the gate of Parappuram house.[46]

This moment, where the novel comes closest to romantic physical expression, is immediately succeeded by a sense of guilt and self-reprobation so severe that even the gesture of the kiss is rehearsed in a seesaw of conflicting desires for expression and expiation. The kiss on the forehead is repeated on the hands, and then feet; followed by non-erotic gestures of respect and worship,

[46] Kurukkal, *Parappuram*, vol. 1, 239.

touching and holding the feet in a prayer for forgiveness; and finally a *pranam* of obeisance at the feet of his beloved, who has now been elevated to an object of non-erotic worship.

A positive expression of the erotic continues to evade Kurukkal's *Udayabhanu* as well. The novel opens with celebrations on Udayabhanu's passing the BA examination. He wears a garland of flowers sent for the occasion by Devi, and the figures of Udayabhanu and Devi in mutual contemplation seem to reflect a painting displayed in the room:

> This picture must have been drawn by a brilliant and fortunate painter specially blessed by God at a unique moment especially blessed by divine grace . . . The images in this picture of a youthful woman and man exchanging glances marked with intense love reflected inside the women and men who assembled in this room for prayers every morning and night, producing the desire and prayer that they be blessed with spouses and children of similar bodily perfection.[47]

The beautiful couple in the painting, the narrator tells us, must have had their origin in the primordial source of all life (*aadimulachaitanyam*); their loving glances must contain the secrets of creation, sustenance, and destruction of the world. The painting, we are told, was given to the family by a *sanyasi* for their protection. The object of worship here is the ideal as it shines through the real, and the non-erotic idealisation of the romantic is already at work in this opening moment of the narrative. Udayabhanu and Devi, from their first appearance in the novel, contain traces of an archetypal significance, freed of the tumultuous passages of worldly desire. The concept of *aadimulachaitanyam* reappears in the third volume of the novel, to protect Devi when she is in danger of sexual assault by the zamindar.

[47] Ibid., 3.

The first two parts of *Udayabhanu*, published in 1911, are set in the domain of worldly life: they begin, as we saw, with Udayabhanu's successful graduation and his leaving for Dharmakshetram to seek employment. We noted earlier that government jobs were at the centre of community mobilisation around the time the novel was written, and were a major theme in mass petitions. Udayabhanu's difficulties are paralleled by those in Devi's life as her relatives try to marry her off to a Nambutiri Brahmin, and to rob her of the wealth that her father has left for her.

Such hardships often appear in novels of romantic love as impediments to the union of the protagonists. Kurukkal's novels adopt and rework these tropes in a significantly different direction. *Parappuram* does conclude by uniting Gomathi and Bhasi, yet it is not romantic consummation but the triumph of virtue over evil that defines narrative telos. In *Udayabhanu* we find a far more incisive redefinition of the trope of reunion. In this novel, as in *Indulekha*, a central moment of misunderstanding obstructs and delays the union of separated lovers: each of them receives misleading intelligence that the other has decided to marry someone else. This turns them away from worldly desires to a journey of spiritual self-anchoring. However, the consequences of the work of separation (or *vipralambham*) for the romantic plot are entirely different. When the lovers reunite, both have been transformed not only by the spiritual turn but also by the anti-colonial national movement. Devi has become part of the Navakanyaka movement of chaste women committed to women's uplift, and Udayabhanu is a prominent nationalist activist of the Swarajya movement.[48] They decide, on Devi's suggestion, to go

[48] The fourth volume of *Udayabhanu* opens with a chapter titled "Navakanyakamar" introducing the reader to the arrival of nine renowned chaste women in Dharmakshetram, accompanied by a large number of

on with their missions rather than unite in marital life. Devi has pledged to work for five years for women's freedom, and her advice to Udayabhanu takes the form of a political address:

> This is not the time for weddings and celebrations. It is the time for women and men to work together. Postpone your weddings and festivals! Work united to destroy Mother India's unfreedom. In Indian territory [*Bharatakhandam*], establish self-rule [*swarajyam*] that gives freedom and equality and self-confidence! Free your mother! Free this mother's children! This is our duty. "Vande Mataram!"[49]

Unlike Chandu Menon's *Indulekha*, which reunites the lover-protagonists after the long interlude of the eighteenth chapter, *Udayabhanu* concludes by inaugurating potentially unending austerities of service, predicated on a constant sacrifice of the erotic.

This metaphysical orientation was prominently developed in the third and fourth parts of *Udayabhanu* which were published in 1925. Bankimchandra Chattopadhyay's *Anandamath* was translated into Malayalam by Parakkal Viswanatha Menon in 1909, and it is very likely to have had a strong influence on Kurukkal's later work, as the stress on "Vande Mataram" appears to suggest. The spiritual nationalist discourse in *Udayabhanu* was developed in the 1910s and 1920s when the third and fourth parts of the novel were written. We noted that an orientation towards an ideal understood in quasi-religious devotional terms

---

women. The word "navam" refers not only to the number nine but also to their youth (*navayauvanam*) as well as to the new, the modern, which looks forward to the nation's future. Kurukkal, *Udayabhanu*, vol. 4, 1–7. The arrival of national leaders and the declaration of swaraj by the sovereign are presented in *Udayabhanu*, vol. 4, chapters 19–21.

[49] Kurukkal, *Udayabhanu*, vol. 4, 298.

was already present in the opening of the first part of the novel. *Parappuram* too contained a movement towards the spiritual, with the appearance of spiritual masters Dharmananda and Yogananda in the latter parts of the novel acting as the fulcrum for an ideal image of sovereignty. In *Parappuram*, this is located in the king of the land, who at the end of the novel establishes a just order after destroying the corrupt rule of Atheri, Aandi, and Kesava Pillai. In *Udayabhanu* the resolution of the political plot is through the resurgence of true sovereign power as the Chakravarti, indifferent and unengaged for a long time, suddenly wakes up and takes control of the administration to put an end to the reign of Duryodhanan and Dhrtarashtrar. He invites national leaders to Dharmapuri and declares the establishment of Swaraj, dedicating it to the people, only to be requested by the national leaders to continue as king.[50] In both these novels, the ideal sense of sovereignty foregrounded at the end has a religious or spiritual character.

This feature may indeed be in tune with a shift in Narayana Kurukkal's thought towards metaphysical preoccupations. His books *Ente Gita* and *Jyotishmati* are early indications of this move. The last political novel that Kurukkal wrote, *Satyagrahi* (1927), moves away from Travancore to the national arena and tracks the spiritual and political evolution of Appukkuttan into the nationalist Brahmadattan and eventually the *sanyasi* Radhakrishnan within the horizons of a Gandhian politics, understood here as the culmination of Indic spiritual traditions originating in the Vedas and the Upanishads. Here too resonances of *Anandamath* may be heard. Vasudevan Pillai notes the similarities between worship of the nation as mother that Brahmadattan participates in on his

[50] Ibid., 245–8.

entry into Satyashram in Nagpur, and Mahendra's introduction to the three forms of the mother goddess in *Anandamath*.[51]

These larger frames, however, have – in effective terms – little to do with the high tenor of political criticism articulated in *Parappuram* and *Udayabhanu*. The warring parties in these novels are all within the Hindu fold, and the criticism of evil forces is not made on the grounds of their transgression of Hindu principles or practices. Unlike C.V. Raman Pillai, who invoked normative structures based on age-old customs in Travancore, Kurukkal's portrayal of politics does not hark back to the past to invoke a "golden past" of Nayar valour or superior morality. Even the spiritual domain is not elaborated in detail through concepts or images from the Vedas, Upanishads, or the Gita. As we saw, the use of the Mahabharata in *Udayabhanu* is far from extensive or comprehensive. Spiritual forces manifest in the guise of wise *sanyasis* and yogis who, instead of withdrawing from the world with ascetic resolution, prompt and guide action – especially that of a political character – within the present. Their vision and principles are elaborated in speeches that remain unintegrated – like the detailing of torture or sexual depravity or corruption that we considered – into the novel's narrative progress.

Although Kurukkal's novels allegorically refer to contemporary Travancore politics, their fictional world gives much importance to historical referencing of the past or to philosophical invocations of tradition. The core of their political work is found in the affective critique of figurations of sovereign power, performed in narrative vignettes that demonstrate the moral depravity and cruelty of the powerful. We noted that characters are not developed through discursive deliberation or expressions of inner emotions. There is little by way of evolution or growth, not only for the villainous

[51] A.M. Vasudevan Pillai, *Novelum Rashtriyavum*, 124–5.

but also for the virtuous. Their demonstrative rather than narrative function makes it unnecessary for them to possess substantial temporal or evolutionary potential. Some of the evil characters in the novel end in pathological self-disintegration, in madness, and in violent acts. They are presented as abandoning all shame, producing further spectacles of scandal and disgust, as was the case with their earlier acts of cruelty.

In opposition to their central image of a morally weak and apathetic sovereign power, Kurukkal's novels do not pitch "subjects of the sovereign" or "communities" or other locally anchored collectivities. A conception of the citizen (*pauran*) is invoked in the Swarajya declaration of the Chakravarti in *Udayabhanu*, but it remains distant from the subjects of Dharmapuri familiar to the reader from the four volumes of the novel. It is not a coincidence that this declaration takes place in an Indian national rather than local frame, in the presence of Indian leaders (*bharata netakkal*) invited from various parts of British India and the Navakanyakamar, again of Indian national rather than regional provenance. The energies pitched against decadent sovereignty are presented in abstract images of virtue embodied in the transparent goodness of the young protagonists and in spiritual masters who supplement the fragility of the new generation. Allegories of vice intensify the force of political address in these novels. Those of virtue by contrast work by statement rather than affect.

It is not accidental that Kurukkal's novels receded into the penumbra of the history of the Malayalam novel. Their erasure of the erotic from the domain of desire separate them from idioms of romantic love which has served as the mainstay for the elaboration of the modern subject, even in novels not thematically focused on romantic love. There is no positive conception of the sexual in Kurukkal's political fiction; the sexual appears as the site where sovereignty reveals its deprivation and predatoriness. This strand of novel writing sought Western models for its aesthetic-political vocation not in the novel of romantic love and domesticity but in popular political serial novels such as G.W.M. Reynolds' *The Mysteries of the Court of London* (1850–6). Reynolds was read widely in colonial India and translated into several Indian languages, including Marathi, Malayalam, Tamil, and Bengali. Priya Joshi notes that Reynolds' novels produced strong hatred against vice and inequality, and his readership in colonial India attributed the features of the decadent aristocracy in these novels to the British.[52] In early political novels in Travancore, it was the king and his coterie of non-native Brahmins and Nayars associated with the palace that become the target of a virulent moral-political critique carried out through the heavily sexualised tropes of corruption, promiscuity, and incest.

Malayalam translations of Reynolds began appearing around the time Kurukkal began publishing his fiction, although the best-known translation by Nalappattu Narayana Menon, titled *London Kottarathile Rahasyangal*, was to appear only in 1914. In his review of this translation, Ramakrishna Pillai debated if it was permissible to depict the private affairs of prominent personages in literature. Arguing against the advice to refrain from the depiction of "unpleasant truths", he noted: "Truth, in itself, is not unpleasant. It can be considered unpleasant only in relation to the person about whom it is said . . . One who indulges in wrongdoing and harms society, whether he is the lowest of the low or the most powerful lord, should be treated like the excrement of the community; there is no need for the community to defer to his sentiments."[53]

The sexual domain stands for the realm of "unpleasant truth"

[52] Joshi, "Culture and Consumption", 214.

[53] Pillai, "London Kottarathile Rahasyangal", 126.

and becomes the key trope of truth telling against decadent forms of sovereign power. The possibility of counter-sovereignty in Kurukkal's novels is gestured at only by abandoning the domain of the sexual altogether.

The mode of address deployed in Kurukkal's political novels disappeared from the mainstream of the Malayalam novel in later decades. Unlike novels which found their discursive anchorage in literary traditions of Sanskrit or vernacular *kavya* or of the English novel, Kurukkal's allegorical novels refer to forms of public writing such as petitioning and political journalism. His work belongs to a time when fiction had a close relationship with the address of scandal journalism as political critique. As we saw, *Udayabhanu* valorises the work of the newspaper as a paradigm for speaking truth to power, which in turn is placed at the core of its conception of virtue. Kurukkal, and K. Ramakrishna Pillai, considered this a matter not only of politics but of ethics. It is perhaps in this sense that the latter described *Parappuram* as his "Holy Bible".

Many of the early novels in India presupposed a readership familiar with the literary pleasures either of poetry or of the English novel. The implied readers of Kurukkal's novels were more importantly defined as readers of newspapers and pamphlets, and as producers and consumers of political-sexual gossip. The sensational tableaux of vice and oblique figurations of abstract virtue offered in these novels disappeared from the centrestage of fictional production in Malayalam, except in some texts of political dystopia such as O.V. Vijayan's *Dharmapuranam* (1977). However, the form of the political novel inaugurated by Kurukkal is likely to have had a longer life in the domain of popular writing, which, if excavated, may help us chart a more adequate history of the Malayalam novel's transactions with political imaginaries of sovereignty and virtue.

References

Aiyer, Ulloor S. Parameswara, *Kerala Sahitya Charitram* (History of Kerala Literature), 4th edn (Trivandrum: University of Kerala, 1990).

Bakhtin, Mikhail, "Epic and Novel", *Dialogic Imagination: Four Essays*, trans. Caryl Emerson and Michael Holquist (Texas: University of Texas Press, 1981), 15–17.

Basheer, Vaikom, *Dharmarajyam* (1938; Kottayam: DC Books, 2013).

Fielding, Henry, *The History of Tom Jones, A Foundling* (London: Penguin, 2005).

Irumbayam, George, *Malayalanovel Pathompatham Noottandil* (The Malayalam Novel in the Nineteenth Century) (Trivandrum: Department of Cultural Publications, 1997).

Jeffrey, Robin, *The Decline of Nair Dominance: Society and Politics in Travancore 1847–1908* (Delhi: Manohar, 2014).

Joshi, Priya, "Culture and Consumption: Fiction, the Reading Public, and the British Novel in Colonial India", *Book History,* 1:1 (1998), 196–220.

Kumar, Udaya, "Ambivalences of Publicity: Transparency and Exposure in K. Ramakrishna Pillai's Writings", *The Public Sphere from Outside the West,* ed. Divya Dwivedi and V. Sanil (London: Bloomsbury, 2015), 79–96.

———, "Dr. Palpu's Petition Writings and Kerala's Pasts", *NMML Occasional Papers, History and Society*, n.s. no. 59 (New Delhi: Nehru Memorial Museum and Library, 2014).

———, "Seeing and Reading: Some Questions of Visibility in the Early Malayalam Novel", in *Early Novels in India*, ed. Meenakshi Mukherjee (New Delhi: Sahitya Akademi, 2002), 161–92.

———, "The Public, the State and New Domains of Writing: On Ramakrishna Pillai's Conception of Literary and Political Expression", *Tapasam: A Quarterly Journal of Kerala Studies*, 2: 3 & 4 (January and April 2007), 413–41.

———, *Writing the First Person: Literature, History and Autobiography in Modern Kerala* (Ranikhet: Permanent Black, 2016).

Kurukkal, K. Narayana, "Author's Introduction", *Parappuram*, pt 3, iv.

———, *Parappuram*, 2 vols (Trivandrum: B.V. Book Depot, 1949).

———, *Udayabhanu* (The Rising Sun), 4 vols (Trivandrum: Kamalalaya Book Depot, 1949).

Mateer, Samuel, *Land of Charity: A Descriptive Account of Travancore and Its People* (London: John Snow and Co., 1870).

Menon, O. Chandu, *Indulekha*, 20th rev. edn (Kottayam: DC Books, 2014).

———, *Sarada* (1892; Kottayam: D.C. Books, 1996).

Mooliyil, Joseph, "Sukumari", in George Irumbayam, ed. *Nalu Novelukal* (Trissur: Kerala Sahitya Akademi, 1985), 271–395.

Nair, P.K. Parameswaran, *C.V. Raman Pillai* (Kottayam: Sahitya Pravarthaka Co-operative Society, 1973).

Nedungadi, Appu, "Preface", *Kundalata* (Calicut: Mathrubhumi Press, 1987), v.

Ouwerkerk, Louise, *No Elephants for the Maharaja: Social and Political Change in Travancore, 1921–1947*, ed. Dick Kooiman (Delhi: Manohar, 1994).

Palpu, P., "Dharma vs Organized Perfidy: Both Priestly and Official", 20 August 1947, Palpu Papers, Speeches and writings by him, Serial no. 3, Nehru Memorial Museum and Library New Delhi.

Paul, M.P., *Novelsahityam*, 3rd edn (Kottayam: National Book Stall, 1953).

Pillai, A.M. Vasudevan, *Novelum Rashtriyavum* (The Novel and Politics) (Trissur: Kerala Sahitya Akademi, 1991).

Pillai, C.V. Raman, *Martandavarma* (1891; Kottayam: DC Books, 1992).

———, *Videshiya Medhavitvam* (Foreign Domination), ed. N.K. Krishna Pillai (Trivandrum: National Printing and Trading Company Ltd., 1922).

Pillai, E.V. Krishna, "Jeevitasmaranakal" (Life-Memories), in *E.V. Yude Teranjedutha Krtikal* (Selected Works of E.V.) (Kottayam: DC Books, 1996), 583–878.

Pillai, K. Bhaskara, *Swadeshabhimani* (1956; Thiruvananthapuram: Department of Cultural Publications, Government of Kerala, 1998).

Pillai, K. Ramakrishna, *Bhayakautilya Lobhangalkkethire!: Swadeshabhimaniyude Sampurna Mukha Prasangangal* (Against Fear, Slyness and Greed!: The Complete Editorials of Swadeshabhimani), vol. 1 of *Swadeshabhimaniyude Sampurna Kritikal* (The Complete Works of

Swadeshabhimani) (Thiruvananthapuram: Kerala Grandhashala Sahakarana Sangham, 2009).

———, "London Kottarathile Rahasyangal" (Mysteries of the London Court), *Atmaposhini*, ME 1090 Karkitakam (1916), reprinted in *Swadeshabhimaniyude Granthanirupanangal Sahityalekhanangal*, 126.

———, "Preface to the First Edition", in K. Narayana Kurukkal, *Parappuram*, pts 1 and 2, rpt. ME 1124 (Thiruvananthapuram: B.V. Book Depot, 1948)

"Prasthavana", *Udayabhanu*, pt 1 (Thiruvananthapuram: Kamalalaya Book Depot, 1949), iv–v.

"Pusthakabhiprayam: Parappuram", *Rasikaranjini*, 5:2 (1906), 110.

Raja, Padinjare Kovilakathu Ammaman, *Indumatiswayamvaram* (1890; Kottayam: DC Books, 1979).

Reynolds, G.W.M., *Mysteries of the Court of London*, 8 vols (London: John Dicks, 1849–56).

Vijayan, O.V., *Dharmapuranam* (Kottayam: DC Books, 1985).

7

Hootum Pyanchar Naksha, Colonial Modernity, and the Making of the Postmodern Novel in India

SAMBUDHA SEN

THIS ESSAY MAKES A counterintuitive argument: that in negotiating the unprecedented transformations of colonial modernity *Hootum Pyanchar Naksha* (1861) – a popular, lowbrow prose work by the Bengali writer Kaliprasanna Sinha – produced far-reaching expressive strategies whose relevance for the future development of the novel form becomes evident only when we read it in relation to a late-twentieth-century work like *Midnight's Children* (1981).[1]

At first sight this argument may seem untenable since *Hootum* is not even, in any sense, a novel. First issued as a cheap pamphlet

[1] My thanks to Aniket Jawaare, Baidik Bhattacharya, Catherine Gallagher, Madhava Prasad, Madhvi Menon, Regenia Gagnier, Rukun Advani, Dipesh Chakrabarty, Udaya Kumar, Pradip Datta, and Upamanyu Mukherjee for their comments on earlier drafts. Thanks, too, to Shyamali Sarkar and Nivedita Sen for their help with the difficult Bangla of *Hootum*. Udayshree Kanungo's inputs as my research assistant were invaluable.

(*choti boi*), it achieved great popularity primarily because the scandalous lifestyles that it exposed could instantly be related to some of Calcutta's best-known babus.[2] With its relentless focus on scandals and salacious gossip and its "low" colloquial Bangla, *Hootum* was very much part of the Naksha (satirical prose) writing tradition. As such it was always liable to the charge that Arun Nag made against Nakshas in general. In the "Introduction" to his definitive Bangla edition of *Hootum*, Nag pointed out that since, as a rule, Nakshas were "extremely obscene" (*nitanto oshlil*) and "without literary merit" (*sahitto guner lesh matro nei*), *Hootum*'s survival, despite the ephemerality of the genre in which it was cast, testifies to it being an exception:

> . . . when the naksha was first written, readers understood the meaning of every word and recognised each disguised character. With time all these [specific references] have sunk into oblivion. Today's readers read with little recognition [of the specific details]. Without doubt the continuing popularity of *Hootum* today testifies objectively to its literary merit.
>
> (*jokhon naksha lekha hoy chi lo pathak ra shokol shabder artha jaanten. Chinten choddobeshi choritro guli ke . . . Dhire dhire bisriti te toliea geche sob. Aaj ke r pathok alpangshoi chine jene porchen. Nirshondhe aaj ker janapriya tar nokshar nirapekhor shahitto gun i promanito hochhe.*)[3]

In this essay I hope to break down Nag's term "literary merit" into the manoeuvres responsible, in my opinion, for producing some of *Hootum*'s most characteristic effects. Unthinkable

[2] See Nag, *Shatik Hootum*, 12.

[3] Ibid., 12 and 9 (excerpts from Nag's "Introduction" are in my translation). However, Nag also suggests that Nakshas sometimes came out of respectable presses and were marked by "*joog lakhan*" (the symptoms of the age): ibid., 12 and 10.

within the dominant realistic mode in which nineteenth-century English novels were written, these manoeuvres, I argue, had far-reaching implications that were to become evident many years later, after the novel had broken free from the stranglehold of realism. Thus I try to show that Kaliprasanna Sinha's situation as a colonial subject enabled him to elude the imperatives of realism's foundational assumption, namely that time moved as a linear and continuous sequence and that it served, moreover, as the essential – if almost invisible – element in relation to which the changing inner lives of characters could be registered. Instead, drawing on the disruption that colonial modernity caused in the indigenous experience of time, Kaliprasanna Sinha conceptualised time as fragmented: several decades before the advent of modernism in Europe, he worked with disparate segments of time to register discontinuities and produce unthinkable juxtapositions. In the process he also fabricated a mode of characterisation that unfolded across the diverse surfaces of the city rather than successively in relation to continuous time. Finally, as someone who experienced in its full intensity the encounter between post-Enlightenment rationality and a traditional society deeply invested in the powers of the supernatural, and between the newly introduced English language and the constantly mutating Bangla, Kaliprasanna Sinha initiated several linguistic possibilities that would acquire great interest in the postmodern second half of the twentieth century. Indeed, throughout this essay I will invoke *Midnight's Children* to demonstrate certain deep genealogical connections between *Hootum* and *Midnight's Children.* Obviously, I am not arguing that Rushdie had read or was directly influenced by *Hootum* – a work which had not even been translated into English when Rushdie published his masterpiece. Nor is it my contention that *Hootum* was uniquely configured and had no parallel either in nineteenth-century Bengal or in any other region in the world that experienced what has come to be called colonial modernity.[4] On the contrary, I'm interested not in the uniqueness of *Hootum* but in its capacity to stimulate our thinking about a more general set of problems: the contribution that colonial modernity may have made to expressive strategies that we have come to think of as characteristically postmodern and, more specifically, the unacknowledged role that the literature in India's regional languages may have had in the late efflorescence of the Indian novel in English.[5]

Colonialism, Time, and the Novel

One of the most remarkable, though not often commented on, features of the canonical, nineteenth-century realist novel in England is how completely its internal arrangement of time came to be determined by Europe's unshakeable belief, over this period, that time – to adapt Dipesh Chakrabarty's words – was "natural,

[4] For two widely dispersed texts that are in many ways comparable to *Hootum*, see Troilokyanath Mukhopadhyay's posthumously published *Damrucharit* (1923) and the Brazilian novelist Machado de Assis' *The Posthumous Memoirs of Bras Cubas* (1881).

[5] Here and throughout this essay I am working with a set of ideas developed by Bakhtin on the ways in which literary works and the expressive strategies that they set into circulation behave across what he calls "great time". Bakhtin summarises these ideas as follows: "We usually strive to explain a writer and his work, precisely through his own time and the most recent past . . . We are afraid to remove ourselves in time from the phenomenon under investigation. Yet the artwork extends its roots into the distant past. Great literary works are prepared for by centuries, and in the epoch of their creation it is merely a matter of picking the fruit that is ripe after a lengthy and complex process of maturation." See Bakhtin, "Response to a Question from *Novy Mir*", 3–4.

homogenous, secular, calendrical": something that nurtured and measured "the story of human evolution/civilization".[6] Thus the most self-consciously modern projects of the English novel – namely, the elaboration of a carefully observed and historically determined social world, and of psychologically complex characters whose inner lives develop gradually across hundreds of pages – would be impossible without the rigorously monitored, continuous, and linear unfolding of time. Crucially, though, the internal arrangement of time that enabled the English novel to project itself as both modern and real was based on an evasion. It was not just that the novel – "the preeminent genre of nineteenth century Europe" – tended not to engage with colonialism – "the preeminent fact about Europe during this period". It was also that the modern impulse which raised the nineteenth-century novel from the telling of marvellous tales to a historically accurate and psychologically probing report on the everyday life of England took the form of what Buzard, extending Mary Louis Pratt's term, calls "metropolitan autoethnography".[7] This orientation, in Buzard's oddly sympathetic explanation, arose from the English

[6] Chakrabarty, *Provincializing Europe*, 74.

[7] The transition from "the marvels that delighted our ruder ancestors" to stories which restricted themselves "more and more to the actual and the possible" was consistently projected by the great Victorian quarterlies – easily the most influential makers of educated opinion in nineteenth-century England – as the sign of the modern. It was a transition that the novel, as the characteristic artistic mode of a "scientific and somewhat skeptical age", had necessarily to make. In a *Westminster Review* essay, attributed by some to George Eliot herself, the author enumerated at some length on the ways in which the novel's embeddedness in "the actual and the possible" would impact on its plot and characterisation. The modern novel, the essay argued, would have to be based on "the carefully wrought story which progresses in orderly, chronological sequence; which unfolds characters according to those

novelist's situation as one "for whom the very expansion of colonial holdings and international entanglements has brought on new anxieties about where and what Britishness or Englishness might be."[8] The result was that the nineteenth-century English novelist found herself replicating the project of the metropolitan autoethnographer: "the *recovery* of an Anglocentric cultural identity during a phase of intensive, imperial, industrial and commercial expansion."[9]

This "provincialism" – to adapt a key term from Dipesh Chakrabarty – encoded paradoxically into England's most modern form of writing, disabled it from engaging with a significant, though not always visible or obvious, effect of the colonial encounter: its disruption of a straightforward and linear conception of time. It is true of course that Europeans habitually thought of their "backward" or "barbaric" colonies as survivals from lower stages of historical development, and in this sense saw the populations of the colonies as part of a linear history that had progressed

---

laws which experience teaches us to look for as well as in the moral and the material world, and which describes outward circumstances in their inexorable certainty yielding to no enchanter's wand."

It is against this "great tradition" of novel writing – that extended from Jane Austen to George Eliot and Henry James – that I juxtapose the alternative set of possibilities *Hootum* was putting into play. On the other hand *Hootum* would have much in common with popular forms of print entertainment that circulated in London through the late-eighteenth and early-nineteenth centuries. Towards the later part of this essay I draw attention to Sinha's debt to the tradition of urban sketches, especially to Dickens' *Sketches by Boz.*

For the quotations from *Westminster Review*, see Unsigned, "Progress of Fiction", 343–4; for "metropolitan autoethnoegraphy", see Buzard, *Disorienting Fiction*, 43.

[8] Buzard, *Disorienting Fiction*, 51.

[9] Ibid., 107 (emphasis in the original).

beyond them.[10] But the colonial encounter also entangled the lives that emerged from dramatically different historical trajectories in what Chakrabarty calls a "constant and shared 'now'." This "synchronicity of the non-synchronous" – to use a phrase that Chakrabarty borrows from Ernst Bloch – would "rend . . . the seriality of historical time and make . . . any particular moment of the present out of joint with itself."[11]

The complications that colonialism produced in the linear unfolding of time are vividly registered in *Hootum*. To begin with, the forward movement of time as seconds, minutes, and hours is understood in Kaliprasanna Sinha's book not as an attribute of nature but rather as an European imposition enforced by newly imported McCabe clocks, and by those unmistakable signifiers of power, the guns stationed at Fort William. Moreover, *Hootum* is organised around a cycle of traditional Bengali festivals precisely to disrupt the temporal regime underpinned by the regular and routinised work schedules of modernity.[12] Yet if its author focuses insistently on festivals it is not because he has any interest or

[10] As the sociologist Johannes Fabian argued, anthropology gave to colonialism "a firm belief in 'natural', i.e. evolutionary Time. It promoted a scheme in terms of which not only past cultures, but all living societies were irrevocably placed on a temporal slope, a stream of Time – some upstream, others downstream. Civilization, evolution, development, acculturation, modernization (and their cousins, industrialization, urbanization) are all terms whose conceptual content . . . derives from evolutionary Time." Fabian, *Time and the Other*, 17.

[11] Chakrabarty, *Provincializing Europe*, 112, 113.

[12] The impositions of clock time on Calcutta's nineteenth-century office-goers is memorably outlined in Sarkar, "Kaliyug, Chakri, and Bhakti". As Sarkar puts it: "Time acquired new meaning and disciplinary authority through an equally abrupt entry of clocks and watches, and there was among some a sense of moving forward in consonance with its linear progress." Ibid., 152.

belief in them as the sites of some slow, cyclical, uncontaminated pre-colonial time. Rather, like the crowd in *Hootum* – perpetually high on alcohol and cannabis, and running helter-skelter in search of distraction and pleasure – time in *Hootum* is both frenetic and directionless.

In a landmark essay on *Hootum*, Ranajit Guha makes an invaluable distinction between this form of time – a "present always on the move along a path going nowhere" as he evocatively calls it – and the continuous time of Europe, "conducive to the sedimentation that history requires". But he also conceptualises "this incessantly unsettled contemporaneity" as a form of native "self-assertion" and, in this sense, gives to it an autonomy which is, in my opinion, illusory. The "shared time out of the sum of short-lived sensations" cannot be understood as an autonomous domain since its existence is crucially predicated, as Guha himself shows, on the printing press and newspapers – that is, on the same colonial modernity that brought the clock to Calcutta. In this sense the "instantaneous exchange of information in myriad bits" cannot be separated from colonial modernity, although, fuelled by wild urbanised festivals, rumours, and gossip, they fragment and deflect the linear and disciplinary time that clocks seek to impose.[13]

Rather than follow Guha's binary between the disciplinary time of European modernity and the chaotic but autonomous time that Guha associates with native self-assertion, it seems more useful to conceptualise the directionless and broken temporal sequences of *Hootum* as the ruptures that colonialism caused in the European notion of linear and continuous time. With its inward turned autoethnographic focus, the English novel did not engage with the complexities that colonialism brought about in the way time

[13] Guha, "A Colonial City", 424, 423, 430.

could be conceptualised. On the other hand, *Hootum* describes a Calcutta where it is impossible to experience time except as fragmented. Thus, even a straightforward description of some aggressive young men collecting subscriptions for the Durga puja cannot free itself from the implications of a time that has, as the central image in the passage suggests, literally been trampled upon by colonialism: "Twenty years back, those who went collecting subscriptions for a baroyari puja were much like a bailiff who had come to enforce Regulation Eight. They would trample over the clay stove in the house and force the householder to pay up, quite like an extortionist persecuting a Brahmin for occupying duty-free land."[14] The interesting thing here is that the festival in honour of the goddess Durga, originally embedded in the slower time of a pre-colonial calendar, is intertwined by Sinha's analogy to the violent intervention of colonialism – which did not so much erase and replace the native calendar as overwrite it. Empowered by Regulation 8 of the Permanent Settlement, the bailiff in this passage may be thought of as the embodiment of a pitiless modernity which does not respect traditional practices, such as the granting of tax immunity to poor Brahmins who received small pieces of land as gifts. But, rather than bring into existence a new, secular, tradition-free time of modernity, the ruthless practices of colonial governance come to inhabit, in contemporary Calcutta, precisely the traditional pre-colonial calendar and its cycle of festivals. Working in an environment where the relationship between the past and the present can only be experienced through a series of interruptions, fragmentations, displacements, and overlaps, Sinha fabricates a discourse where time has become

[14] Sinha, *Hootum Pyanchar Naksha*, trans. Basu, 48. All references to *Hootum* are to this text except where indicated otherwise.

unstable and directionless but free of the compulsion to present itself as a linear and continuous sequence.

Hootum and the "Modernism of Underdevelopment"

The denaturalised and fragmented time of colonial modernity that *Hootum* captures cannot, of course, be compared to the time that was radically reorganised in the modernist novels of Europe. In the work of Proust and Joyce the shattering of linear time is triggered by consciousness and often by memory. In this sense, time is reorganised in relation to a preoccupation that had always been at the heart of the novel as it developed in the West: interiority. The fragmented time of *Hootum*, on the other hand, works its effects entirely on the surface: by registering the chaotic jostling of the modern and non-modern played out in the streets and festivals it exemplifies for me what has been called the "*avant garde* . . . in backward cultures".[15] Later I will try to show that this configuration had the potential to produce a range of far-reaching novelistic possibilities. Paradoxically, however, this potential often remained unnoticed because modernism in underdeveloped situations has often been inseparable from locations that seem to fly against the very notion of the aesthetic. Here for example is Marshall Berman's description of underdeveloped modernity as it unfolded in nineteenth-century St Petersburg:

> It is suited perfectly to an urban society that stimulates modern patterns of consumption even as it represses modern modes of production and action . . . that fills people with the need and the desire to communicate while restricting communication to official celebration

[15] Berman, *All That is Solid*, 43.

> or escapist romance. In such a society, life in the street takes on a special weight, because the street is the only medium in which free communication can take place.

In the Calcutta of *Hootum*, too, modernity unfolds in a frenzy of consumption that scatters thoughtless urban subjects in multiple unrelated directions. Moreover, unlike what happened in St Petersburg, modernity in Calcutta was inextricable from the violence and subjection of colonialism. This only deepened and exacerbated the fissures that Berman uncovers within the "modernism of underdevelopment".[16]

> The bells and gongs indicating the arrival of evening had stopped ringing . . . The liquor shops were shut, in keeping with the laws of the excise department, but it was not as if the customers went back [empty-handed]. Soon, it was dark enough to conduct business under cover. It was difficult to tell the bhadraloks on the street from the lowly folks. They all wore English shoes, striped wraps from Santipur and Simla-style dhotis. Smart-assed *yaars* went around in groups, knocking on people's doors, laughing raucously and spitting out English words, fast and furious. (*Hootum*, 17)

There is plenty of evidence in this passage to justify Kaviraj's assertion that the modernity brought to Calcutta by the British unfolded most of all as "travesty".[17] Thus, excise laws – attributes of modern administration – are enacted only so that they may be flouted, English shoes are worn in combination with traditional dhotis, and the mutilated bits of the English language that are thrown around along with Bangla words can do no better than arouse raucous laughter. Above all, in contrast to visions of

[16] Berman, *All That is Solid*, 231, 232.

[17] Kaviraj, *Invention of Private Life*, 268.

self-development encoded in the English *bildungsroman*, every character in *Hootum* comes to a sticky end – overwhelmed inevitably by the boozing and whoring to which the quoted passage refers and which, together with the imbibing of cannabis and opium, takes up a major part of their lives.

In its cynical exposure of the sordidness of modern life *Hootum* may indeed be said to both inaugurate and exemplify a species of urban literary modernism that continued to be treated, until the early decades of the twentieth century, with extreme hostility within Bangla literary history.[18] In a couple of influential essays written several decades after the publication of *Hootum*, Rabindranath Tagore linked what he saw as a lack of aesthetic value in early-twentieth-century modernist poetry emanating from the West precisely to the disenchanting effects of colonialism in India, and in this sense to the conditions that produced *Hootum*. In the first of these essays, "Bengali National Literature" (1895), Tagore argued that colonialism broke up the "primordial stream" of Bengali literary culture, making it impossible to distinguish between its "ancient water" from "the rain puddles [of] recent popular convention". The idea of muddying the "primordial stream" – of desacralisation – is taken further in "Modern Poetry" (1932), an essay in which Tagore combines strident criticism of modernist poetry emanating from England and America with an array of evocative images embedded in Indian life. The project of the English and American modernists is, in his view, to rob the world of its enchantment, but typically Tagore picks on an Indian

[18] For Kaviraj this revulsion towards the city and its culture took the form of an "embarrassment about the city, the place which was the theatre of the most immediate and intense experience of modernity, but which seemed to defy aestheticisation . . ." Ibid., 274. See also Sarkar, *Writing Social History*, 176–7.

image to elaborate his point. Modernism, he says, is interested above all in exposing the "goddess' broken image with its timber and straw stuffing [to] full view". This "convulses" the modernist poets with "laughter" and provokes "[s]harp talk which stabs at the clay and the wood and the straw".

Clearly, then, "the besmirched modernity" of the 1920s affects the cultural life of India in exactly the same way as the "rain puddles of recent convention" brought on by colonialism had affected the "ancient water" of Indian literary culture. In both cases the modern spills into and disenchants the sacred. But Tagore's criticism of modern poetry goes further. With its "sharp talk" and "stabs", such poetry ends up draining its object of aesthetic value itself – reducing it to "clay and wood and straw", mere "rubbish" without form or shape.[19]

The disenchanting encounter between the modern and the sacred is evident everywhere in *Hootum*. Here, for example, is Kaliprasanna Sinha's description of the massive idol of the goddess Bhagawati that presides over the baroyari puja:

> The boroyari idol was almost 20 cubits tall. The frame was decorated with images of Scottish highlanders on horseback, fairies, birds of all kinds, lotus and other flowers made of pith. Mother Bhagawati, the world's nurturer, appeared at its centre. The lion's body was coated with silver foil and the elephant's with green velvet. The idol's face was that of a European woman; her figure and complexion resembled authentic Jewish and Armenian styles. The Gods – Brahma, Vishnu, Shiva and Indra – put their hands together and prayed to her. Little English fairies played the horn above the idol, carrying the Union Jack. The royal crest with the Queen's lion and unicorn appeared in between. (59–60)

[19] Tagore, *Selected Writings on Literature and Language*, 180 and 290.

Tagore would have no difficulty recognising this image as an early example of the modernism that he was fighting, since "modernity", as he declared early on in "Modern Poetry", "is more about ideas than about periods".[20] Indeed, in a different part of his book, Kaliprasanna Sinha had accompanied the description of an as-yet-unformed idol of Durga with something worse than modernism's "sharp talk", "stabs", and "cynical laughter". As the goddess awaits the last layer of clay, "[f]rogs that inhabit the field began to sing a welcome song for the Goddess: croak, croak, croak, they went on" (217).

And yet, though never free from irony, the elaborate description of the completed idol just quoted suggests expressive and – provided we free the word from the obligation to connote only beauty – even aesthetic possibilities. Specifically, the criticism of colonial modernity – as something that merely broke up and corrupted the "primordial stream" of Bengali literary culture – does not account for the expressive possibility enabled by the diversity of time frames that go into the representation of the Bhagawati tableau. It was paradoxically the very need to negotiate between the modernising impulses of colonialism and a primordial pantheon of gods that enabled Kaliprasanna Sinha to break, decades before postmodernism, the indispensable and constraining set of conditions within which the realistic scene was shaped. Thus, at a time when the canonical English novel could only look inwards to discursively produce that internal consistency and recognisability necessary for what has been called the "effect of the real",[21] *Hootum*, as the description of the Bhagawati tableau suggests, was already fabricating an extraordinarily supple prose

[20] Ibid., 280.

[21] On the "effect of the real", see Barthes, *S/Z*, 22.

capable of registering and generating multiple relations between objects, emblems, ways of thinking, and languages that had originated in dramatically disparate cultures.

The Aesthetic of Admixtures and Literary History

This aesthetic of admixtures, which has until recently been understood in South Asia as an attribute of a "'weak' or 'mistaken' modernity, always already flawed by the shamed circumstances of its origin under colonial subjugation",[22] was also written out of literary histories emerging from the West. Kaviraj's incisive comments on the "unprecedented" configurations to come out of India's "flawed" modernity, and on the failure of Western sociology to engage with these configurations – far less to sense their relevance in the internationalised future of the world – are incisive. They help to explain the general obliviousness to the expressive strategies in *Hootum*, which sidestepped the methods of English realism and showed the path to those deployed in a novel like *Midnight's Children*. Discussing modern and traditional attitudes to privacy in India, Kaviraj says:

> Often enthusiastic supporters of the ideologies of the modern and the traditional declare their undying hostility to the other side but are forced by historical circumstances to negotiate and modify what their own practical concepts mean to them. Both ideologies are displaced and troubled by the proximity and subtle invasion of the other, and this leads often to configurations unsanctioned and unprecedented, for which there are no standard sociological names and which are consequently conjured out of existence by the pressing vocabulary of Western sociology. In a strange inversion of the relation

[22] Chaudhuri, *The Literary Thing*, lxv.

> of reference, the vocabulary devised to describe the historical world of Europe is confused with the ontology of all possible social worlds. Such historical refigurations of ideas and practices are wiped out conceptually rather than seriously registered.[23]

It is clear that (among so much else) Kaliprasanna Sinha's Bhagawati, "with the face of a European woman" and a "figure and complexion [that] resembled authentic Jewish and Armenian styles", exemplifies "the unsanctioned and unprecedented" configurations to which Kaviraj draws our attention. Like Western sociologists, literary critics have never really engaged with the kind of forms that *Hootum* brings into play. They have not therefore uncovered this concealed literary history that lies roughly between *Hootum* and Rushdie's novel, a history not of documentable influence but of the astonishing afterlife of expressive possibilities that, emerging out of colonial modernity, gained recognition only in our present postmodern, post-colonial situation. The most obvious among these possibilities relate to the shared experience of worlds constituted by time frames, objects, and ideas that had their origins in dramatically disparate cultures. *Hootum* had not been translated into English when Rushdie published *Midnight's Children*. But even if it had been Rushdie, given his disdain for regional literatures from India, would not have read it, and far less have imagined a connection between his magnum opus and an obscure nineteenth-century book of sketches in old Bangla. Yet "the stereoscopic vision" with which he claimed to have revolutionised the Indian novel was already in play in *Hootum*.

There are of course obvious and important historical differences between the situations of Rushdie and Kaliprasanna Sinha. In the important opening essay of *Imaginary Homelands*, Rushdie

[23] Kaviraj, "Filth and the Public Sphere", 93.

attributed his "double perspective" to a contemporary experience – his condition as part of a "post-diaspora community". By contrast Kaliprasanna Sinha was not a free migrant to England but a subject of British colonialism. Despite this Rushdie, like Kaliprasanna Sinha, found in his mixed identity a discursive energy that was not, he claimed, available to realism's "whole sight". Specifically, Rushdie repeatedly spoke of the many ways in which his work drew on the fragments from diverse cultures that could coexist, in a taken-for-granted sense, only in everyday worlds of migrants cursed (or blessed) with multiple identities. The song from Bombay films in which Raj Kapoor proclaims he wears Japanese shoes, English trousers, and a Russian hat, but has an Indian heart, may have served, Rushdie tells us, as Saleem Sinai's "theme song".[24]

Rushdie's celebration of Saleem's hybrid constitution suggests to me the possibility of recovering the broken lines of connection that lead from *Hootum* to *Midnight's Children*. Thus, although it is cast in the synchronic mode as part of a book of independent sketches rather than a novel, Kaliprasanna Sinha's Bhagawati itself suggests that the "stereoscopic vision" has, in *Hootum*, already entered into the depths of Bengali culture and mediated the representation of Bengal's gods and goddesses. The Union Jack and royal crest that hover around the Bhagawati idol do, of course, suggest colonial domination, but these emblems of the conqueror are by no means allowed to overwhelm the centrality of Bhagawati and the panoply of Indian gods who accompany her in the author's description. Rather, the humiliation of conquest is, in his description, subsumed by a set of highly productive tensions that seem capable of proliferating in many directions: between the Bangla in which *Hootum* was originally written and English

[24] Rushdie, *Imaginary Homelands*, 19, 15, 11.

words like the Union Jack; the processes of secular power and magical world of gods and goddesses; the internal integrity due to Bhagawati, "the world's nurturer", and the alien tints (Armenian, Jewish) that have seeped into her complexion.

I will argue, indeed, that *Hootum* uses these tensions to set into motion at least three powerful impulses that would attain full realisation only in post-realist forms of novel writing. First, the coexistence within *Hootum* of what Chakrabarty would call "the nonmodern and the modern [in] a shared constant 'now'" enabled Kaliprasanna Sinha to produce powerful fictional effects based on the grotesque intertwining of traditional and modern attitudes.[25] It enabled him also to draw, in a matter-of-fact (and often ironic) way, on the magical resources of the gods and goddesses that were never far from the everyday lives of Calcutta's inhabitants. The novelistic possibilities generated by this freedom from what a highbrow journal, the *Westminster Review*, normatively described as the "actual and the possible", should, I argue, be related not to "the marvels that delighted our ruder ancestors" but to the expressive breakthroughs with which "magic realism" transformed the novel through the second half of the twentieth century.[26] Second, Kaliprasanna Sinha's Bhagawati – a Hindu goddess who is nevertheless given the features and complexion of European women – looks forward, I argue, to a mode of characterisation that would enable a novelist like Rushdie to disregard the distinctive sense of self demanded by psychological realism, and to spread his Saleem Sinai across a bewildering diversity of geographical space rather than develop his inner life through time. Finally, I will show that more than a century before Rushdie "Indianised" English, Kaliprasanna Sinha, drawing on an already well-developed

[25] Chakrabarty, *Provincializing Europe*, 112.

[26] Unsigned, "Progress of Fiction", 343.

dynamic, worked with the acoustic, rhyming, as well as expressive potential of both English and the Bangla street slang of nineteenth-century Calcutta to fabricate a prose that anticipates, by more than a century, the hybridising impulse of postmodern styles.

Hootum and the Limits of Realism

Hootum reconfirms a problem noted by some of the most influential scholars on the early novel in India: the "mismatch" between realism – a foreign form – and the formal requirements of indigenous novels. But Priya Joshi and Meenakshi Mukherjee focused on India's "affinity for melodrama" and its nationalist quest to retrieve a golden past – which in turn took the form of the historical novel – in their tracking of the anti-realist lines along which the early Indian novel developed.[27] Neither of them took cognizance of the powerful anti-realistic possibilities that the messy encounter between European modernity and different forms of indigenous life held for the future of the novel. These possibilities, already present in the figure of the goddess Bhagawati, are also capable, in *Hootum*, of taking diachronic forms.

This happens when the radical split inseparable from colonial modernity is embodied in – to adapt Chakrabarty – the "bodily habits" of people, their "unselfconscious collective practices", their "reflexes", and the ways in which people "relate to objects in the world as . . . human being[s] and together with other human beings".[28] Set into the motion thus by the behaviour of people, the intertwined unfolding of the modern and not-modern takes in *Hootum* the form of proto-novelistic sequences that are far beyond the scope of nineteenth-century British realism.

[27] Joshi, *In Another Country*, 137; Mukherjee, *Realism and Reality*, 41–2.
[28] Chakrabarty, *Provincializing Europe*, 66.

One such sequence revolves around Danu Mitra – the son of an accountant turned money-lender – whose progress in the English system of education has been so slow that he has grown-up sons and a married daughter by the time he gets to college. What Danu has picked up, though, through the course of his progressive education, is a fondness for English liquor. And it is in the drunken behaviour of Danu and his friends that Kaliprasanna Sinha finds the means of uncovering the chaotic unfolding of Indian modernity, as well as the diversity and range of conflicting elements that this modernity brings into play – and therefore the infinite possibilities of elaboration that are available to it.

The evening when Danu and his friends get "wildly drunk" begins quietly enough: "the bottle was uncorked very carefully, and the drink sipped very cautiously . . . (like cats lapping up stolen milk)." But the situation escalates quickly, the men lose all restraint, they begin to "hoot . . . and howl" and make "speeches in English". Danu's money-lending father, who is also a devout Hindu, is in the Chandimandap (prayer room) when his ritual evening worship is inundated by the alcohol-fuelled, English-laden hullabaloo raised by his son's friends. He is infuriated and in the confrontation that ensues Danu's father is felled by one of the drunken men with a "'Young Bengal' style punch". Apprehending that the old man may have died, the friends beat a hasty retreat, and amidst the chaos and laments of not only Danu's mother but all the women of a traditional joint family, Danu makes an extraordinary speech: "Ma, long live Vidyasagar. What do you have to fear? Let the old fool die. We never wanted him. Now I will get you a kind of father with whom you and I could sit together and drink to our health. Let the old fool die. I want a father who is quite reformed" (69).

The complexity of Kaliprasanna Sinha's darkly satiric story

stems from the inextricable but radically unstable ways in which tradition and modernity are mixed up within it. On the one hand Danu's father has happily abandoned the prohibitions of caste to grasp the financial opportunities offered by the British. He works as an accountant in a British firm, lends money charging high interest, and has ensured that his son is educated in the English style. On the other hand the modernity that he participates in (but also keeps out of his personal, religious, and domestic practices) not only overwhelms him but proves also to be radically unstable. It is without shape or direction and, following Danu's drunken associative logic, is ready to take in everything. Indeed, a modernity that can stretch from parricide and drunken behaviour to Vidyasagar's reforms and widow marriage can only be the object of satire. But, like the tradition which it pressurises and destabilises, Kaliprasanna Sinha's unstable modernity is capable of infinite discursive proliferation. By uncovering both the instability and potential for discursive elaboration inherent within both the traditional and the modern as they are played out in India, the author demonstrates the possibility of a novelistic universe expanding beyond the familiar and predictable processes of "ordinary domestic relationships" to which realistic novels in England had become increasingly confined.[29]

Reality in *Hootum* is complicated not only by the multiple levels at which it unfolds but by its coexistence with – in a matter-of-fact and everyday sense – the magical world of gods and goddesses. The work is filled with characters who invoke divine visitations to justify all kinds of activities: to extract large contributions from rich patrons for a local festival, to persuade whole communities that Yama, the god of death, has decided to

[29] Stephen, "The License of Modern Novelists", 125.

allow a batch of dead people to return to their homes because the god wants to mark the wedding of his son. Many of *Hootum*'s stories, such as the one about Yama, are merely tall tales meant to entertain, or at most to expose the gullibility of the crowd. But, as we know from the vantage point of the twenty-first century, it was precisely by working with magic as an ingrained, taken-for-granted element in the everyday lives of his characters, that Gabriel Gárcia Márquez rescued the novel from the burden of a denuded realism that had reduced itself to – as Márquez put it contemptuously – registering the "price of tomatoes and eggs".[30] Rushdie did not hesitate to acknowledge that he had learned from Márquez (and contemporaries of Márquez) the art of using the magical and the impossible as a means "of finding new angles at which to enter reality".[31] But Sinha's story about the Afghan child-lifters demonstrates Rushdie had a more indigenous predecessor, and one who, a century before Márquez, was perfecting discursive strategies by which the prodigious exaggerations and fantastic improvisations of rumours and gossip could be brought within the domain of writing to produce "new angles at which to enter the real".

In Kaliprasanna Sinha's retelling of the fantastic story that circulated in the streets of Calcutta, Kabuliwallas who trade in dry fruit kidnap children from Calcutta and transport them to Afghanistan. The children are then let loose in magnificent orchards and allowed to gorge without restraint on low-hanging fruit. When their cheeks are plump and they acquire a complexion that has the colour of milk mixed with lac, they need only be scratched to overflow with delicious nutrients like ripe fruit. At this

[30] Márquez and Mendoza, *The Fragrance of Guava*, 35.

[31] Rushdie, *Imaginary Homelands*, 15.

stage the children are hung upside down over boiling cauldrons until all their blood drains in large drops out of their bodies. The yield is then mixed with dry fruit and other candy and served as a rare and delicious dessert to the Muslim aristocracy.

What distinguishes this story from a simple tall tale is that every magical or impossible element within it works to intensify the reality of prejudice. Specifically, these elements isolate and metonymically improvise on the internal details of the life of a community in ways that demonise the community. Thus the meat-eating habits of Muslims are, in the Kabuliwalla story, tipped over into cannibalism. Similarly the practice of halal – separating the meat from the blood – is both replicated and made to undergo a startling inversion. Above all, these details are connected with others (for example, the perverse but fascinating luxuries of a dissipated aristocracy that once ruled India) by a logic that holds together the fantastic story but at the same time replicates the very real process by which communal prejudices are produced. Drawing thus on expressive strategies that could germinate only in the multicultural cauldron of nineteenth-century India, *Hootum* anticipates a form of novel writing quite beyond the scope of nineteenth-century realism.

Midnight's Children, Time, and the Postmodern

The simultaneous presence of the modern and non-modern responsible for producing so many of the effects described is integral to *Midnight's Children* as well. Like *Hootum*, *Midnight's Children* reflects, metatextually, on the doubleness of time as it is experienced in the subcontinent. Like the Calcutta of *Hootum*, where cannons stationed at Fort William go off at hourly intervals, the world of *Midnight's Children*, especially in its early stages, is marked by "Mountbatten's tick tock . . . English-made time [which] beats with relentless accuracy."[32] The inexorable forward movement of Mountbatten's time is of course towards India's independence, and in this sense points to the marginalisation of all things British, including presumably "English-made time". But the Englishman Methwold's optimistic and brilliantly bilingual refrain – "Subkuch tictoc hai" (129) – suggests that linear, progressive "English" time with its connotations of Western modernity will have been internalised by a sufficient number of Indians for it to remain active in post-Independence India.

What Methwold does not take into account, however, is the heterotemporality that colonial modernity encoded into the Indian experience of time. Thus Rushdie juxtaposes against the inexorable forward movement of "English-made" time "the crippled hours" and "the rusted time" (239) of the clock tower that he associates with Bombay as a whole. The complexity with which Rushdie handles time has figured prominently in contemporary criticism. But critics have most often discussed the sheer variety of the ways that time is used in *Midnight's Children* as a feature of postmodern aesthetics.[33] What British and American critics who write on Rushdie, and perhaps Rushdie himself, do not take into account is that several decades before even Proust destabilised the temporal continuity that the realist novel took for granted, colonial modernity had fragmented time in India, and that a text such as *Hootum* had already registered the experience of that fragmentation. Relating time in *Midnight's Children* to the

[32] Rushdie, *Midnight's Children*, 142. All subsequent references to the novel are to this edition and page numbers appear in parenthesis.

[33] See for example O'Brien, "Both Masters and Victims", esp. 165–6.

temporal complexities encoded historically in India's evolution since colonialism would enable us to read the novel in terms not of some vague, purely discursive "decentring", but a historically determined configuration where the modern and non-modern jostle for space in a "shared, constant now". Like the drama in *Hootum*, which moves wildly between Danu Mitra's drunken exhortations in support of widow remarriage and his father's performance of rituals in their Chandimandap, the tetrapod of the scientifically minded Dr Narlikar – whose instrument is placed on Marine Drive at the edge of the Arabian Sea – becomes both "an icon pointing the way to the future" and emblem of "old dark priapic forces of ancient, procreative India". Dr Narlikar, we're told,

> had arranged a single, symbolic tetrapod to be placed along the sea wall, as a kind of icon pointing the way to the future; and here he noticed a thing that made him lose his reason. A group of beggar-women had clustered around the tetrapod and were performing the rite of puja. They had lighted oil lamps at the base of the object . . . they were chanting prayers as they gave the tetrapod a thorough and worshipful wash. Technological miracle had been transformed into Shiva-lingum. (244)

The tension between the persistence of "ancient . . . India" and the unsteady, eccentric emergence of the modern provides a diachronic energy for the unfolding of the novel at many levels. For example, the modern-minded Dr Aziz – recently back from England – has to negotiate the practice of purdah when he is repeatedly invited to examine Naseem, the local landlord's daughter, for her various ailments. Confronted with a patient who will not come out of purdah, Dr Aziz examines different parts of her body through seven-inch holes in a mutilated sheet until "the phantasm of a partitioned woman" (26) begins to haunt him.

Rushdie uses the resources of the fully developed novel form to elaborate the idea of partitioning that haunts Dr Aziz through the entire length of *Midnight's Children*. This is, of course, impossible in a collection of discrete sketches such as *Hootum*. What *Midnight's Children* carries forward from *Hootum*, however, is the persistence of the ancient and, with it, the continuing presences of gods and goddesses in its everyday world. It is not just that the beggar-women at Marine Drive can effortlessly find in the physical features of a scientific instrument the corresponding features of Shiva's linga. What is more, like Kaliprasanna Sinha before him, Rushdie does not hesitate to work with the habits of mind that the beggar-women bring into play when they transform a scientific instrument into an embodiment of the divine. Thus he unknowingly follows Kaliprasanna Sinha in deploying the metonymic logic of "unenlightened" India as well as its disregard of "the actual and the possible" to produce some powerful perspectives on the real.[34] If we were looking for a precedent of the magical disintegration that Saleem suffers on the last page of *Midnight's Children* we would have to turn not to the fiction of Jane Austen, whose influence Rushdie acknowledges, but to the story of the Kabuliwallas in *Hootum*.[35]

Hootum, Midnight's Children, and the Problem of Characterisation

Despite its violation of probability, and therefore of a basic tenet of realism, Saleem's disintegration in the final scene of the book

[34] Stephen, "Progress of Fiction", 343.

[35] See Rushdie, "Introduction", *Midnight's Children*, xii.

remains an effective novelistic device because, in a paradoxical way, it makes material and real a potential that the novel sees as inherent in the situation that Saleem embodies. This suggests that the aesthetic logic of embodying the diversity and violent contradictions of a newly independent India in the figure of Saleem must necessarily differ from that which is embedded in the "deep", psychologically complex, yet sharply individualised "life-like" character at the heart of the realistic novel.

As it happens, several scholars have commented on the irrelevance of Western ideas of individuality not just for Rushdie but also for the emerging novel in nineteenth-century India. Kaviraj has drawn attention to the strangeness of "the aesthetic idea of the novel itself" in the "context of caste society and its ordering of individual lives". Similarly, Priya Joshi has reinforced Meenakshi Mukherjee's argument that conditions in nineteenth-century India were hostile to what lay at the heart of the nineteenth-century English realistic novel – the attainment of a distinct personhood.[36]

There can be no doubt that the aesthetic values associated with realism – and projected as normative by the great Victorian quarterlies – complicated the emergence of the early Indian novel. But realism, although understood as the sign of the modern in the 1860s, was not the only mode available even to Victorian novelists. What current criticism on the early Indian novel seems unaware of is the development in eighteenth- and nineteenth-century England of a city-based mode of characterisation that resonated in interesting and positive ways with conditions in colonial Calcutta. This mode, integral to the powerful English tradition of urban sketches, extended all the way from William Hogarth to George Cruikshank in the domain of visual representation and from Pierce

[36] Kaviraj, *Invention of Private Life*, 29; Joshi, *In Another Country*, 130–1.

Egan to Charles Dickens in the domain of the literary.[37] In an extremely interesting description of a scene that he observed in a low tavern, Cruickshank offers an insight into the dynamics that underlay a mode of characterisation which has more in common with Kaliprasanna Sinha's figures than with the introspective and sharply individuated realistic character. While passing through one of the poorer quarters of London, Cruickshank spotted "a small bust of Shakespeare placed over the chimney piece, with a short pipe stuck in its mouth" in a low public house. This, he says, "struck me to be the perfection of the human picturesque; it was a palpable meeting of the Sublime and the Ridiculous; the world of Intellect and Poetry seemed thrown open to the meanest capacity; extremes had met; the highest and lowest had united in harmonious fellowship."[38]

Cruikshank's Shakespeare, with a short pipe stuck in his mouth, flies against the rules of realistic characterisation: it corresponds to what Cruikshank's contemporary G.H. Lewes had contemptuously described as "a pug-nosed Apollo or Jupiter in a great coat".[39] Both Cruikshank's Shakespeare and Lewes' Apollo violate the internal consistency necessary for any represented figure to attain lifelikeness. Yet it is precisely by violating the integrity of Shakespeare's image, adding to it new and incongruous features, that the London coal heavers could transform it into a figure whose significance lay not in its lifelikeness but in its capacity to encompass the dramatically different elements that came together in the city. Put another way, anything in the bust of Shakespeare that might convey a sense of flesh-and-

[37] See Sen, *London, Radical Culture*, esp. 106–11.

[38] Quoted in Jerrold, *The Life of George Cruikshank*, 39.

[39] Lewes, "Realism in Art", 493.

blood individuality – a facial expression or a look in the eye that might suggest some facet of inner life or even a distinctive physical profile – is consciously blanked out or distorted. But what Shakespeare's image loses in terms of psychological depth it gains semantically in the unrestrained play of surfaces. This form of characterisation – produced by that "complex kind of training" to which, as Walter Benjamin argued, the experience of urban modernity subjected "the human sensorium"[40] – moves horizontally across social space rather than vertically through time, and was consistently understood by the quarterly press, and by some of the nineteenth century's most influential novelists, as unworthy of what Thackeray called "the Art of Novels".[41] Yet the "flat" character, energised by the fragmented multiplicity of the city rather than an evolving interiority, continued to develop in many novels – most significantly in the novels of Dickens.

It was not a literary critic but the historian Ranajit Guha who took serious cognizance of the echo from Dickens' *Sketches by Boz* in the (English) subtitle of the second edition of *Hootum*.[42] For Guha, though, the connection between Dickens and Kaliprasanna Sinha is an opportunity to probe not the literary problem of characterisation but the historical problem of time. Specifically, he picks on the "Everyday Life" common to both subtitles to set up an opposition between the ways that everyday time plays out in London and Calcutta. My essay, as should be obvious, owes a great deal to Guha's insights on colonial time, but I am interested also in the word "Sketches" that Kaliprasanna Sinha borrows from the subtitle of Dickens' first published book – because it signifies

[40] ". . . technology has subjected the human sensorium to a complex kind of training", Benjamin, *Writer of Modern Life*, 191.

[41] Quoted in Tillotson, *William Makepeace Thackeray*, 128.

[42] See Guha, "A Colonial City and its Times", esp. 414–15.

a non-realistic, popular English tradition of representing scenes and people from the big city.[43] Moreover, unlike Guha, who locks *Sketches by Boz* and *Hootum Pyanchar Naksha* in a set of all-pervasive oppositions, I believe that while colonial difference does break up linear time in *Hootum*, this difference cannot invariably determine every element in the relationship between *Hootum* and *Sketches*. In fact I am arguing that Dickens' first book exposed Kaliprasanna Sinha to the tradition of city sketches and provided him with a set of basic strategies with which to focus in the figure of the babu a dizzying multitude of social signs marking his frenetic movement through the unstable diversity of life in Calcutta. Mutating always in conditions that were far more complex in Calcutta, these resources enabled the fabrication of figures from social surfaces who, in their internal diversity, produce a range of tensions far more socially resonant than those that Cruikshank's hybridised Shakespeare had put into play.

Characters in *Hootum*, shaped often by the inherently contradictory impulses of colonialism, cry out for the grotesque embodiment of which Shakespeare's bust is a somewhat mild example. For example, the babu who does everything in the English style – smokes cigars, drinks brandy from decanters, and has "The Englishman" and "The Phoenix" within easy reach – is embodied in an image within which an English sculpting style and mode of presentation combine with an excretory substance that is habitually moulded and dried for various purposes in everyday Indian life.

[43] On the tradition of urban sketching, see Grey, "Views and Sketches London", 43. On the connection between the sketching tradition and ·ban mode of characterisation, see Reid, *Bucks and Bruisers*; and Sen, ·, *Radical Culture*, esp. 65–94.

Kaliprasanna Sinha's "cowdung busts of well-bred babus"[44] (in Swarup Roy's translation) seems to suggest the author's inevitable implication in what Kaviraj calls "the self-ironical" tradition of nineteenth-century Bangla writing – the necessary consequence of having to choose between "autonomy without modernity or modernity with the acceptance of subjecthood".[45] Yet Kaliprasanna Sinha's figures expand considerably beyond the merely satiric when we move away from the problem of the self and read them in relation to what Baudelaire called "the external life of [an] age".[46]

Like Baudelaire's anonymous "Painter of Modern Life", Kaliprasanna Sinha never misses a chance to pick up and comment on the dress, accessories, fashions, hairstyles, postures, and styles of conversation set into circulation by colonial modernity. Moving

[44] *The Observant Owl*, 15.

[45] Kaviraj, *The Invention of Private Life*, 227. It is significant though that Kaviraj glances at *Hootum* and then sets it aside in his discussion on "the self ironical tradition" in Bangla literature of the nineteenth century. His reason for excluding Sinha from a serious "self-ironical tradition" of Bangla literature is, in fact, related to a familiar preoccupation: interiority. It is true that the interiority Kaviraj discusses differs significantly from the ways in which subjective life is represented in dominant forms of the English novel such as the *bildungsroman* and domestic realism. Rather than moving the protagonist towards maturity, "self understanding" for the subject of colonial modernity is inseparable from "self ironical laughter". What does not change as we move from the English votaries of psychological realism, from G.H. Lewes and F.R. Leavis to Sudipta Kaviraj, is the focus on interiority as privileged terrain of serious literature. Discerning accurately that *Hootum* lacks the capacity to register the inward turned self-division that he believes to be an essential element in serious literary responses to the contradictions of colonial modernity, Kaviraj sets it aside as minor, "too frivolous to raise serious discussion".

[46] Baudelaire, *Painter of Modern Life*, 14.

horizontally across the crowded streets of Calcutta rather than vertically through a developing individual consciousness, *Hootum* registers everything from the fad for the Prince Albert hairstyle that has pushed the traditional turban into oblivion, to the spouting of badly pronounced English words by young men about town, to the gait of clerks returning home after work. None of these, however, function as mere trivia. Rather, the relationship between the people who inhabit the world of *Hootum* and the detachable appendages that circulate incessantly through it is generative and productive. Thus, characters will grasp or discard a headgear, a style of dress or speech, or a set of etiquettes to facilitate their movements through the bewilderingly varied and even contradictory social domains that make up the world of colonial modernity.

A typical character in *Hootum* is Pyalanath Babu.

> The babu was a staunch Hindu who fasted on the eleventh day of the waxing moon . . . He had studied English for . . . three months at Sherburne's school . . . So far he had managed to get by with what he learned there . . . His favourite outfit comprised churidar trousers cut in the Lucknow style (which made him look a bit like a baiji's servant), a long loose shirt, a dupatta tied across the middle and of course the tilted cap. He was held in high esteem in the baiji and khyamta circles . . . (55)

There is no attempt in this representation to produce a divided interiority through the accretion of successive experiences as he moves through the contradictory social worlds that he inhabits. Rather, what drives Pyalanath Babu is his incessant capacity for ·lf-fashioning. His willingness to superimpose the attributes of ·slim and British culture on his relatively unchanging body ·s to the most dynamic element in his characterisation: his capacity to move across what is potentially an unlimited social expanse.

Characterisation and Social Space in *Midnight's Children*

The figure of Pyalanath Babu receives only limited elaboration in *Hootum* and, for reasons I will turn to in the last part of this essay, the mode of characterisation that he exemplifies did not have much of an afterlife in the mainstream Bangla novel as it developed after *Hootum*. But the propensity for cultural intermixtures that went into his making became a potent resource for a novel like *Midnight's Children*. Rushdie himself attributed his commitment to an aesthetic of cultural mixtures to his situation as a diasporic Indian; his more recent critics have gone even further in their casual disregard for how much he drew on conditions that developed *within* the subcontinent ever since the advent of colonialism. Rushdie's characters, writes Vassilena Parashkevova, are "in line with the post-structuralist emphasis on the decentered, plural, constantly changing self as opposed to the essentialist notion of identity as an inherent, ever-present sameness."[47] Disregarding for the moment that no realist novel ever conceptualised "identity as an inherent, ever-present sameness", it seems incredible to me that Parashkevova does not even consider the possibility that colonialism could have produced a modernity where it would be completely possible to conceptualise the self as "decentered", "plural", and "constantly changing".

More important, though, is a second possibility that the figure of Pyalanath Babu holds for the internal workings of *Midnight's*

[47] Parashkevova, "Turn Your Watch Upside Down", 12.

Children. One way to understand this possibility would be to focus on an important sequence that occurs halfway through the novel. In this sequence, Saleem hides himself in the boot of the family car that is carrying his mother to a secret rendezvous. As he imagines the car moving rapidly northwards "past Breach Candy Hospital and Mahalaxmi Temple, north along Hornby Vellard past Vallabhbhai Patel Stadium and Haji Ali's island tomb", his consciousness is reduced in his "pell-mell tumble of a brain" to a tiny "white dot" that "jumped about like a wild flea from one thing to another" (297).

Drawn rapidly, and under uncertain circumstances across the length of Bombay, Saleem loses his social moorings at Methwold Estate and the sense of self it sustained. His consciousness which, were it embedded in a realist novel would enjoy an elaborate and psychologically complex development, is reduced to an unstable dot. His transformative car journey is thus designed to pull him out from the parameters within which the realistic hero develops after he is, in Bakhtin's words, "assigned to a plot as someone fully embodied and strictly localised in life, as someone dressed in the concrete and impenetrable garb of his class or social station, his family position, his age, his life, his biographical goals."[48] Freed by the logic of Rushdie's characterisation from the "impenetrable garb of his class or social situation", Saleem can be moved through a range of contradictory incarnations – from a boy growing up in a posh Bombay locality to the inmate of a Delhi slum; from someone who becomes part of the Pakistani elite to a Buddhist mendicant lost in the Sunderbans. It seems to me that Pyalanath Babu – adept at moving comfortably from a devout Hindu home the world of Muslim courtesans and English officials – had

ıkhtin, *Problems of Dostoevsky's Poetics*, 104.

set in motion, many years before the postmodern celebration of multiculturalism, a mode of characterisation oriented towards exploring not so much the depths of individuality but the contradictory, tense, fissiparous multiplicity of the subcontinent.

Hootum Pyanchar Naksha, *Midnight's Children*, and "the Efflorescence of Language"

In an insightful "Foreword" to the Chitralekha Basu edition of *Hootum*, Amit Chaudhuri argues that the modern in Kaliprasanna Sinha's book should be understood in terms not of "description" or "subject matter" but predominantly of "the efflorescence of language" that it is able to sustain.[49] A similar linguistic efflorescence, driven primarily by the synergy between English and Indian languages, turns out to be the most powerfully distinguishing feature of Rushdie's *Midnight's Children* as well. I contend here that the linguistic energy with which Rushdie revolutionised the English novel in India was already available for Kaliprasanna Sinha and other regional writers of the nineteenth century, and that their improvisations in a linguistic universe being incessantly churned by the arrival of English can be understood as the legacy that Rushdie inherited.

There is, of course, one crucial difference between Kaliprasanna Sinha and Rushdie. As an international writer working with the English language in a cultural climate that privileged the hybrid over the "pure", *Midnight's Children* resonated across the world in a way *Hootum* could never manage. Moreover Rushdie saw himself, and was seen by others, as having overcome the multiple problems that had inhibited Indian novelists from writing in English ever

[49] Chaudhuri, "Foreword", x.

since Bankim Chandra Chatterjee discarded it after his first novel. Many Indian novelists, as Rushdie knew, were reluctant to use the coloniser's unfamiliar language, which reinforced the native's inferiority and which was, in any case, incapable of registering the colloquialism, idioms, and metaphors that incessantly circulated through the writer's mother tongue.[50]

Rushdie's response, in *Midnight's Children*, was to radically reinvent English as a new "literary idiolect that allowed the rhythms and thought patterns of Indian languages to blend with the idiosyncrasies of 'Hinglish' and 'Bambaiyaa', the polyglot street slang of Bombay." He hoped in this way to "conquer" English and wipe out the humiliation of colonialism, and at the same time remake the language "for our own purposes".[51] By all accounts he succeeded brilliantly. One reader's exultation that Rushdie had "represented my world in a language totally unprecedented in the history of English literature" also represents, as Priya Joshi has shown, a real consensus.[52]

The hybridising orientation of Rushdie's language, often announced metatextually within the body of the novel itself, resonated well with the postmodern and multicultural climate of the 1980s. Saleem's proclamation "that the fishmarket cacophony of my voices" is determined by the "polyglot frenzy in my head" (233) is picked up enthusiastically, though somewhat pompously,

[50]As Meenakshi Mukherjee put it: "For a long time it had seemed that English writing in India was destined to remain an one-stringed instrument, because the normal ground conditions of literary production – where a culture d its variations, a language and its dialects, centuries of oral traditions and ·en literature,, all interact to create a new text – do not exist in the case ·lish in India." Mukherjee, *Perishable Empire*, 172–3.

shdie "Introduction", xii, and *Imaginary Homelands*, 17.

ım Bharucha, quoted in Joshi, *In Another Country*, 254.

by critics like Robert Bennett and those who write about the "heteroglot polyphonic voices" in Rushdie's "poststructuralist" narrative.[53]

Rushdie's massive impact on the Indian novel in English, his international reputation, and the existence of a critical vocabulary to celebrate his "literary idiolect" have all worked to constitute his achievement as unique and unprecedented, and to sever any connection it might have had to a long and rich tradition of linguistic intermixtures that flourished continuously in many Indian languages from the nineteenth century. And yet the significant and sustained influence of other tongues has been a persistent feature in the development of many, if not most, Indian languages.

For example, many historians have shown that, in addition to emerging out of and borrowing crucial elements from Sanskrit, Bangla continuously drew on the vocabulary of Persian and Arabic. Moreover, as Meenakshi Mukherjee has confirmed, citing her own research, it is no longer possible to assume that English, when it arrived, remained confined to the domain of official dealings. She acknowledges that she had begun with the prevailing assumption about English, but that research led her to revise her position as she began to discover the many ways English entered into and influenced the language of intimacy.[54] Rosinka Chaudhuri elaborates in much greater detail and depth the infiltration of tropes, conventions, idioms, phrases, and words from the English language and English literature into literary Bangla.[55] Her

[53] Bennett, "National Allegory or Carnivalesque Heteroglossia?" 178, 189.

[54] For example, see Chakravorty, "Purity and Print"; Ghosh, *Power in Print*; and Banerjee, *The Parlour and the Street*. Mukherjee discusses this revision of opinion in *Perishable Empire*, 44.

[55] See Chaudhuri, *The Literary Thing*.

analyses of nineteenth-century Bangla poetry, together with Sumanta Banerjee's work on popular culture, suggests that the interaction between Bangla and English was by no means orderly, and what Bangla appropriated was a hodge-podge of English words, phrases, and literary conventions. But the very fragmented and distorted nature of the English that found a home in Bangla facilitated literary effects unavailable to the pure forms of either language. This polyglot Bangla could, for example, produce a range of effects from the comic to the profound by conjuring unexpected rhymes or alliteration that worked only on multilingual levels. Similarly, it could awaken a derisive connotation in an authoritative English word or phrase of colonial administration via a bilingual pun intelligible only to Bangla readers.

In *Hootum* the experience of colonial modernity is articulated in a prose that has absorbed English words and phrases, overlaid them with accents of Bangla speech, and joined them to other words, in this way creating an unprecedented allusive and semantic reach. *Hootum* may be embedded in an earlier and more subservient phase of India's unequal relationship with England than is *Midnight's Children*, but, incorporated into Bangla, English words lose their status as part of the master's language and become elements of a new hybrid vocabulary that can mockingly reflect the unassimilated mixtures of colonial modernity. If anything, Kaliprasanna Sinha's mixture of English and Bangla is sharper than anything in Rushdie in its indictment of the Anglicised gentleman. Saleem's father has an unacknowledged ancestor in *Hootum* – the babu who finds his most appropriate representation the "goborer bust" – a bust in the classical Western style made wdung (*Shatik*, 50).

we might expect, it was in the process of negotiating the new commodity culture brought into existence by colonialism that the Bangla language absorbed and indigenised large numbers of English words. *Hootum* improvises brilliantly with the mixed-up language of commodity culture to capture at many levels the transformation of a world gripped by a frenzy of consumption. The alliterative *cha* (tea) and cheroot leaves open the possibility of a harmonious relationship between the new commodities that the babu has recently learned to consume (*Shatik*, 50). More often, though, the world of commodities both embodies and stimulates a new language for the most unexpected configurations. Kaliprasanna Sinha draws on two foreign languages to describe a typical garment to emerge out of the cauldron of new commodity culture. He calls this garment a "*cuff o collar er kameez*" (the traditional long shirt fitted with the English-style cuffs and collar: *Shatik*, 52). In a more elaborate description, he deploys fragments of English and other languages to embody on the surface of a phrase the strange, half-formed situations that colonialism had brought into existence. Babus who seek to replace the traditional floor arrangement with English-style seating when getting together with friends spawn a situation whose grotesque modernity can only be described by an unprecedented Bengalisation of foreign words: the "*table chairer majlis*" (the get-together on chairs and tables: *Shatik,* 50).

The rough overlay of English words and phrases spills over in *Hootum* from the language of commodities to that of colonial administration. Moreover, far from remaining confined within officialdom – as an older generation of historians had argued – English or English-inflected appellations such as the section *lekhar kerani* (section officer) and the "head writer", "the warren" (the warrant) and the grand jury, have in *Hootum* penetrated so deep into everyday Bengali life that its author can effortlessly use them in combination with the most indigenous forms of Bengali culture. For example, a metaphor from the pre-colonial Bengali lunar calendar is a taken-for-granted part of what Rushdie would call Kaliprasanna Sinha's "idiolect" in the latter's description of a musically inclined "superintendent Saheb" who prefers the company of his piano- and harmonium-playing friends over that of his official associates. The inspector, the author says, is as rarely sighted in "inspector *mahol*" (society of inspectors) as "*amabarshae brihashpati*" (the new moon in the house of Jupiter: *Shatik*, 46). Drawing on the other end of the spectrum, he finds in the language of English law the means of fabricating the familiar tone that a drunken babu uses in his harangue with the goddess Jagadhatri. Jagadhatri's failure to reform her ways will drag her, the babu intones, to the "grand jury" (*Shatik*, 74).

We could thus argue that the hybrid style of colonial modernity looks forward to that moment in the late-twentieth century when the Indian novel, drawing on the resources of local dialects, would reinvent the English language for its own purposes. In this *Hootum* embodies an important and productive impulse that has been associated with the cultural world of the colonised: "The colonized cannot continue to be conceived as victims of a triumphant Englishness imposing its rule and civility on its racial other. On the contrary the colonial space was to reconstitute itself in response to the imposition of Englishness; in inventing itself, the colonial space would also reinvent the structure and meaning of the core term Englishness . . ."[56] In fact, as I have tried to show, *Hootum* contains in embryonic form a whole set of such forward-looking impulses that would, over the years, outflank the development of English realism and in this way not just reinvent "the structure and meaning of the core

[56] Gikandi, *Maps of Englishness*, xviii.

term Englishness" but also make it irrelevant. *Hootum* paved the way not only for the hybrid "idiolect" that *Midnight's Children* celebrated as an appropriate literary language in our globalised world, but also for some of the characteristic "postmodern" features of *Midnight's Children*: its organisation of time and character, and indeed for a whole aesthetic based on unthinkable but socially resonant intermixtures.

Unfortunately, these possibilities became marginal to the Bangla novel as it developed through the nineteenth and most of the twentieth century. The fundamental reason for this is that Kaliprasanna Sinha died young. Unlike Dickens he did not get the time to make a transition to novel writing. But even if he had produced a full-blown novel from the expressive strategies that *Hootum* put in play, such a novel would have had little chance of influencing the future development of Bangla literature – just as Dickens' fiction had no influence on what F.R. Leavis called "the great tradition" of the English novel. One of Kaliprasanna Sinha's most far-reaching achievements – his fabrication of a complex, multilayered, and polyglot literary Bangla – was already becoming discredited by the late 1860s. The attack on Kaliprasanna Sinha was led by Bankim Chandra Chatterjee, who denigrated the *Hootum* variety of carefully crafted prose – which could effortlessly mix Sanskritic poetic conventions, street slang, and Bengalicised English – as "*oshlil*": "not seldom disfigured by obscenity", as Chatterjee put it.[57]

Bankim's unusually harsh response to *Hootum* ought to be related to what Anindita Ghosh, drawing on Norbert Elias, has called the "civilising drive" aimed at rescuing Bangla from what was seen as "loose colloquial forms, allegedly polluted by rusticity

[57] Quoted in Guha, *Small Voice of History*, 414.

and abundant sexuality."[58] Moreover, stalwarts like Ishwar Chandra Vidyasagar, who could not, understandably, have anticipated the relevance that Kaliprasanna Sinha's polyglot Bangla would have for a postcolonial world, believed that modernising Bangla meant, as Sumit Sarkar has shown, fabricating a "prose capable of tackling in a creative and attractive manner a much wider range of themes than had been possible or necessary in precolonial times."[59] The enthusiastic support which Vidyasagar's efforts received from British educators suggests the gradual convergence between the opinions of the Bengali *bhadralok* and British administrators on what counted as modern. This notion of the modern, underpinned by the idea of propriety and purity, came to encompass *bhadralok* print culture as a whole.[60] And it pushed not only the polyglot language that Kaliprasanna Sinha fabricated, but the whole range of expressive strategies that *Hootum* had developed, to the margins of what could be considered literary. To be sure, *Hootum*'s sardonic tone and startling juxtapositions continued to survive in some forms of poetry written through the second half of the nineteenth century.[61] But in general it was Lord Napier's call for refinement, and specifically his advice to Indian painters that they deploy modern European techniques to explore Indian subjects, that came to determine the course of the canonical nineteenth-century novel in Bengal.[62]

The result has been a certain ambivalence towards *Hootum*. *Hootum*, says Partha Chatterjee, has "enjoyed a steady popularity in Bengal" ever since its first publication, but has also carried the stigma of the "disreputable and the prohibited". It is almost as

[58] Ghosh, *Power in Print*, 4.

[59] Sarkar, *Writing Social History*, 250.

[60] See Ghosh, *Power in Print*, 4–5.

[61] See Chaudhuri, *The Literary Thing*.

[62] On Napier's advice, see Mukherjee, *Perishable Empire*, 100.

if, Chatterjee concludes, "the educated *bhadralok*, ever in search of bourgeois respectability . . . has kept the pleasures of *Hootum's* sketches firmly to itself, like a family secret that must not be revealed to the outsider."

And yet Chatterjee's "Foreword" itself testifies to a rapid breaching of the relatively confined domain within which *Hootum* circulated through most of its 150-odd years of life. Indeed, in the last ten years alone it has been the subject of an English-language graphic novel, apart from being twice translated into English. This revival promises much to the historian" "Our . . . post-colonial confidence," Chatterjee writes, "might allow contemporary Indian culture to recognize and recover much that is of value from the neglected remains of popular cultures of the past."[63]

For the literary critic, I believe, the stakes are even higher. The current expansion of interest in *Hootum* suggests that the book speaks to us in a way that it did not to nineteenth- and early-twentieth-century readers. In this sense it reinforces one of the arguments I've been making: that *Hootum* (and other texts like it) articulated a modernity far in advance of the modern as it was understood both in nineteenth-century English literature and by its votaries in Bangla. And that the enormous relevance of Kaliprasanna Sinha's hybridising aesthetics to our current literary environment might enable us to think of *Hootum* as embodying what Bakhtin conceptualised as "generic memory"[64] – on which a

[63] Chatterjee, "Foreword", ix, xii.

[64] This conceptual category remained active throughout Bakhtin's work. In *Problems of Dostoevsky's Poetics* he elaborates it: "A literary genre . . . reflects the most stable . . . tendencies in literature . . . A genre is always the same and yet not the same, always old and new simultaneously . . . A genre lives in the present but always *remembers* its past, its beginning. Genre is a representative of creative memory in the process of literary development." Bakhtin, *Dostoevsky's Poetics,* 106.

future novelist like Rushdie could draw, elaborate, and disseminate to an international audience. Seen in this way, *Hootum* enables us to shift the sources of *Midnight's Children* from general categories such as the "diasporic" and the "postmodern" to linguistic innovations, forms of conceptualising time and characters, and a general aesthetic based on unprecedented juxtapositions circulating in vernacular literary cultures ever since the rude shock of colonialism began producing mixed and messed-up urban cultures in India.

References

Bakhtin, M.M., *Problems of Dostoevsky's Poetics*, trans. Caryl Emerson (Manchester: Manchester University Press, 1984).

———, *Speech Genres and Other Late Essays*, trans. Vern W. McGee (Austin, TX: University of Texas Press, 1986).

Banerjee, Sumanta, *The Parlour and the Streets: Elite and Popular Culture in Nineteenth Century Calcutta* (Calcutta: Seagull, 1989).

Barthes, Roland, *S/Z: An Essay*, trans. Richard Miller (New York: Hill and Wang, 1977).

Baudelaire, Charles, *The Painter of Modern Life and Other Essays*, trans. Jonathan Mayne (New York: Phaidon, 1995).

Benjamin, Walter, *The Writer of Modern Life: Essays on Charles Baudelaire* (Massachusetts: Harvard University Press, 2006).

Berman, Marshall, *All That Is Solid Melts into Air: The Experience of Modernity* (London: Penguin, 1988).

Blanchard, Jerrold, *The Life of George Cruikshank in Two Epochs* (London: Chatto and Windus, 1898).

Bennett, Robert, "National Allegory or Carnivalesque Heteroglossia? *Midnight's Children*'s Narration of Indian National Identity", *Bucknell Review* 43.2, 2000.

Buzard, James, *Disorienting Fiction: The Autoethnographic Work of 19th-Century British Novels* (Princeton: Princeton University Press, 2005).

Chakrabarty, Dipesh, *Provincializing Europe: Postcolonial Thought and Historical Difference* (Princeton: Princeton University Press, 2000).

Chakravorty, Swapan, "Purity and Print: A Note on Nineteenth Century Bengali Prose", in Abhijit Gupta and Swapan Chakravorty, ed., *Print Areas: Book History in India* (New Delhi: Permanent Black, 2004).

Chatterjee, Partha, "Foreword", in Kaliprasanna Sinha, *Hootum Pyanchar Naksha*, trans. by Swarup Roy as *The Observant Owl: Hootum's Vignettes of Nineteenth-century Calcutta* (Ranikhet: Permanent Black/Black Kite, 2008).

Chaudhuri, Amit, "Foreword", in Kaliprasanna Sinha, *Hootum Pyanchar Naksha*, trans. by Chitralekha Basu as *Sketches by Hootum the Owl: A Satirist's View of Colonial Calcutta* (Calcutta: Samya, 2012).

Chaudhuri, Rosinka, *The Literary Thing: History, Poetry and the Making of a Modern Cultural Sphere* (New Delhi: Oxford University Press, 2013).

Fabian, Johannes, *Time and the Other: How Anthropology Makes Its Object, With a New Postscript by the Author* (New York: Columbia University Press, 2002).

Ghosh, Anindita, *Power in Print: Popular Publishing and the Politics of Language and Culture in a Colonial Society, 1778–1905* (New Delhi: Oxford University Press, 2006).

Gikandi, Simon, *Maps of Englishness: Writing, Identity in the Culture of Colonialism* (New York: Columbia University Press, 1996).

Grey, Donald, "Views and Sketches of London in the Nineteenth Century", in Ira Bruce Nadel and F.S. Schwarzbach, ed., *Victorian Artists and the City* (New York: Pergamon Press, 1980).

Guha, Ranajit, "A Colonial City and its Time(s)", in idem, *The Small Voice of History: Collected Essays*, edited and with an introduction by Partha Chatterjee (Ranikhet: Permanent Black, 2009), 409–35.

Joshi, Priya, *In Another Country: Colonialism, Culture, and the English Novel in India* (New York: Columbia University Press, 2002).

Kaviraj, Sudipta, *The Invention of Private Life: Literature and Ideas* (New York: Columbia University Press, 2015).

———, "Filth and the Public Sphere: Concepts and Practices about Space in Calcutta", *Public Culture* 10: 1 (1997), 83–113.

Lewes, G.H., "Realism in Art: Recent German Fiction", *Westminster Review*, 70 (1858).

Márquez, Gabriel García, and Plinio Apuleyo Mendoza, *The Fragrance of Guava* (London: Verso, 1983).

Mukherjee, Meenakshi, *Realism and Reality: The Novel and Society in India* (New York: Oxford University Press, 1994).

———, *The Perishable Empire: Essays on Indian Writing in English* (Delhi: Oxford University Press, 2000).

O'Brien, Sean P., "'Both Masters and Victims of their Times': Engaging Aporetic Time in *Midnight's Children*", *The Journal of Commonwealth Literature*, 2015, vol. 50 (2), 164–78.

Parashkevova, Vassilena, "'Turn Your Watch Upside Down in Bombay and You See the Time in London': Catoptric Urban Configurations in Salman Rushdie's *The Satanic Verses*", *Journal of Commonwealth Literature*, 2007, vol. 42 (3), 5–24.

Reid, J.C., *Bucks and Bruisers: Pierce Egan and Regency London* (London: Routledge and Kegan Paul, 1971).

Rushdie, Salman, *Midnight's Children* (London: Vintage, 2013).

———, "Introduction", *Midnight's Children* (London: Vintage, 2013).

———, *Imaginary Homelands: Essays and Criticism, 1981–1991* (London: Granta, 1991).

Sarkar, Sumit, *Writing Social History* (Delhi: Oxford University Press, 1997).

———, "Kaliyuga, Chakri, and Bhakti: Ramakrishna and His Times", in idem, *Essays of a Lifetime* (Ranikhet: Permanent Black, 2018).

Sen, Sambudha, *London, Radical Expression and the Making of the Dickensian Aesthetic* (Columbus: State University of Ohio Press, 2012).

Sinha, Kaliprasanna, *Hootum Pyanchar Naksha* (1862), ed. Arun Nag, in *Shatik Hootum Pyanchar Naksha* (Calcutta: Ananda Publishers, 2008).

———, *Hootum Pyanchar Naksha*, trans. by Swarup Roy as *The Observant Owl: Hootum's Vignettes of Nineteenth-century Calcutta* (Ranikhet: Permanent Black / Black Kite, 2008).

———, *Hootum Pyanchar Naksha*, trans. by Chitralekha Basu as *Sketches by Hootum the Owl: A Satirist's View of Colonial Calcutta* (Calcutta: Samya, 2012).

Stephen, James Fitzjames, "The License of Modern Novelists", *Edinburgh Review*, CVIII, 18 July 1857.

Tagore, Rabindranath, "Bengali National Literature" (1895), and "Modern Poetry" (1932), trans. and reprinted in Sukanta Chaudhuri and Sisir Kumar Das, ed., *Selected Writings on Literature and Language: Rabindranath Tagore* (New Delhi: Oxford University Press, 2001).

Tillotson, Geoffrey, ed., *Willaim Makepeace Thackeray: The Critical Heritage* (London: Routledge, 1968).

Unsigned, "The Progress of Fiction", *Westminster Review* LX, October 1853.

Note on Contributors

Baidik Bhattacharya is Assistant Professor of English at the University of Delhi. He is the author of *Postcolonial Writing in the Era of World Literature: Texts, Territories, Globalizations* (Routledge, 2018), and co-editor of *The Postcolonial Gramsci* (Routledge, 2012). His essays have appeared in *Critical Inquiry, New Literary History, Boundary 2, Interventions*, and *Postcolonial Studies* among other places. He serves on the editorial board of the journal *Postcolonial Studies.*

Vasudha Dalmia is Professor Emerita of Hindi and Modern South Asian Studies at the University of California, Berkeley. Her monograph, *The Nationalization of Hindu Traditions: Bharatendu Harischandra and Nineteenth Century Banaras* (1997; new edition, Ranikhet: Permanent Black, 2010), has been widely acclaimed as one of the monumental classics of Indian history. Her finest essays have appeared as *Hindu Pasts: Women, Religion, Histories* (Ranikhet and New York: Permanent Black and SUNY Press, 2015). Her latest book is about the Hindi novel, *Fiction as History: The Novel and the City in Modern North India* (Ranikhet and New York: Permanent Black and SUNY Press, 2017).

Udaya Kumar is Professor, Centre for English Studies, Jawaharlal Nehru University, New Delhi. He has previously worked at the University of Delhi, Centre for Studies in Social Sciences, Calcutta, and Nehru Memorial Museum and Library. His recent research focuses on death and contemporary culture, forms of life-writing, cultural histories of the body, and idioms of vernacular social thought. His publications include *The Joycean Labyrinth: Repetition, Time and Tradition in 'Ulysses'* (Oxford: Clarendon, 1991), *Writing the First Person: Literature, History, and Autobiography in Modern Kerala* (Ranikhet: Permanent Black, 2016), and papers on literary and cultural theory and modern literature from Kerala, India.

Rochelle Pinto was Research Fellow at the Nehru Memorial Museum and Library, New Delhi, 2015–17. Her current research is titled Land and Narrative – The Culture of Economy in Colonial Goa. A recent article by her in the *Journal of World History* is "The Foral in the History of the Comunidades of Goa".

M. Madhava Prasad is Professor of Cultural Studies at E.F.L. University, Hyderabad. He is the author of *Ideology of the Hindi Film: A Historical Construction* (Delhi: Oxford University Press, 1998), *Cine-Politics: Film Stars and Political Existence in South India* (Hyderabad: Orient Blackswan, 2014), and numerous essays on literature, popular culture, and Indian society and democracy. He is currently completing a manuscript on language and democracy in India.

Sambudha Sen is Professor of English, Shiv Nadar University, Uttar Pradesh. He has published essays on the print and visual culture of Victorian England in *Representations, Victorian Studies, English Literary History*, and *Nineteenth Century Literature*. He is the author of *Dickens's Novels in the Age of Improvement* (Delhi: Manohar, 2003), and *London: Radical Culture and the Making of the Dickensian Aesthetic* (Columbus: Ohio State University Press, 2013). He is currently researching the ways in which contagion was understood in nineteenth-century England, especially in relation to the poor. He is also beginning a project on the development of English literary prose in India.